DANIEL MULHALL is a retired diplo
Ambassador in Kuala Lumpur, Ber
and was a member of the Irish G
negotiations that produced the Go
Since his retirement in 2022, he has been Global Distinguished
Professor of Irish Studies at Glucksman Ireland House, New York
University, Parnell Fellow at Magdalene College, Cambridge
University, and a Fellow at the Institute of Politics, Harvard
University. Throughout his diplomatic career, he lectured and
published widely on Irish history and literature and, in 2022, he
produced the bestselling and critically acclaimed *Ulysses: A Reader's
Odyssey* (New Island Books). He is a consultant with the global law
firm DLA Piper and Honorary President of the Yeats Society, Sligo.

**Praise for**
***Ulysses: A Reader's Odyssey***

'He writes about *Ulysses* with exuberance and evident enjoyment.'

*Dublin Review of Books*

'An excellent guide through daunting terrain.'

*Hot Press*

'Cleverly decodes all 18 episodes of the novel.'

*Irish Central*

'An informed, enjoyable guide, it homes in on *Ulysses*' emotional core.'

*Irish Independent*

'Powerfully, [Mulhall] argues that Joyce and Ireland for him are
indissociable and that he retains a burning relevance today.'

*Irish Times*

'Releases the great masterpiece from its reputation of
impenetrability. An affectionate, accessible tribute.'

*Sunday Independent*

'Highly readable, personable and well researched.'

*The Times*

PILGRIM SOUL
First published in 2023 by
New Island Books
Glenshesk House
10 Richview Office Park
Clonskeagh
Dublin D14 V8C4
Republic of Ireland
www.newisland.ie

Print ISBN: 978-1-84840-881-4
eBook ISBN: 978-1-84840-882-1

Set in 11.5 on 15.5pt Baskerville Display PT
Typeset by JVR Creative India
Edited by Neil Burkey, neilburkey.com
Cover design by Jack Smyth, jacksmyth.co
Cover image: W.B. Yeats by George Charles Beresford © National Portrait Gallery, London and 'Easter 1916' (detail), by permission of United Agents and Caitríona Yeats. Printed by L&C, Poland, lcprinting.eu

New Island Books is a member of Publishing Ireland.

10 9 8 7 6 5 4 3 2 1

# Pilgrim Soul

W.B. Yeats and
the Ireland
of His Time

## Daniel Mulhall

NEW ISLAND

*To Greta, my 'pilgrim soul' and lifelong companion, and to my latest grandchild, Arthur Tibor Mulhall, born while I was completing this book.*

# Contents

# Abbreviations

## Works by Yeats

| | |
|---|---|
| *Au.* | *Autobiographies* |
| *CL1* | John Kelly & Eric Domville (eds), *The Collected Letters of W.B. Yeats, Vol. 1, 1885–1895* |
| *CL2* | Warwick Gould et al. (eds), *The Collected Letters of W.B. Yeats, Vol. II, 1896–1900* |
| *CL3* | John Kelly & Ronald Schuchard (eds), *The Collected Letters of W.B. Yeats, Vol. III, 1901–1904* |
| *CL4* | John Kelly & Ronald Schuchard (eds), *The Collected Letters of W.B. Yeats, Vol. IV, 1901–1904* |
| *E&I* | *Essays and Introductions* |
| *Exp.* | *Explorations* |
| *Ideals* | Lady Augusta Gregory (ed.), *Ideals in Ireland* |
| *Letters* | Allan Wade (ed.), *The Letters of W.B. Yeats* |
| *LNI* | *Letters to a New Island* |
| *Mem.* | Denis Donoghue (ed.), *W.B. Yeats Memoirs* |
| *SC* | *Selected Criticism* |
| *Sen.* | Donald R. Pearce (ed.), *The Senate Speeches of W.B. Yeats* |

| | |
|---|---|
| *UP1* | John P. Frayne (ed.), *Uncollected Prose by W.B. Yeats: 1, First Reviews and Articles, 1886–1896* |
| *UP2* | John P. Frayne & Colton Johnson (eds), *Uncollected Prose by W.B. Yeats: reviews, articles and other miscellaneous prose, 1897–1939* |
| *Var.* | Peter Allt & Russell K. Alspach (eds), *The Variorum Edition of the Poems of W.B. Yeats* |
| *YGL* | Anna MacBride White & A. Norman Jeffares (eds), *Always Your Friend: the Gonne-Yeats Letters, 1893–1938* |
| *YY* | Edward Callan (ed.), *Yeats on Yeats: the last introductions and the 'Dublin' Edition* |

## WORKS ABOUT YEATS

| | |
|---|---|
| *Chron.* | John S. Kelly, *W.B. Yeats: A Chronology* |
| *Foster 1997* | R.F. Foster, *W.B. Yeats: A Life: I: The Apprentice Mage 1865–1914* |
| *Foster 2003* | R.F. Foster, *W.B. Yeats: A Life: II: The Arch-Poet 1915–1939* |
| *NC* | A. Norman Jeffares, *A New Commentary on the Collected Poems of W.B. Yeats* |

# Introduction

I wrote this book in New York, Cambridge and Dublin in the year after my retirement from Ireland's Department of Foreign Affairs. I did so to mark the 100th anniversary of W.B. Yeats's receipt of the Nobel Prize for Literature in December 1923. In many ways, this project is the consummation of a lifelong interest in Yeats's 'indomitable Irishry', which, in 'Under Ben Bulben', he urged us 'in coming days' to embrace. Yeats certainly followed that precept and was, through the twists and turns of his life and work, always indomitably Irish, even if not all of his contemporaries always saw him in that way.

I first became interested in Yeats's Irishness during my college days, when I wrote an MA thesis on the poet's nationalism. His significance as a witness to Irish history during a transformative era for Ireland continued to occupy my attention during four decades of diplomatic life spent in nine countries across the globe. I came to see Yeats as an asset in telling the complex story of Ireland's struggle for freedom in the opening decades of the twentieth century. His poetry also attracted interest and admiration from people around the world with no ancestral connection to Ireland, but who developed an affinity with us. That is all part of Yeats's bounteous literary legacy. Ireland captures far more attention than it would if it did not have writers of Yeats's calibre to help brand us in the eyes of the world. Over the years, I have spoken at Yeats Societies in India, Western Australia and Korea, whose members were drawn to Yeats for different reasons.

I had the privilege of representing Ireland as a diplomat for forty-four of the Irish state's first hundred years. Thus, for me, 1922 is the pivotal year in modern Irish history, the moment when Irish independence went from being a long-held aspiration to a lived reality. As a student of history, I have always been intrigued by the manner in which Ireland broke free from Britain, which, having been among the victors in World War I, remained one of the world's leading powers. How did a people that had been so Famine-damaged and demographically depleted keep the flame of independence alight? And against a backdrop of the failure of successive nineteenth-century efforts to secure self-government, how did early twentieth-century nationalism manage to pull it off? Was it that the times had changed and become more propitious for Ireland, or were there new elements in the nationalist mix that paved the way for independence? Was the literary revival that Yeats pioneered part of the explanation for Ireland's political transformation?

Was it pure coincidence that Irish literature flowered so brilliantly during those same years, with the publication of James Joyce's three great works, *Dubliners* (1914), *A Portrait of the Artist as a Young Man* (1916) and *Ulysses* (1922), alongside two major Yeats collections, *The Wild Swans at Coole* (1919) and *Michael Robartes and the Dancer*

(1921)? My sense is that the Irish political and literary achievements of that era were linked, as both were the output of an accomplished, impatient generation that came to the fore at the turn of the century and sowed seeds of revolution and artistic creativity. James Joyce was, after all, an exact contemporary of Ireland's longest-serving political leader, Éamon de Valera.

Yeats was born fifteen or so years before the leading lights of the revolutionary generation, but he was witness to their deeds and a contributor to the milieu from which they emerged. By his own account, he became an Irish writer when he was just twenty and, despite the temptation he must occasionally have felt to follow the path trodden by Oscar Wilde and George Bernard Shaw in the mainstream of English literature, Yeats stayed the course.

Yeats's Irish *turas* (the Irish word for journey and pilgrimage) was a winding one. Born into a family that was part of Ireland's Anglo-Irish Protestant community, he was not an obvious candidate for a role as the premier poet of nationalist Ireland. His discovery during the 1880s of the Gaelic tradition in literature and mythology turned out to be a life-changing event. It caused him to become the prime proponent and advocate of an Irish national literature in the English language. Yeats was part of a wider cultural revival, involving also the Gaelic Athletic Association(GAA) and the Gaelic League, that helped remake Irish identity at the turn of the century. This, coupled with his enduring fascination with Maud Gonne, caused him to become a fairly robust nationalist in the closing years of the nineteenth century. Indeed, he was probably sworn in as a member of the oath-bound, clandestine Irish Republican Brotherhood at that time, an unusual distinction for a major poet.

The first decade of the twentieth century was difficult for Yeats, with the shock of Maud's impetuous marriage to John MacBride, followed by its tempestuous disintegration. Those upheavals in his private life occurred alongside the exacting labours entailed in steering the Abbey Theatre during its formative years. He was also troubled by the emergence of more vehement brands of nationalism rooted in Catholic and Gaelic identities hostile to Yeats's preference for a hybrid version of Irishness that would blend Gaelic and English elements.

Having proclaimed the death of Romantic Ireland in 1913, Yeats resurrected his Irish engagement in response to the 1916 Rising and spent most of the rest of his life living in Ireland, as a Senator and an internationally celebrated Irishman. His concern about rising lawlessness peaked during the Irish Civil War, which he observed at close quarters. It brought his incipient conservative inclinations to the fore. Due to his frustration with developments in Ireland, he conjured up a cult of the Anglo-Irish tradition, which exposed him to accusations that his nationalism lacked proper native roots. And in the 1930s, he had a regrettable brush with fascism and dabbled disgracefully in eugenics. Despite being out of tune with 'the sort now growing up' in Ireland, at the end of his life he insisted that 'Ancient Ireland knew it all' and paid homage to the 'seven heroic centuries' of struggle against outside domination of Irish affairs.

In the pages that follow, I try to chart Yeats's elongated, meandering Irish journey. This exercise has three connected aims: to establish a deeper understanding of

Yeats's Irishness, to view Ireland through his eyes and to plot the manner in which his engagement with Ireland affected his writing. By exploring Yeats's involvement with the Ireland of his time, I am also probing the puzzle of how Yeats, the quintessential late-romantic, became one of the essential modern poets of his time and ours.

# 1

# 'Those masterful images'

## Yeats's Ireland

# The Circus Animals' Desertion

### I

I sought a theme and sought for it in vain,
I sought it daily for six weeks or so.
Maybe at last being but a broken man,
I must be satisfied with my heart, although
Winter and summer till old age began
My circus animals were all on show,
Those stilted boys, that burnished chariot,
Lion and woman and the Lord knows what.

### II

What can I but enumerate old themes?
First that sea-rider Oisin led by the nose
Through three enchanted islands, allegorical dreams,
Vain gaiety, vain battle, vain repose,
Themes of the embittered heart, or so it seems,
That might adorn old songs or courtly shows;
But what cared I that set him on to ride,
I, starved for the bosom of his fairy bride?

And then a counter-truth filled out its play,
'The Countess Cathleen' was the name I gave it;
She, pity-crazed, had given her soul away
But masterful Heaven had intervened to save it.
I thought my dear must her own soul destroy,
So did fanaticism and hate enslave it,
And this brought forth a dream and soon enough
This dream itself had all my thought and love.

And when the Fool and Blind Man stole the bread
Cuchulain fought the ungovernable sea;
Heart mysteries there, and yet when all is said

It was the dream itself enchanted me:
Character isolated by a deed
To engross the present and dominate memory.
Players and painted stage, took all my love
And not those things that they were emblems of.

### III

Those masterful images because complete
Grew in pure mind, but out of what began?
A mound of refuse or the sweepings of a street,
Old kettles, old bottles, and a broken can,
Old iron, old bones, old rags, that raving slut
Who keeps the till. Now that my ladder's gone
I must lie down where all the ladders start,
In the foul rag and bone shop of the heart.[1]


## 'To engross the present and dominate memory'

In his last years, beset by ill health and often restricted to a diet of fruit and milk, W.B. Yeats's poetry became more autobiographical as he delved into his memory, looking back over his eventful life as poet, playwright, essayist and public figure. In 'The Municipal Gallery Revisited' he gathered around him 'the images of thirty years', peopled by members of his personal pantheon – Lady Gregory, John Millington Synge, Hugh Lane, Hazel Lavery and, among the political clan, Arthur Griffith ('staring in hysterical pride') and Kevin O'Higgins ('a soul incapable of remorse or rest') – with all of whom, he insisted, you could:

Ireland's history in their lineaments trace;
Think where man's glory most begins and ends
And say my glory was I had such friends.

Another late poem, 'Beautiful Lofty Things', continues this celebration of his own inner circle – John O'Leary, Maud Gonne, Standish O'Grady and his father John B. Yeats – 'All the Olympians; a thing never known again'. They became Olympian because that was what W.B. Yeats, master image-maker, declared them to be.

'The Circus Animals' Desertion' does something different. It casts the mind back over Yeats's writing life from the 'enchanted islands, allegorical dreams' of his younger days, to the 'themes of the embittered heart' and the 'players and the painted stage' from his middle years, and on to 'the foul rag and bone shop of the heart', where the aged poet 'must lie down' now that his 'ladder's gone' and he is no longer busy climbing Mount Parnassus. That 'rag and bone shop' is a far cry from the 'crowd of stars' in which his imagination hid its face in 'When You Are Old', the early Yeats poem that contains the term 'pilgrim soul'. At the heart of Yeats's story is how he progressed with his poetry from inhabiting the late-romantic 'bee-loud glade' in 'The Lake Isle of Innisfree' to being stalked by decidedly modernist images like 'a mound of refuse or the sweepings of a street' that might have migrated from T.S. Eliot's *The Waste Land.*

Many of 'those masterful images' that run through Yeats's poetry offer insight into the Ireland of Yeats's time. And, while he believed that you could trace Ireland's history in the 'lineaments' of his friends' faces, for me Yeats's poetry possesses that same capacity. The 'masterful images' Yeats created act as signposts to Irish history. His poetic insights have shown themselves to possess the kind of permanence he hoped would attach to the words he had 'carved on a stone at Thoor[2] Ballylee', his west of Ireland summer base for the most productive decade of his writing life, 1918–1928:

> I, the poet William Yeats,
> With old mill boards and sea-green slates,
> And smithy work from the Gort forge,
> Restored this tower for my wife George;
> And may these characters remain
> When all is ruin once again.

This book seeks to do what Yeats did with those late-life poems. It covers biographical ground, as does 'Municipal Gallery' and the literary terrain mapped out in 'Circus Animals'. It is written with a focus on Yeats's poetry and his Irishness, the 'indomitable Irishry' he wrote about in his poetic epitaph, 'Under Ben Bulben'. I have approached Yeats's life and work with the general reader in mind, and have drawn heavily on Yeats's poetry and prose, believing that his 'words alone are certain good'.[3] During my travels over the years, I have been asked to recommend a manageable, accessible account of Yeats's life and work, but often struggled to come up with an answer. This book sets out to explore Yeats through an Irish lens, drawing attention to his status as the paramount Irish literary chronicler of his age. It is written for readers with an interest in Yeats, or a curiosity about him, but who are disinclined to dip into the deep scholarly pool that wells around his literary career.

# Stockholm 1923

I begin my Yeats story long before I was born, in the life-time of my fervently republican paternal grandparents (who probably would not have cared too much for the Free State-supporting Senator Yeats), at a time when a newly independent Ireland had just emerged from a damaging, divisive civil war. The year was 1923 and the place, Stockholm.

When the Swedish Academy announced its 1923 Nobel literature laureate in the autumn of that year, it opted for a writer who had produced what the Academy described as 'always inspired poetry, which in a highly artistic form gives expression to the spirit of a whole nation'. The poet's name was William Butler Yeats[4] and his nation had the previous year achieved a measure of self-government as the Irish Free State, which had been formed at the end of a six-year struggle for freedom that began with the Easter Rising of 1916, an event that the poet had elegised in his magisterial history poem, 'Easter 1916'. Yeats modestly acknowledged the wider context in which he was being awarded the Nobel Prize, remarking that, 'I consider that this honour has come to me less as an individual than as a representative of Irish literature, it is part of Europe's welcome to the Free State.'[5]

Yeats learned of his Nobel Prize one night in November 1923 when he was telephoned by Bertie Smyllie, an *Irish Times* journalist and future editor of the paper who was asked by the then editor, John Healy, to inform Yeats about the award and to record his response. Yeats's reaction, demonstrating that he had down-to-earth pre-occupations alongside his more ethereal ones, was 'And tell me, Bertie, how much is it worth?'[6] The answer was

£7,000, a tidy sum in the early 1920s, which would have a current value (2023) of almost €400,000.

Yeats later recalled that news of his success reached him between 10 and 11 p.m., after which he and his wife George celebrated with a plate of sausages, having failed to find a bottle of wine in their cellar. The following evening, during a presumably more elaborate dinner at the Shelbourne Hotel, a congratulatory telegram arrived from James Joyce, who, for the remaining eighteen years of his life, never managed to find favour with the Nobel Committee.

A few weeks later, Mr and Mrs Yeats set off by ferry for Sweden, where the coveted prize was conferred on this almost '60-year-old smiling public man' by King Gustav V at a ceremony in Stockholm on 10 December. It came at a time of great achievement in Irish literature. Joyce's *Ulysses* had been published almost two years before, while Sean O'Casey's first great play, *The Shadow of a Gunman*, premiered at the Abbey Theatre in April 1923. Yeats himself, who had lately returned to Ireland and been appointed to the Senate, was in full creative flow. Two years before he had published *Michael Robartes and the Dancer*, containing 'Easter 1916' and 'The Second Coming', and had recently written 'Meditations in Time of Civil War', containing that quintessentially evocative Yeats line, 'caught in the cold snows of a dream'. This was also a time of huge turmoil in Irish life, with the ending of the Civil War and the fraught consolidation of the Irish Free State.

At the award ceremony on 10 December, Yeats spoke about the Irish literary movement, in which he had played a leading role:

Thirty years ago a number of Irish writers met together in societies and began a remorseless criticism of the literature of their country. It was their dream that by freeing it from provincialism they might win for it European recognition. I owe much to those men, still more to those who joined our movement a few years later, and when I return to Ireland these men and women, now growing old like myself, will see in this great honour a fulfilment of that dream. I in my heart know how little I might have deserved it if they had never existed.

Per Hallström, Chairman of the Nobel Committee of the Swedish Academy, spoke perceptively about Yeats's identification with his homeland. He noted that:

> Yeats's association with the life of a people saved him from the barrenness which attended so much of the effort for beauty that marked his age. Around him as the central point and leader arose, within a group of his countrymen in the literary world of London, that mighty movement which has been named the Celtic Revival and which created a new national literature, an Anglo-Irish literature.
>
> The foremost and most versatile poet of this group was Yeats. His rousing and rallying personality caused the movement to grow and flower very quickly, by giving a common aim to hitherto scattered forces or by encouraging new forces, previously unconscious of their existence.

And that 'mighty movement' was the subject of Yeats's Nobel lecture, delivered on 15 December 1923. In 'The Irish Dramatic Movement', Yeats sought to claim his share of the credit for the coming of Irish independence. The words he spoke on that occasion went all out to highlight the significance and the influence of the literary movement he had come to personify. It is an illustration of Yeats's sense of history and of his powers as a gifted prose stylist, at his brilliant best in this opening salvo:

> The modern literature of Ireland, and indeed all that stir of thought which prepared for the Anglo-Irish War, began when Parnell fell from power in 1891. A disillusioned and embittered Ireland turned away from parliamentary politics: an event was conceived and the race began, as I think, to be troubled by that event's long gestation. Dr. Hyde founded the Gaelic League, which was for many years to substitute for political argument a Gaelic grammar, and for political meetings village gatherings, where songs were sung and stories told in the Gaelic language. Meanwhile I had begun a movement in English, in the language in which modern Ireland thinks and does its business; founded certain societies where clerks, working men, men of all classes, could study those Irish poets, novelists, and historians who had written in English, and as much of Gaelic literature as had been translated into English.[7]

This is an example of Yeats's ability to take hold of Ireland's history and to trace its 'lineaments' in accordance with his own imaginative vision. As his fellow poet T.S. Eliot once wrote, Yeats was 'one of those few whose history is the history of their own time, who are part of the consciousness of an age which cannot be understood without them'.[8]

Let me parse the image of Ireland's recent past that Yeats conjured up in his Stockholm lecture. In his view of things, the political demise and subsequent death of Charles Stewart Parnell had caused the Irish people to turn away from parliamentary politics and devote more attention to cultural movements. Those movements were part of a 'stir of thought' that had radicalised Ireland, unleashing forces that delivered Irish independence in 1922 on the back of a war of independence waged between 1919 and 1921. Mind you, this is not a set of ideas that Yeats first came up with when he sat down to write his Nobel lecture. He had been banging the drum about Parnell's fall giving space for the emergence of cultural movements since shortly after the death of Ireland's 'uncrowned king' in October 1891.

Yeats's historical schema attributes considerable political and societal influence to the Irish cultural revival of the late nineteenth and early twentieth centuries. Now, let me be clear, Yeats's thesis can be, and has been, challenged. Yeats's biographer, Roy Foster, writing in his influential study of modern Ireland, wondered if 'given the circumstances of the time, the activities of the intelligentsia were really more significant than the actions of the politicians and the "agitators"'.[9]

Another study of the prelude to Irish independence, Patrick Maume's *The Long Gestation: Irish Nationalist Life, 1891–1918*, though it takes its title from Yeats's Nobel lecture, barely mentions the poet or the literary movement he personified. Yeats's ideas about the course of Irish history during his lifetime, the notion that a post-Parnell vacuum resulted in political energy being diverted into cultural channels, attests to the value of what we now call 'soft power' – that 'stir of thought', as Yeats worded it – in bringing about transformational political change.

The centenary of Yeats's Nobel Prize, the first to be won by an Irish figure, seems like an opportune time to take a look at Yeats's life and work against the background of the country in which he was born and by which at different stages of his life he was inspired and exasperated. But, at all times, Ireland preoccupied him. Early in his life he was gripped by Irish folklore and mythology, and the grip that Ireland had on him never relaxed although its density changed with the passage of time. Now that more than eight decades have passed since Yeats's death and the Ireland he knew has been 'transformed utterly', it may be asked, why does Yeats continue to warrant biographical and critical attention? My answer is that the words he pieced together in his poems still speak to us, and that Yeats's time, coinciding with the birth of modern Ireland, remains parental to ours.

## New York 2022

As I was busy writing this book during my time teaching Irish Studies at Glucksman Ireland House, New York University, in the closing months of 2022, one day I wandered into Strand Books, a New York institution located at the edge of Greenwich Village. Among the titles on prominent display that caught my eye that day were Cormac McCarthy's *No Country for Old Men*, Chinua Achebe's *Things Fall Apart* and J. Bradford DeLong's *Slouching Towards Utopia: An Economic History of the Twentieth Century*. All three titles were clearly inspired by Yeats's writing, and they testify to his extraordinary ability to craft phrases that were destined to stand the test of time.

Books about Northern Ireland abound with Yeatsian echoes; take, for example, Jonathan Powell's *Great Hatred, Little Room. Great Hatred* is also the title of Ronan McGreevy's book on the assassination by the IRA of Field Marshal Sir Henry Wilson in London in June 1922. Wilson was a contemporary of Yeats's, having been born in Dublin into a Protestant family a year before him, but Wilson, who became a staunch Unionist, developed a radically different response to developments in their ruffled homeland of the late nineteenth century.[10] In 1976 Jill and Leon Uris called their book on Ireland *A Terrible Beauty.* But it is not just books on Ireland that reach for Yeats's words for their titles. In 1998 Roger Cohen chose *Hearts Grown Brutal: Sagas of Sarajevo* as the title for a book about the war in Bosnia-Herzegovina, while Elizabeth Dore called her study of the Cuban revolution *How Things Fall Apart.* I could go on. My point is that Yeats's words have had a lengthy and influential afterlife that few writers manage to achieve.

In my teaching at NYU I sought to explore Ireland's history using Yeats, Joyce, O'Casey, Synge and others as guides. Although written while I made the transition from a 44-year career with Ireland's Department of Foreign Affairs to what I hope will be a fruitful and satisfying retirement, there is a sense in which this book is the culmination of a lifelong project aimed at understanding Ireland's greatest English-language poet, and through him the Ireland in which he lived.

What I am offering here is not a full-scale biography, but a selective biographical exploration that looks at Yeats's dialogue with Ireland during an era of profound political transformation, which he observed with his keen poet's eye and his gift for conjuring up some truly 'masterful images'. Throughout his life he drew inspiration from Ireland and, in his writings, set out to reimagine and, in any way he could, to reshape the country of his birth, a country for which he maintained an undying affection.

Although lacking the kind of imagination needed for creative writing, I have long been under the spell of Yeats and the history of Ireland during his lifetime. Since 2019 I have enjoyed the privilege of being Honorary President of the Sligo-based Yeats Society, which celebrates the life and works of Yeats and his talented family in a place that meant so much to the poet and was a source of inspiration for him, especially in his early writings.

## Cork 1975

Yeats died in January 1939, a decade and a half before I was born, and I have only ever met one person who could remember encountering him in person. The former Irish rugby international Des O'Brien, a member of the Grand Slam-winning team of 1948, when I met him in Edinburgh in 1999, recalled how as a boy he had been playing with his father at Rathfarnham Golf Club when they came across Yeats out walking and young Des was duly introduced to the famous poet.

I first came across Yeats's poetry as part of the Irish Leaving Certificate English syllabus during the early 1970s. At Mount Sion School in Waterford I was fortunate to have a talented and far-sighted English teacher, Sean Crowe, who inspired in his pupils an enthusiasm for literature. This boyhood interest in writing, and especially in poetry, has persisted through the many changes the decades have brought. I have never written a poem, but have always admired the power of a well-tempered verse and have been posting lines of Irish poetry daily on my Twitter account @DanMulhall since 2015. I value poetry for its capacity to enable us to 'see into the life of things', including into the elongated byways of our history.

I was a student at University College Cork when I became absorbed with Yeats's poetry. One day in the college bookshop, I picked up a copy of Yeats's *Selected Poetry*. I still have that book, with its introduction by the Yeats scholar A. Norman Jeffares. Back in the 1970s I underlined some of Jeffares's words, including his comment that Yeats had set out 'to write for an Irish audience and about Ireland' and 'to re-create a specifically Irish literature'.[11]

Even with the passage of almost half a century, I have a vivid recollection of the impression Yeats's poems had on me during the summer of 1975, when I was preparing for my undergraduate examinations and considering what I might do in the way of postgraduate study. Enthralled by Yeats's poems, I temporarily shelved other course reading. That experience left me with an abiding impression of the power and historical importance of his writing. I was struck especially by the poems that addressed aspects of twentieth-century Irish history, 'No Second Troy', 'September 1913', 'Easter 1916', 'Nineteen Hundred and Nineteen', 'The Second Coming' and 'Meditations in Time of Civil War', to name but a few.

It seemed to me that Yeats's work offered a precious insight into that seminal era of Irish history, the two decades between the turn of the century and the attainment of independence in 1922. His was a selective view, of course, shaped by personal preoccupations and prejudices, but no less compelling for that limitation. Yeats's story and the story of Ireland in the closing decades of the nineteenth century and the first third of the twentieth are fortuitously intertwined. That entanglement has yielded a rich harvest of 'masterful images' of Ireland's cultural and political *belle époque.*

The literary critic Seamus Deane observed that, 'Yeats began his career by inventing an Ireland amenable to his imagination. He ended by finding an Ireland recalcitrant to it.'[12] The following pages explore Yeats's imaginative inventiveness and also grapple with Ireland's recalcitrance; what he might have seen as a cussed unwillingness to bow to his romantic urgings. Yeats yearned for what he envisioned as a romantic Ireland, but what came out of the mill of history was a chequered Ireland: a stable democracy but also a reservoir of disappointed idealisms. In his final play, *The Death of Cuchulain,* he wrote that he was 'out of fashion and out of date like the antiquated romantic stuff'.[13] It is true that the Ireland of the 1930s was not the one he had dreamt of, but he could nonetheless look back with satisfaction at having, in the words of one scholar, 'helped bring a regenerated nation into being'.[14]

Inspired by this reading of Yeats's poems as a form of historical narrative, I decided to devote my postgraduate study at University College Cork to a literary-historical topic. Two years later, having studied under the guidance of Professor Joe Lee at UCC, I ended up calling my thesis *'The indomitable Irishry': writers and politics in Ireland, 1890–1939.* It looked at the evolution of Yeats's nationalism from the 1890s to the 1930s, that of his contemporary and lifelong friend George William Russell (Æ) (1867–1935), poet, painter, mystic and editor, and of the short-story writer and commentator Sean O'Faolain.

As a young man in the years after the death of Parnell in 1891, Yeats devoted huge effort to the creation of a national literature for Ireland. After 1900 his vision of Ireland darkened as he grappled with what he termed the 'seeming needs of my fool-driven land'. This caused him considerable frustration, as did 'the day's war with every knave and dolt / Theatre business, management of men', when he strove to develop the Abbey Theatre and pushed back against its detractors, notably those who were offended by Synge's *The Playboy of the Western World.*

The prime source of Yeats's disenchantment was the emergence of what he saw as a narrower brand of nationalism from that which he had espoused during the 1890s. Beset by multiple frustrations, Yeats composed his dirge for the death of 'romantic Ireland' in 'September 1913', but less than three years later he was mesmerised by the 'terrible beauty' of Easter 1916, which revived his interest in Ireland's potential. On the back of the events of 1916, and seemingly excited about the prospect of contributing to Ireland as it moved towards independence, Yeats returned from London to reside in Ireland, where he spent most of the next decade and a half.

Yeats experienced renewed disenchantment during the 1920s and 1930s as he faced the realities of literary censorship and the intensely Catholic atmosphere of independent Ireland. In search of refuge, his response was to immerse himself in the Anglo-Irish tradition, which saw him develop a cult-like devotion to the great Anglo-Irish figures of the past: Swift, Burke, Grattan, Goldsmith, Berkeley and Parnell. Then there were the deeply conservative views he espoused in the 1920s and 1930s, a kind of haughty, aristocratic nationalism, which drew him into an unfortunate but fleeting association with Ireland's homegrown fascist movement, the Blueshirts, and to the expression of some wildly unappealing political views in *On the Boiler*, published in the year of his death.

Despite the ups and downs of his engagement with Ireland, to the end of his days Yeats remained absorbed with the affairs of the country of his birth. Indeed, in his poetic epitaph, 'Under Ben Bulben', written in the final months of his life, Yeats returned to the source of his late nineteenth-century Irish idealism, writing that 'ancient Ireland knew it all'.

There is something deeply fascinating about those decades between the fall of Parnell in 1890 and the death of Yeats in 1939. That was a time when Ireland was transformed from a restless province of the United Kingdom to an independent state in a position to assert its neutrality during the greatest crisis in modern Irish history, World War II. That same period also witnessed the emergence of a distinctively Irish tradition in literature, which became one of the glories of twentieth-century Ireland.

During this time, writers of the calibre of Yeats, John Millington Synge, Sean O'Casey, James Joyce, Samuel Beckett and Flann O'Brien emerged from an Ireland that was undergoing a fraught transition from the Victorian world of Charles Stewart Parnell to the Ireland of Éamon de Valera. Those writers were not all part of Yeats's movement (indeed Joyce sought to distance himself from the Irish literary revival, and Flann O'Brien frequently poked fun at it), but the influence of Yeats runs through this entire era of exceptional literary achievement. Any effort to understand Ireland's evolution between the failure of the Fenian rebellion of 1867 and the outbreak of war in 1939 will, I believe, profit from a study of Yeats's life and work.

## New Delhi 1982

My favourite reminiscence to do with Yeats comes from a distinguished Indian woman I met in 1982. She was indeed 'old and grey', although she was certainly *not* 'full of sleep'. I was still a young man in my mid-twenties when I had this experience, one that made me fall under the spell of W.B. Yeats's poem 'When You Are Old'.

I recall the occasion as if it were yesterday. The location was a house in New Delhi's Hanuman Road, belonging to a renowned Indian figure, Mrs Vijaya Lakshmi Pandit (1900–1990). At that time I was based in India and had come to know Mrs Pandit's granddaughter, Gita Sahgal, at whose wedding I was to act as best man. In the lead-up to her granddaughter's wedding Mrs Pandit had kindly invited my wife, Greta, and me to lunch at her residence.

Then in her early eighties, Mrs Pandit was the sister of India's first Prime Minister, Jawaharlal Nehru (1889–1964), one of the outstanding political figures of the twentieth century. She herself had had a long innings in public life, as India's Ambassador to the Soviet Union, the United Nations, Ireland and Britain. Amongst her many achievements, Mrs Pandit had been the first woman ever to preside over the annual United Nations General Assembly. When I met Mrs Pandit, her brother's daughter, Indira Gandhi, was India's serving Prime Minister, although the two women were by that time estranged because of political disagreements.

It was a memorable lunch in the company of this still formidable woman, who had accumulated a wealth of experience and life's wisdom. Also at lunch were various family members and friends, and the conversation centred on Indian history, culture and politics. When she discovered I was Irish, Mrs Pandit spoke of her fondness for Ireland and the country's influence on India's struggle for independence.

In her autobiography, Mrs Pandit recalls that the outbreak of World War I had not had much of an impact on her generation of Indians, but that she had followed the Easter Rising of 1916 with an 'emotional interest'. A few years later, the death of Cork Lord Mayor Terence MacSwiney had 'caused a tremendous wave of indignation in India', and the young Vijaya Lakshmi Nehru entered a competition with an essay entitled 'On the Meaning of Terence MacSwiney's Death', for which she won a gold medal. As Ambassador in Dublin many years later, she said that her greatest enjoyment had been to visit the Abbey Theatre.[15]

During this memorable lunch, Mrs Pandit launched into an impressive, word-perfect recitation of 'When You Are Old' and 'The Lake Isle of Innisfree', poems she informed me she had memorised while interned with her brother during the 1930s, when both were participants in the struggle for Indian independence. Yeats's work, she said, had been a source of inspiration and strength to the Nehru family during their incarceration as opponents of British rule in India.

Several members of her family, including her daughter, the novelist Nayantara Sahgal, who were gathered around the lunch table, joined in the recitation, revealing that Yeats's work was a source of shared enthusiasm across the generations. There was something deeply moving about being 4,500 miles from home, in a very different cultural environment, and learning that an Irish poet was so revered by this distinguished Indian family.

That afternoon in the company of Mrs Pandit and her family was not the only time during my years in India when Yeats's international renown was brought home to me. I came across many Yeats enthusiasts there, some of whom founded a Yeats Society of India and invited me to be their inaugural speaker. It was Yeats's reputation as a nationalist, his advocacy of Rabindranath Tagore and his abiding interest in Eastern philosophy and mysticism that mainly attracted his many Indian admirers.

On another unforgettable occasion I heard Karan Singh, son of the last Maharaja of Jammu and Kashmir, and a leading Indian politician, address a literary conference in New Delhi. He spoke about the importance of poetry, quoting freely from Yeats's work, all from memory, to illustrate his arguments. His knowledge of Yeats's work was deeply impressive and, through Yeats and other Irish writers, he had acquired a high regard for, and extensive knowledge of, Ireland.

Such was the appeal of Yeats's work in 1980s India that I was asked to deliver a paper on 'Yeats and the idea of a national literature for Ireland' to the annual gathering of the All-India English Teachers' Association, an audience of some 1,500 conference participants. This topic had a resonance in India, which, like Ireland, had had to grapple with issues of language and identity. The teachers I met during that conference had never left India, but Irish writing had given them a window through which they could peer into our faraway 'green island'.

When I met Greta in New Delhi in 1980, I often read Yeats's poems to her. Born in Australia, she had at that time never been to Ireland, and I considered Yeats's work as good an introduction as any to the charms of my homeland. At our wedding ceremony in Delhi in 1982 I recited 'He Wishes for the Cloths of Heaven' and 'The Lake Isle of Innisfree'. 'When You Are Old' would not have been a suitable choice for such an occasion! A few years later, while living in Greta's homeplace, Perth, Western Australia, we became involved with the local Yeats Society. I can fondly recall one particular evening when I talked about Yeats at the home of one of the leading Australian novelists of her generation, Mary Durack, in her garden on the banks of the Swan river. That Australian Yeats Society later presented ornamental door handles to the church at Drumcliff in the form of a West Australian black swan and one of the 'wild swans at Coole'.

## Yeats's 'indomitable Irishry'

In the English language at least, Yeats is a rarity in being a nineteenth-century writer (born in 1865) whose writing continued to flourish in the period after World War I. His nineteenth-century lyric poems, with their delicate, musical phrases that many poetry lovers can readily quote, are probably his best-loved works. They tend to pop up whenever people in Britain and Ireland are asked to choose their favourite poems. In a list of *One Hundred Favourite Poems* chosen some years back by listeners of the UK's Classic FM radio station, Yeats had two poems in the top twenty most popular choices, with only Shakespeare being similarly represented.[16]

While works like 'When You Are Old' enjoy enduring popularity, Yeats's reputation as a major writer rests
primarily on the poems he wrote during the twentieth
century. It has always been an interest of mine as to how
Yeats went from writing lines like:

> And walk among long dappled grass,
> And pluck till time and times are done
> The silver apples of the moon,
> The Golden apples of the sun.

to the distinctively twentieth-century tones of such poems
as 'Sailing to Byzantium', in which he rages against life's
infirmities:

> An aged man is but a paltry thing,
> A tattered coat upon a stick, unless
> Soul clap its hands and sing, and louder sing
> For every tatter in its mortal dress,
> Nor is there singing school but studying
> Monuments of its own magnificence; ...

George Russell (Æ) put his finger on this aspect of Yeats's
achievement, 'the new and strange beauty' of his later
poetry. Æ wrote:

> So many poets labour to make a style for themselves,
> and then become the slaves of their style ... But in the
> case of Yeats we find that the later poet is not only
> intellectually the lord of the earlier poet, but that as
> a stylist there is an amazing advance, yet without any
> diminution of emotion or imagination ... It is his habit
> of continual intellectual adventure which has kept

his poetry fresh ... It is that untiring energy of mind which has made his later poetry as we read it seem new and strange and beautiful, and the plain words seem many-coloured, as if they had been dusted over with powdered jewels, not less glowing for all their absence of that vivid colour he used so lavishly in *The Wanderings of Oisín* or *The Shadowy Waters*.[17]

I want to argue that at least part of the explanation of the miracle of Yeats's never-ending poetic vigour lies in his immersion in Irish affairs. That was probably a curse for Æ as he enmeshed himself in the rigours of weekly political journalism, which made him a popular figure but deprived him of the time to get the best out of his own, admittedly lesser, poetic talent. I take the view that Yeats's own brand of indomitable Irishness helped keep him fully creative into old age. Disenchantment with aspects of Irish life in the twentieth century helped harden his poetry. Yeats's verse allows us to plot his changing responses to the Ireland of his time. Some of his finest poems deal with key moments in modern Irish history. His words still shape how many readers view Ireland's past.

I fully accept that Yeats is a vaster subject than can be encompassed by his Irishness, crucial though I believe that is to making a rounded assessment of his achievement. I know that I am skirting around vast expanses of Yeats territory, his interest in theosophy, magic and the occult, which consumed much of his time and energy, especially during those years when he was active in London's Hermetic Order of the Golden Dawn, even though his literary occultism was invariably 'both radiant and questioning', 'subtle' and 'circumspect'.[18]

I am also steering away from his interest in Indian philosophy, not to mention his theories of history and his complicated love life, through which, in the words of my friend Joe Hassett, 'passionate relationships with women would provide a necessary emotional impetus to poetry'.[19] In doing this, I am guided by something that Sean O'Faolain observed about Yeats when he considered writing his biography:

> I found that W.B. had, in his time, dived down so many caverns of knowledge and as quickly returned, bringing so many pearls with him, that if I were to write about him with any authority of knowledge, I should have to dive down the same caverns, stay much too long and bring back very little – all to write about his voyagings with an assurance about things I could not be interested in for their own sakes.[20]

That captures my position perfectly. O'Faolain, someone whose work I examined in my MA thesis on account of his engagement with what he saw as the 'dreary Eden' of independent Ireland, ultimately decided not to write Yeats's biography. Faced with the same dilemma posed by the encyclopaedic nature of Yeats's life, I resolved to write this one, but on terms that reflect my own knowledge and interests.

## 'Wisdom is a butterfly'

From the time I first came across 'When You Are Old', the phrase about loving 'the pilgrim soul' made a particular impact. I saw it as an invocation of the importance of always being a seeker after wisdom and enlightenment.

The idea of a 'pilgrim soul' seems to me to offer an insight into Yeats's own life. It captures something of his unending search for meaning, of the intense mutability of his life, successively as a dreamy aesthete, an active nationalist, a member of literary societies, a dabbler in occult, magic and spiritualism, the founder of a national theatre, a senator, controversialist and passing admirer of right-wing ideologies. The Yeats pilgrimage that I set out to probe here is what I call, using an Irish word, his *turas*,[21] his lifelong Irish journey.

In India during the early 1980s I received a letter from a woman named Padmini Manchander, offering me some books for sale from her late father's library. Her father, G.K. Chettur, had met Yeats during the 1920s in Oxford, where he had studied history and literature. One of the volumes I acquired from her was Yeats's *Plays for an Irish Theatre*, published in 1912. The book was signed by its author (on 23 July 1920) and inscribed with a verse couplet:

> For wisdom is a butterfly
> And not a gloomy bird of prey.

That volume remains one of my most precious possessions. I have no idea why Yeats chose those lesser-known lines from his vast oeuvre. They come from 'Tom O'Roughley', which first appeared in *The Wild Swans at Coole*. Yeats explained the image of the hawk and the butterfly as symbolising 'the straight road of logic ... and the crooked road of intuition',[22] which was always his personal preference. Perhaps he was trying to give this young Indian student some sage advice. The butterfly is known for moving from flower to flower, collecting nectar and pollen. By contrast, the bird of prey stalks its target and then strikes decisively and definitively. Yeats seems to be saying that the road to wisdom lies in flitting butterfly-like from task to task, just as he did throughout his life. His concern is with life's pilgrimage, the endless search for understanding, rather than its ultimate destination.

Yeats's life brought him into heated engagement in Irish affairs at what turned out to be a seminal era for modern Ireland. The historian F.S.L. Lyons once remarked that 'We in Ireland are all in a sense children of the revolution' of the revolutionary decade 1912–22,[23] which was also a crucial decade in Yeats's evolution as poet and public man. The following chapters dwell on the key staging posts on Yeats's *turas*, his dedicated journey. Much of his life was a kind of secular pilgrimage through the public life of the Ireland of his time. That is why I have chosen to call this book about Yeats's 'indomitable Irishry' *Pilgrim Soul.*

# 2

# 'That sang, to sweeten Ireland's wrong'

## Yeats and the Literary Revival

## To Ireland in the Coming Times

Know, that I would accounted be
True brother of a company
That sang, to sweeten Ireland's wrong,
Ballad and story, rann and song;
Nor be I any less of them,
Because the red-rose-bordered hem
Of her, whose history began
Before God made the angelic clan,
Trails all about the written page.
When Time began to rant and rage
The measure of her flying feet
Made Ireland's heart begin to beat;
And Time bade all his candles flare
To light a measure here and there;
And may the thoughts of Ireland brood
Upon a measured quietude.

Nor may I less be counted one
With Davis, Mangan, Ferguson,
Because, to him who ponders well,
My rhymes more than their rhyming tell
Of things discovered in the deep,
Where only body's laid asleep.
For the elemental creatures go
About my table to and fro,
That hurry from unmeasured mind
To rant and rage in flood and wind;
Yet he who treads in measured ways
May surely barter gaze for gaze.
Man ever journeys on with them
After the red-rose-bordered hem.
Ah, faeries, dancing under the moon,
A Druid land, a Druid tune!

While still I may, I write for you
The love I lived, the dream I knew.
From our birthday, until we die,
Is but the winking of an eye;
And we, our singing and our love,
What measurer Time has lit above,
And all benighted things that go
About my table to and fro,
Are passing on to where may be,
In truth's consuming ecstasy,
No place for love and dream at all;
For God goes by with white footfall.
I cast my heart into my rhymes,
That you, in the dim coming times,
May know how my heart went with them
After the red-rose-bordered hem.


## 'When time began to rant and rage'

'To Ireland in the Coming Times' first appeared in 1892, when what has become known as the Irish Literary Revival was coming into its own, with Yeats as its chief exponent and most energetic advocate.[1] At that time, Yeats was busy developing his craft as an Irish writer while devising and articulating his own distinctive brand of cultural nationalism. As one source has put it, Yeats's 'towering figure' also helped write that era's history, 'establishing a settled narrative of the cultural revival'.[2]

What is meant by cultural nationalism? I see it as representing the idea of Ireland as a separate cultural realm in which the country's distinctive history, language, literature and traditions serve to underpin claims for political independence. Its focus is on national character rather than territory, with Irish culture being seen as a central component of a separate political identity. Neither the parliamentary nationalism championed by Parnell in the 1870s and 80s nor the Fenians of that era had given much attention to the cultural dimension of Irish nationality, although that was part of the legacy of the Young Ireland movement of the 1840s.

The pragmatic parliamentarians and the hard-nosed Fenians had their focus on Home Rule, land reform and political freedom. The new movements that graced the last two decades of the nineteenth century succeeded in making Irish culture a primer of *fin-de-siècle* nationalism. Those movements did not have an explicit political aim, but it was impossible to avoid the wider implications of Ireland's distinctiveness, its separate identity and destiny.

Whatever their objectives might have been, the GAA, the Gaelic League and the Literary Revival were grist to the mill for advanced nationalists, who naturally savoured their unmistakable separatist potential. Vivian Mercier has made the valid point that 'the Anglo-Irish literary revival, which saw itself at first as an alternative to, or even a denial of, politics, helped to foster a new separatist political tradition'.[3]

In 'To Ireland in the Coming Times', Yeats stakes his claim to a place alongside the Young Ireland leader Thomas Davis, poet James Clarence Mangan and poet and antiquarian Sir Samuel Ferguson as writers who had sung 'to sweeten Ireland's wrong'. But the poem also insists that its rhymes will explore 'things discovered in the deep', thus committing its writer to maintaining high artistic standards while serving what he saw as Ireland's need for a national literature of which its people could be proud. And he wants his readers to brood about Ireland with 'a measured quietude', an ambition that would become difficult to sustain as the atmosphere of public life in Ireland grew more impassioned as the twentieth century dawned.

Even if somewhat self-regarding, it was no great exaggeration when Yeats later observed that 'I practically planned and started this whole Irish literary movement'.[4] In those halcyon days, Yeats envisaged a hybrid identity for Ireland with the country's folklore and the lure of the Gaelic past as its inspiration, and the English language as its medium of communication.


## 'Come away, O human child'

With his family background and childhood experience, Yeats might have been expected to follow in the footsteps of Oscar Wilde and George Bernard Shaw and become a mainstream English writer, but he took a very different track. He was not an obvious candidate for a role as Ireland's national poet in the English language, 'the greatest poet since Shakespeare' in the opinion of Michael Longley, or since Milton according to the American critic William York Tindall. Resolving to be an Irish poet was a courageous choice for a young man of conspicuous literary talent, but that is what Yeats did.

William Butler Yeats was born in a house at 6 George's Ville in Sandymount on the southern shores of Dublin Bay on 13 June 1865, not far from Sandymount Castle, home of his great-uncle, Robert Corbet, who had fought against Napoleonic France during the Peninsular Wars at the beginning of the nineteenth century. At one time Corbet was reputed to have been one of the richest men in Dublin,[5] but Yeats grew up in a family that was invariably financially straitened.

Yeats was born into an Ireland that would change beyond recognition during his lifetime. The shifting landscape in Irish affairs, which alarmed many of his family's co-religionists who were devoted to the union with Britain, excited Yeats, who made his own contribution as poetic chronicler of, and participant in, the emergence of modern Ireland. A feature of late nineteenth-century Irish nationalism was its capacity to attract accomplished individuals such as Yeats, Augusta Gregory, Douglas Hyde and Roger Casement, whose backgrounds might have been expected to point them in a different political direction.

Within two years of Yeats's birth, the Fenian movement, which aspired to the creation of an Irish Republic, triggered an unsuccessful uprising. He later recalled being told as a child about the Fenians and of rifles being handed out to local Orangemen for defence against the insurgents. This made him imagine he might in his future life die fighting the Fenians.[6] As it happened, Yeats became some semblance of a Fenian, following, of course, his own idiosyncratic version of that separatist creed.

When Yeats was just four years old the Church of Ireland, the confessional pillar of Anglo-Ireland, was disestablished by an Act of the British Parliament, and in 1870 Gladstone's administration passed a modest land act as part of the Prime Minister's determined effort to pacify Ireland. Over the following four decades a succession of land acts resulted in a gradual transfer of ownership from Anglo-Irish landlords to their largely Catholic, politically nationalist tenants.

Yeats came from a line of Church of Ireland clergy-men on his father's side and merchants on his mother's. Yeats's biographer, Roy Foster, has styled his paternal and maternal lineage as 'two clans quintessentially of the Irish Protestant middle class'.[7] According to Yeats's first biographer, Joseph Hone, 'the Pollexfens were loyal Protestants and active Freemasons, who suspected, and looked down upon, Roman Catholics and Nationalists; yet they too seemed to have an anti-English prejudice ... The attitude was common enough among the Protestant and Unionist minority in the nineteenth century.'[8] Yeats undoubtedly inher-ited a goodly measure of anti-English sentiment that remained with him despite the many years he spent contentedly living in London.

Yeats's father, John Butler Yeats (1839–1922), the son of a Church of Ireland rector, was born in County Down and went on to study at Trinity College Dublin. An impres-sive individual in his own right, John Butler Yeats might have been expected to follow his father and grandfather into religious life, but he became a profound sceptic. As he later explained, 'I came in time to recognise natural law, and then lost all interest in a personal god, which seemed to me merely a myth of the frightened imagina-tion.'[9] Yeats was forever pushing back against his father's secularism, while at the same time being influenced by his rich mind and especially the weighty opinions voiced in his letters from New York, where John Butler Yeats spent the last thirteen years of his life.

Yeats's mother was born Susan Pollexfen and hailed from a Sligo merchant family. Her father, William Pollexfen, arrived there from England in 1832 and married the daughter of the 'old merchant skipper' in Yeats's verse, his Sligo great-grandfather, William Middleton (1770–1832). William Pollexfen went on to become the family patriarch ('the silent and fierce old man' in *Responsibilities*) who loomed over Yeats's childhood days in Sligo. As Yeats later wrote, 'He was never unkind, and I cannot remember that he ever spoke harshly to me, but it was the custom to fear and admire him.'[10]

Susan Pollexfen met her future husband when he visited Sligo to see her brothers, who were his schoolfriends. John Butler Yeats, who was inclined to look askance at his purse-proud in-laws, had his own family ties with Sligo, where his grandfather had been rector at Drumcliff Parish from 1811 to 1846 – 'An ancestor was rector there / Long years ago', as Yeats wrote in 'Under Ben Bulben'.

After graduating from Trinity College, John Butler Yeats took the risky (some would say reckless) decision to abandon the law and move his family to London so that he could pursue his artistic ambition. His career as a painter never reached its potential heights, but it has been said of him that, though he was carelessly inefficient at managing his personal affairs, he had 'an extremely rounded philosophy of life'.[11]

Yeats's early years were spent shuffling back and forth between Dublin, London and Sligo, living at a variety of addresses as part of a family that was always financially stretched due to his father's chronic inability, on account of what Yeats termed his 'infirmity of will', to earn a consistent living, and in which his father and mother were evidently on different wavelengths. His mother, who died in 1900, suffered a debilitating stroke in 1887 and was largely housebound for the last decade of her life.

Yeats's happiest childhood times were spent amidst 'the waters and the wild', during long summers in Sligo, which he came to see as 'more dear than any other place'.[12] As Nicholas Allen wrote, 'the Sligo of Yeats's early imagination is a place of overlapping attachments on the shoulder of Ireland's Atlantic coast, a seaport open to the movement of people ... It was also a gateway to the interior which Yeats ... romanticised as the basis of a folk culture whose beliefs were to be the foundation of the Revival's self-image.'[13] The first poem Yeats wrote that became part of his canon, 'The Stolen Child', published initially in 1886, is replete with Sligo place names familiar to Yeats from his childhood:

> Where dips the rocky headland
> Of Sleuth Wood in the lake ...
> Far off by furthest Rosses
> We foot it all the night ...
> Where the wandering water gushes
> From the hills above Glen-Car,
> In pools among the rushes
> That scarce could bathe a star ...
> We seek for slumbering trout
> And whispering in their ears
> Give them unquiet dreams; ...

Yes, that is a spectacular piece of writing in which Yeats comes across as already a deeply accomplished poet in the late romantic tradition.

Yeats spent the bulk of his childhood in London, being educated at the Godolphin School in Hammersmith, where he was by no means an outstanding pupil. There is a sense in which Yeats was a 'stolen child' spirited away from an idyllic Sligo and forever yearning for it. The Yeats clan may have been the most talented Irish family ever to live in Britain for father, sons and daughters were all artistically gifted – Jack as a painter, Lollie as a printer and Lily as an embroiderer – but their life there was a perpetual struggle to make ends meet.

But for the financial necessity that drove John Butler Yeats to return to Dublin in 1881, when Yeats was sixteen, his son might have grown into a mainstream English poet, his work influenced perhaps by some Irish notes. Instead, he spent a formative six years in Ireland finishing his studies at the High School in Rathgar, where, curiously, he was good at geometry, algebra and botany, and was known as a committed Darwinist,[14] and then at the Metropolitan School of Art. A school contemporary confessed that his fellow pupils had no inkling of 'the embryo genius we barely tolerated in our midst'.[15] His schoolfriend Charles Johnston remembered the youthful Yeats as 'markedly good looking and very talkative'.[16]

At art school he met his lifelong friend George Russell (Æ), who went on to become a major figure in early twentieth-century Ireland as editor for twenty-five years of two influential journals, *The Irish Homestead* and *The Irish Statesman*.

## 'Sing of old Eire and the ancient ways'

Yeats's early verses were often set in Arcadia and India rather than Ireland. His verse play *The Island of Statues: An Arcadian Faery Tale* is a story of shepherds, a shepherdess, a hunter and an enchantress. It was written in the manner of Spenser, Keats and Shelley, and showed no trace of Irish influence.

> The whole world's sadly talking to itself.
> The waves in yonder lake where points my hand
> Beat out their loves lamenting o'er the sand ...[17]

Arcadia and such fanciful realms might easily have continued to be Yeats's favoured locale, and he was fortunate to escape the derivative grip of those 'gracious woodland joys' and to find creative vigour in an embrace of Irish themes as in 'The Madness of King Goll':

> And now I wander in the woods
> When summer gluts the golden bees,
> Or in autumnal solitudes
> Arise the leopard-coloured trees;
> Or when along the wintry strands
> The cormorants shiver on their rocks;
> I wander on, and wave my hands,
> And sing, and shake my heavy locks.

He was correct to advise his first literary ally, Katharine Tynan, to substitute 'the landscapes of nature for the landscapes of art' and to 'make poems on the familiar landscapes we love, not the strange and glittering ones we wonder at'.[18] That is sage counsel for any writer, which recalls for me Declan Kiberd's description of Yeats as 'the greatest poet-critic in the English language since Coleridge'.[19]

Katharine Tynan (1859–1931) was for a number of years his chief correspondent, and he may even have proposed marriage to her, although such a liaison would probably not have worked. Yeats's heterodox religious leanings could scarcely have been at peace with Tynan's devout Catholic faith. The two drifted apart after Tynan's marriage in 1893 to the Dublin-born lawyer, writer and classical scholar, Henry Hinkson. Tynan became an enormously prolific writer, churning out some hundred books, mainly popular fiction.

Yeats confided in Tynan about his desire to build a school of poetry 'founded on Irish myth and History – a neo-romantic movement'.[20] With that in mind, and with an undoubted element of cynicism, he encouraged her to write on Irish subjects because 'by being as Irish as you can you will be the more original and true to yourself and in the long run more interesting even to English readers'.[21] The future, he thought, depended on Ireland 'developing writers who know how to formulate in clear expressions the vague feelings, now abroad'.[22] Yeats certainly took that advice to heart in his own literary career.

In her autobiography, Tynan remembered Yeats as 'a boy, very simple, passionately generous to his friends, absorbed in his art'. She recalled that he had deployed a 'superhuman energy' in sweeping away the whole fabric of what the Young Ireland 'versifiers' had left behind and to rebuild 'the nation's poetry'.[23] She reminisced that the young Yeats would walk five miles in wintry weather to her home in Clondalkin 'so long as he found at the end a fire, a meal, a bed and a talk about poetry'. She remembered him in front of a blazing hearth 'chanting poetry to himself with a slow delight'.[24]

Despite the long stretch of time he spent in London, hardly any of Yeats's poems have a specifically English theme. And while he grappled with what was happening in Ireland, the public life of England seems scarcely to have bothered him. From the time he was twenty, Yeats's 'subject matter became Irish'.[25] This shift of focus was due in large part to an encounter he had in 1885 with the Fenian John O'Leary, who remained an influence on Yeats long after his death in 1907 – indeed, late in life, Yeats would describe himself as a Fenian of the school of John O'Leary. Born in 1830 into a prosperous Tipperary family, O'Leary spent five years in prison for Fenian activities and then sixteen years in exile, mainly in France, before returning to Ireland in January 1885, when he settled in the Dublin suburb of Rathmines with his sister, the poet Ellen O'Leary, and became an iconic figure in Dublin literary and political circles.

Yeats admired O'Leary's 'lofty character'[26] and was impressed with his brand of nationalism, typified by comments like: 'There are things that a man must not do to save a nation' and 'never has there been a cause so bad that it has not been defended by good men for good reasons'.[27] In his *Autobiographies* published in 1915, Yeats offered a fulsome account of O'Leary's importance to him:

> ... from O'Leary's conversation, and from the Irish books he lent or gave me has come all I have set my hand to since. I had begun to know a great deal about the Irish poets who had written in English. I read with excitement books I should find unreadable today, and found romance in lives that had neither wit nor

adventure ... I began to plot and scheme how one might seal with the right image the soft wax before it began to harden. I had noticed that Irish Catholics among whom had been born so many political martyrs had not the good taste, the household courtesy and decency of the Protestant Ireland I had known, yet Protestant Ireland seemed to think of nothing but getting on in the world. I thought we might bring the halves together if we had a literature that made Ireland beautiful in the memory and yet had been freed from provincialism by an exacting criticism, a European pose.[28]

Although written thirty years after the events it describes, that seems a fair summary of what Yeats was attempting to do as he set out on his literary journey: to use literature as a uniting force in a divided society and to combine popular appeal with elevated literary standards. In Yeats's view of things, a high-quality literature could be of real value to Ireland as it made its way towards some measure of self-government, which had seemed a likely prospect in the late 1880s and early 1890s.

In his poem of disenchantment, 'September 1913', Yeats presents O'Leary as an embodiment of 'romantic Ireland' under threat from the allegedly philistine values of Dublin's middle class. As late as 1937, Yeats wrote about 'Beautiful lofty things: O'Leary's noble head'. At a more grounded level, O'Leary was someone Yeats often turned to for a loan of a pound or two to tide him over when the need arose.

## 'With Davis, Mangan, Ferguson'

O'Leary encouraged Yeats to take an interest in the patriotic writers of the Young Ireland tradition. In his autobiography, *Recollections of Fenians and Fenianism*, O'Leary credited the Young Irelander Thomas Davis (1814–1845) with transforming his view of Ireland, 'for all that is Irish in me, and, above all, for the inspiration that made me Irish, the fountain and the origin must always be sought in Davis'.[29]

Although Davis was a much-beloved figure among Irish nationalists, when Yeats asked to be 'numbered' with him as a writer he was being more than a little disingenuous, for he already knew, as did O'Leary, that Davis was not a poet of the first or even second rank. Davis came to be seen by Yeats as 'a potent maker of opinion' rather than a true poet, and he ultimately aspired to a de-Davisisation of Irish writing in order to expunge those mundane patriotic verses that did not meet Yeats's standards.[30]

The title of the first book that bore the unmistakable stamp of the literary revival, *The Poems and Ballads of Young Ireland* (1888), deliberately evoked the memory of the romantic nationalist scribes of the 1840s (who, in addition to Davis, included Oscar Wilde's mother, Lady Jane Wilde, writing under her pen-name, Speranza). Yeats contributed four poems to the collection, including 'The Stolen Child'.

Samuel Ferguson was a more substantial figure than Davis, and Yeats was much taken with his work. He was just twenty-one years old when he published a gushing endorsement of 'The Poetry of Samuel Ferguson'. Yeats's essay begins with a bang:

> In the garden of the world's imagination there are seven great cycles. The seven great cycles of legends

– the Indian; the Homeric; the Charlemagnic; the
Spanish, circling round the Cid; the Arthurian;
the Scandinavian; and the Irish – all differing
one from the other, as the peoples differed who
created them. Every one of these cycles is the voice
celebrating itself, embalming forever what it hated
and loved.[31]

Such imperious authority is wonderfully impressive
from the pen of one so young. It confirms that, while
rightly famed as a poet, Yeats was also a master of prose.
Too bad if you came from a background excluded from
Yeats's imaginary garden, for example the Japanese,
the Chinese and all of Africa, to name just some of the
absentees. His core argument was that the legends of
ancient Ireland were on a par with the great jewels of
global literary history, an important assertion for a
country whose native culture had often been derided
and devalued. Yeats credited Ferguson with bringing
those legends to light for nineteenth-century readers.
Seeing the Gaelic past as an unrivalled source of inspiration for Irish writers, Yeats hoped that others would
follow Ferguson's example and use the materials of the
Irish mythological cycle to 'bring thence living waters
for the healing of the nation, helping us to live the
larger life of the spirit'.[32]

Ferguson, who is now probably best remembered
for his 'Lament for Thomas Davis' (which I recall study-
ing at school in Ireland in the early 1970s), had learned
Irish in Belfast at the Ulster Gaelic Society in the 1830s,[33]
which goes to show that the language had at that time
the capacity to bring people together across the sectarian

divide. Seamus Deane describes Ferguson as someone who sought to forge an alliance between the Catholic and Protestant strands in Irish life. For Ferguson, as Deane views him, this was 'the only alliance which can effectively put a halt to the degradation of the national character by a populist nationalism which would sharpen sectarian strife and a provincial, philistine culture'.[34] While Yeats's politics contrasted with Ferguson's unionism, the younger poet later came to recoil from populist Irish nationalism, turn-of-the-century style, with its scarcely hidden sectarian overtones.

## 'Ballad and story, rann and song'

Yeats saw Irish ballads as 'the poem of the populace', a literary form that had been allowed to die in England but was still a vital element in Irish life. Although he had many reservations about its literary quality, he sought to master the genre, thus aspiring to create a popular literature of high artistic merit. Yeats took the view that, 'Behind Ireland fierce and militant, is Ireland poetic, passionate, remembering, idyllic, fanciful and always patriotic.'[35] His early work contains many ballads, a good example being 'The Ballad of Father O'Hart' (1888), an eighteenth-century priest who:

> In penal days rode out
> To a shoneen who had free lands
> And his own snipe and trout.
> ...
> But Father John went up,
> And Father John went down;

And he wore small holes in his shoes,
And he wore large holes in his gown.

Yeats's mastery of the ballad form came to fruition with one of his best-loved poems, 'The Fiddler of Dooney' (1892):

For the good are always merry,
Save by an evil chance,
And the merry love the fiddle,
And the merry love to dance:

And when the folk there spy me,
They will all come up to me,
With 'Here is the fiddler of Dooney!'
And dance like a wave of the sea.

Yeats's first substantial publication was not a book of poetry but a product of his interest in Irish folk and fairy lore. *Fairy and Folk Tales of the Irish Peasantry* appeared in 1888 with an introduction by the poet explaining the omnipresence of fairies in rural Ireland. The tales from the Irish countryside – about trooping fairies, the banshee, the pooka, ghosts, witches, fairy doctors and so forth – were, he wrote:

full of simplicity and musical occurrences, for they are the literature of a class for whom every incident in the old rut of birth, love, pain and death has cropped up unchanged for centuries: who have steeped everything in the heart: to whom everything is a symbol. They have the spade over which man has leant from the beginning.[36]

Thus, for Yeats, Irish folklore provided access to a bygone

world, the revival of whose values he saw as an antidote to the utilitarian materialism of the late Victorian era.

## 'The woods of Arcady are dead'

With the appearance of *The Wanderings of Oisin and Other Poems* (1889) Yeats became indisputably a poet of substance and boundless promise. In a review of the collection, John Todhunter judged Yeats to have 'the true poet's instinct', with many passages that 'pleasantly haunt the ear and the imagination'.[37]

The collection contained a mix of Arcadian, Indian and Irish-themed poems. It opens with 'The Song of the Happy Shepherd':

> The woods of Arcady are dead,
> And over is their antique joy;
> Of old the world on dreaming fed;
> Grey Truth is now her painted toy;
> Yet still she turns her restless head:
> But O, sick children of the world,
> Of all the many changing things
> In dreary dancing past us whirled,
> To the cracked tune that Chronos sings,
> Words alone are certain good.

Don't get me wrong, that is perfectly fine poetry but there is nothing distinctively Irish about it. With this collection, Yeats's interest in the woods of Arcadia waned. His poetry grew in power and wisdom when he turned to Irish themes. It matured against the background of his often-fractious encounters with the Ireland of his time. In those early days he was aware of the frailties of his poetry, unduly influenced by the pre-Raphaelite movement, and he wanted to develop a hardier style.

The title poem, a thousand lines of verse, tells the story of the Fenian Oisin and his centuries-long sojourn with Niamh in Tír na nÓg, the land of youth. Oisin is in dialogue with St Patrick, who opens the poem:

> *S. Patrick.* You who are bent, and bald, and blind,
> With a heavy heart and a wandering mind,
> Have known three centuries, poets sing,
> Of dalliance with a demon thing.

But it is Oisin and his yearning for his fellow Fenians who thereafter captures most of the poet's attention:

> *Oisin.* Sad to remember, sick with years,
> The swift innumerable spears,
> The horsemen with their floating hair,
> And bowls of barley, honey, and wine,
> Those merry couples dancing in tune,
> And the white body that lay by mine;
> But the tale, though words be lighter than air,
> Must live to be old like the wandering moon.

When Oisin falls from his horse, he meets his fate:

> And my years three hundred fell on me, and I rose,
>     and walked on the earth,
> A creeping old man, full of sleep, with the spittle on
>     his beard never dry.

Of the Irish poems in this collection, only 'The Stolen Child', 'Down by the Salley Gardens' and 'The Meditation of the Old Fisherman' made it into fellow Nobel Prize-winner Seamus Heaney's selection of Yeats's poetry.[38] The latter poem, less familiar than the other two, harks back to Yeats's childhood experiences in the west of Ireland:

> You waves, though you dance by my feet like children
>     at play,
> Though you glow and you glance, though you purr
>     and you dart;
> In the Junes that were warmer than these are, the
>     waves were more gay,
> *When I was a boy with never a crack in my heart.*

## 'One man loved the pilgrim soul in you'

In January 1889 a young woman arrived by carriage at the Yeats's London home at Blenheim Road in Bedford Park. She came with an introduction from John O'Leary. Yeats later wrote about that landmark day:

> I was twenty-three years old when the troubling of my life began. I had heard from time to time in letters from Miss O'Leary, John O'Leary's old sister, of a beautiful girl who had left the society of the Viceregal Court for Dublin nationalism ... I had never thought to see in a living woman so great beauty. It belonged to famous pictures, to poetry, to some legendary past. A complexion like the blossom of apples, and yet the face and body had the beauty of lineaments which Blake calls the highest beauty because it changes least from youth to age, and a stature so great that she seemed of a divine race.[39]

Although I said in the previous chapter that I did not intend to explore the byways of Yeats's love life, an exception has to be made for Maud Gonne because Yeats's infatuation with her and his engagement with Ireland were utterly intertwined. For Yeats she became a mix of the classical beauty, Helen of Troy, and the patriotic Irish symbol, Cathleen ní Houlihan. The daughter of a British Army officer, by the time she met Yeats she had become a committed Irish nationalist.

Gonne quickly became an obsession for Yeats. The lawyer and scholar Joe Hassett has described Yeats's life-long devotion to Gonne as 'the most sustained and fully developed tribute to a Muse in the history of literature in English'.[40] She stood in the way of other relationships, as he was convinced that 'I love the most beautiful woman in the world'[41] and was disinclined to settle for anyone who might be deemed second best. He saw Gonne's politics as his 'one visible rival' for her affections.[42]

Writing to Katharine Tynan, Yeats acknowledged that Gonne was 'very good looking' and professed to admire 'her love of the national idea', even if he pretended not to care for her flamboyance (when that was probably just what attracted him to her).[43] By then, he had already made the first of his many marriage proposals to Gonne, who had inspired 'When You Are Old', Gonne being 'the pilgrim soul' of that beautiful 1891 poem.

In an essay published in July 1892 in the *Boston Pilot*, a newspaper edited by the Fenian John Boyle O'Reilly, Yeats composed a prose rhapsody for Gonne, 'the new Speranza', seeing her as following in the footsteps of the Young Ireland poet who became Lady Wilde, Oscar's mother. For Yeats, Gonne was 'a beautiful woman who makes speeches' of a 'sincere and simple eloquence'.[44] No doubt this essay was meant for Gonne's eyes and designed to impress her. Corresponding with John O'Leary, he offered a less flattering assessment that was clearly not intended to be shared with Gonne, who, Yeats wrote, was 'kindly & well-meaning & ardently Irish but has not a big intellect or anything of that kind'.[45]

One of the many strands in Gonne's character that attracted Yeats was their shared interest in mysticism. Gonne later reminisced about dreams the two shared about building 'a shrine of Irish tradition' in the middle of a lake, where 'only those who had dedicated their lives to Ireland' would be permitted to stay for short periods 'for rest and inspiration'.[46] In the early years of their friendship, she enthused about his poetry, which she saw as 'so wild and fascinatingly Irish'.[47]


## 'His memory is a tall pillar'

Unlike James Joyce, Yeats came from a family that had little regard for Charles Stewart Parnell, who dominated the Irish political universe throughout the 1880s. Indeed, John Butler Yeats blamed Parnell and his followers for the political demise of his predecessor, Isaac Butt, a Yeats family friend. When the Irish party split in 1890 over Parnell's involvement in a divorce case, Yeats supported the Parnellites, as did many others who had advanced nationalist views. He relished the prospect of Irish politics being shaken up by the dispute that pitted Parnell against some of the more conservative elements in Irish society. In December 1890 he told John O'Leary that he found this 'Parnell business ... most exciting.' He hoped that Parnell would hold on, because the controversies exposed 'no end of insincerities'.[48] When Parnell died in 1891, Yeats penned an unspectacular poetic lament, 'Mourn – and then Onward':

> ... there is no returning,
> He guides ye from the tomb;
> His memory is a tall pillar, burning
> Before us in the gloom.

This was not vintage Yeats and, although he thought the poem had been a success when it appeared in a nationalist paper, it never surfaced in any published Yeats collection.

In the wake of Parnell's fall and early death, Yeats was quick to argue that the literary movement could hold out 'the flag of truce to all Nationalists', who could perhaps find peace working together on the cultural front.[49] When Parnell died, Yeats claimed to have been seized 'by the sudden certainty that Ireland was to be like soft wax for years to come'. This revelation was for him 'a moment of supernatural certainty'.[50]

## 'No nationality without literature'

Just two months after Parnell's death, Yeats was busy in London conceiving the Irish Literary Society, an organisation that still exists. Writing in May 1892 as he was about to launch a Dublin-based National Literary Society, Yeats explained the rationale behind his literary activism. 'Ireland,' he insisted, 'is between the upper and nether millstone – between the influence of America and the influence of England.' Those influences were bringing about the denationalisation of Ireland. To resist this push, Ireland needed 'all our central fire, all our nationality'.[51] He added that 'no man who deserts his own literature for another's can hope for the highest rank. The cradles of the greatest writers are rocked among the scenes they are to celebrate.' His imperious conclusion was that 'there is no nationality without literature, no literature without nationality'.[52]

Yeats's assertion about literature and nationality can certainly be contested, but it was at the heart of everything he did during these years as he stretched every sinew in making an exhaustive case for an Irish national literature in the English language. Although undoubtedly more nuanced in his Anglophobia, Yeats's position was not that far removed from that of those who argued for the de-anglicisation of Ireland through a revival of the Irish language and who flocked to join the Gaelic League after it was established in 1893.

The veteran Young Irelander Charles Gavan Duffy became the Irish Literary Society's President on its foundation in 1892. Elected as MP for New Ross in 1852, Duffy had subsequently emigrated to Australia, where he rose to be Premier of Victoria and Speaker of the Victorian Parliament. Duffy returned to Europe in 1880, living mainly in France. A figure from a bygone world, Duffy became a troublesome presence in Yeats's orbit. One of Yeats's goals was to make quality Irish writing available to the reading public. His scheme for publishing a Library of Ireland led him into an arm-wrestle with Duffy about what books should be included in the series. Yeats feared that an Irish library shaped by Duffy risked making Irish literature 'the scullery maid of politics'.

When Yeats discovered that Duffy and T.W. Rolleston were discussing the library project with a London publisher, he complained that the two were 'West British' and 'Whiggish'. By contrast, the young men of Yeats's generation were, he said, 'Parnellites'. In a letter to the *Freeman's Journal*, Yeats argued that Duffy was badly out of touch with contemporary Ireland,[53] which was probably true enough. For all of Yeats's criticism of him, Duffy won the day, but it hardly mattered as the publishing project quickly petered out while Yeats had the consolation of producing volumes that left Duffy's efforts trailing in the dust.

As a young writer making his way in the literary world, Yeats made a living chiefly by contributing essays to British and American journals, in which he argued that a revival of Ireland's ancient traditions could bring forth a new national literature of real consequence. As he put it in his *Autobiographies*, 'we had in Ireland imaginative stories which the uneducated classes knew, and even sang, and might we not make these stories current among the educated classes' and 'so deepen the political passion of the nation that all, artist and poet, craftsman and day labourer, would accept a common design'.[54] That was an ambitious aspiration, easier said than done. Has such an alliance between the artist and the labourer been achieved anywhere in the world?

Ireland's legends were, he believed, 'the mothers of nations' and their 'high companionship' could save Ireland from 'that leprosy of the modern'. He cut loose against 'the shoddy society of "West Britonism"' and was critical of those who were 'servile to English notions'.[55] He looked to the 'young men clustered here and there throughout our land, whom the emotion of Patriotism has lifted into that selfless passion in which heroic deeds are possible and heroic poetry credible'.[56] Thus, even before the emergence of the Gaelic League, Yeats was busy calling for Ireland to turn away from English influences, employing language that anticipated the Anglophobic rhetoric of subsequent Irish Ireland enthusiasts.

Ironically, while Yeats was winding himself up against English influence in Ireland, he was living mostly in London. Although he professed an intense dislike for 'hateful' London, 'where you cannot go five paces without seeing some wretched object broken either by wealth or poverty',[57] he continued to live there. He felt that 'nothing in the world can make amends for the loss of green field and mountain slope & for the tranquil hours of one's own country side'.[58] As a London resident, he became part of various literary coteries, centred round William Morris, Lady Wilde and the Rhymers' Club, which he helped found, and where he is reported to have 'intoned' his verse 'with a musical voice and very haunting cadence'.[59]

## 'Made Ireland's heart begin to beat'

Yeats first met Douglas Hyde in the mid-1880s at Dublin's Contemporary Club, a place where nationalist and Unionist opinions could be debated in an amicable atmosphere. Hyde, who went on to serve as the first President of Ireland (1938–45), became infatuated with the Irish language when he first encountered it among the local people in his home place in County Roscommon, where his father was a Church of Ireland clergyman. Like Yeats, Hyde sought inspiration in Ireland's Gaelic past, which led him to believe in the vital importance of reviving Irish as a spoken language.

Yeats was present at a meeting of the National Literary Society in November 1892 when Hyde delivered one of the most influential speeches in modern Irish history, on the 'Necessity of De-Anglicising Ireland'. The Gaelic League, founded the following year, and which Hyde led until 1915, certainly made Ireland's heart beat more robustly.

Yeats maintained a mixed view of Hyde. In his *Autobiographies*, he commented that Hyde had 'no critical capacity' but that he possessed an 'uncritical folk genius' that no other educated person in Ireland had ever acquired. He conceded that Hyde had created 'a great popular movement, far more important in its practical results than any movement I could have made'.[60] Yeats commended Hyde's speech for 'its learning, its profound sincerity, its passionate conviction'. But he also doubted the viability of reviving the Irish language. Could Ireland not de-Anglicise without setting aside the English language?

'Can we not', Yeats wrote, 'build up a national tradition, a national literature, which will be none the less Irish in spirit from being English in language?'[61] 'Let us,' he pleaded, 'by all means prevent the decay of that tongue where we can, and preserve it as a learned language to be a fountain of nationality in our midst, but let us not base upon it our hopes of nationhood.'[62]

In October 1892 Yeats wrote an important essay on his 'Hopes and Fears for Irish Literature', in which he summed up his dilemma. His life in literary London was lived in the company of his fellow members of the Rhymers' Club, for whom poetry was an end in itself and has 'nothing to do with life, nothing to do with anything but the music of cadence, and beauty of phrase'. He, on the other hand, believed in the dependence of 'all great art and literature upon conviction and the heroic life'.[63]

Comparing the contemporary literature of Ireland and England, Yeats saw the English tradition as an ageing one, while Ireland was 'living in a young age, full of hope and promise'.[64] As he put it, 'We have the limitations of dawn. They have the limitations of sunset.' Ireland had legends and lofty passions to draw on and, 'If,' he wrote, 'we can but take that history and those legends and turn them into dramas, poems, and stories full of the living soul of the present, and make them massive with conviction and profound with reverie, we may deliver that new great utterance for which the world is waiting.'[65] No pressure there!

## 'In the bee-loud glade'

If *The Wanderings of Oisín* (1889) announced Yeats's arrival as a poet of substance and promise, *The Countess Kathleen and Various Legends and Lyrics* (in Yeats's *Collected Poems*, these poems appear under the title of 'The Rose, 1893') provided convincing evidence that he was a major writer. This volume contained 'The Lake Isle of Innisfree' and 'When You Are Old', two poems that are among the best known and most popular in the English language. It also features such moving lines as these from 'To the Rose upon the Rood of Time':

> *Come near, that no more blinded by man's fate,*
> *I find under the boughs of love and hate,*

*In all poor foolish things that live a day,*
*Eternal beauty wandering on her way.*

His infatuation with Maud Gonne was having a real effect on his writing, where:

A pity beyond all telling
Is hid in the heart of love:
The folk who are buying and selling,
The clouds on their journey above,
The cold wet winds ever blowing,
And the shadowy hazel grove
Where mouse-grey waters are flowing,
Threaten the head that I love.

Now that's a sophisticated love poem.

The Irish mythological theme is also taken forward with 'Cuchulain's Fight with the Sea' and 'Fergus and the Druid', where Fergus wants to:

Be no more a king
But learn the dreaming wisdom that is yours.

'Dreaming wisdom' sounds like a good description of Yeats's Celtic twilight poetry.

The collection also included the magnificent 'Who Goes with Fergus', which was James Joyce's favourite Yeats poem to the point where it features in the opening episode of *Ulysses*:

And no more turn aside and brood
Upon love's bitter mystery;
For Fergus rules the brazen cars,
And rules the shadows of the wood,

And the white breast of the dim sea
And all dishevelled wandering stars.

The collection strikes a political note with 'To Ireland in the Coming Times' and 'The Dedication to a Book of Stories selected from the Irish novelists':

There was a green branch hung with many a bell
When her own people ruled this tragic Eire;
And from its murmuring greenness, calm of Faery,
A Druid kindness, on all hearers fell....
Gay bells or sad, they bring you memories
Of half-forgotten innocent old places:
We and our bitterness have left no traces
On Munster grass and Connemara skies.

His fellow member of the Rhymers' Club, Lionel Johnson, purred with enthusiasm about his friend's second collection, lauding Yeats's ability to 'write Celtic poetry, with all the Celtic notes of style and imagination, in a classical manner'. Johnson praised the poems for their 'haunting music' and 'some incommunicable beauty felt in the simplest words and verses'.[66] By means of determined effort, a dash of genius and a bit of friendly logrolling, Yeats was well on his way to Mount Parnassus via its Irish foothills.

In 1893 Yeats published *The Celtic Twilight*, which gave his literary movement its most evocative name. He wrote of a desire 'to show in a vision something of the face of Ireland to any of my own people who care for things of this kind'.[67] Yeats collected the stories in his book from Paddy Flynn from the village of Ballisodare in County Sligo. Flynn was, in Yeats's description, 'a great teller of tales, and unlike our common romancers, knew how to empty heaven, hell, purgatory, fairyland and earth, to people his stories. He did not live in a shrunken world, but knew of no less ample circumstance than did Homer himself.'[68] As he approached the end of his third decade, Yeats was still no Homer, but he was developing Homeric themes of his own carved out of the legacy of the Irish past, its troubled present and his thickening personal journey in love and life.

## 'A Druid land, a Druid tune'

What influence did Yeats's literary nationalism have on the Ireland of that time? Declan Kiberd has written of the Irish renaissance as 'an attempt ... to restore elements of the old Gaelic order'.[69] Yes, through Yeats's work and that of others, the literary revival gave figures from Gaelic mythology like Cuchulain, Oisín, Deirdre, Niamh, Fergus and many others a new lease of life, bringing them vividly to mind for late nineteenth-century readers in Ireland and beyond. Yeats had a particular fascination with Cuchulain, who populates his work from 'Cuchulain's Fight with the Sea' (1892), where he 'fought with the invulnerable tide', to his last work, 'The Death of Cuchulain' (1939). Although it was not all of Yeats's doing, Cuchulain came to be deeply associated with the Easter Rising, to the point where the memorial at Dublin's General Post Office contains an image not of the Rising's leaders but of Cuchulain. As Yeats once asked:

> What stood in the Post Office
> With Pearse and Connolly?
> ...
> Who thought Cuchulain till it seemed
> He stood where they had stood?

...

A statue's there to mark the place,
By Oliver Sheppard done. ('The Death of Cuchulain').

It would be foolish to argue that Yeats's literary nationalism had a paramount influence on the dramatic events of 1916 and their aftermath. The Home Rule Crisis of 1912–14 and the outbreak of World War I were undeniably the prime and immediate movers of the Irish revolution. But events can have more than one root and Yeats was a significant figure in pre-revolutionary Ireland. From almost the beginning of his writing life, he made Ireland his theme, sprinkling around many 'masterful images' of Ireland's heroic past that helped alter the mentality of the Ireland of his time. Revolutions depend on mentalities as well as motives.

What is abundantly clear is that Irish opinion shifted dramatically during Yeats's prime. Up to 1914 Ireland remained enthusiastic about Home Rule, but by 1918 a great number of Irish people were demanding a more complete form of self-government. Much of that change was brought about by 'the facts on the ground' created by the Easter Rising and all that followed it, but mindsets were also reshaped. Part of that reshaping was enabled by the 'stir of thought' that Yeats referenced in his Nobel Prize lecture.

As chief progenitor of the Irish Literary Revival, Yeats contributed to the cultural churn that helped change Ireland in the decades before independence. His literary movement, though it was significantly less influential than the Gaelic League or the GAA, talked up the uniqueness of Ireland's past in a manner that made it inconceivable that such a people could settle for a subordinate political status.

As an advocate of a national literature for Ireland, Yeats provided a poetic strand to the rich late nineteenth-century tapestry that helped reformulate notions of Irish identity. Yeats later explained that the Irish romantic movement's aim was to make Ireland, as she had been in ancient times, 'a holy land to her own people'.[70] Such an aim could not escape having political connotations. It was all part of the country's transformation in the decades that followed the death of Parnell. In his mature output, Yeats went on to chronicle that transformation three decades after he first embraced his destiny as an Irish writer when he was twenty years of age in 1885.

# 3

## 'The noisy set'

### Yeats at the Turn of the Century, 1896–1904

# Adam's Curse

We sat together at one summer's end,
That beautiful mild woman, your close friend,
And you and I, and talked of poetry.
I said, 'A line will take us hours maybe;
Yet if it does not seem a moment's thought,
Our stitching and unstitching has been naught.
Better go down upon your marrow-bones
And scrub a kitchen pavement, or break stones
Like an old pauper, in all kinds of weather;
For to articulate sweet sounds together
Is to work harder than all these, and yet
Be thought an idler by the noisy set
Of bankers, schoolmasters, and clergymen
The martyrs call the world.'

And thereupon
That beautiful mild woman for whose sake
There's many a one shall find out all heartache
On finding that her voice is sweet and low
Replied, 'To be born woman is to know—
Although they do not talk of it at school—
That we must labour to be beautiful.'
I said, 'It's certain there is no fine thing
Since Adam's fall but needs much labouring.
There have been lovers who thought love should be
So much compounded of high courtesy
That they would sigh and quote with learned looks
Precedents out of beautiful old books;
Yet now it seems an idle trade enough.'

We sat grown quiet at the name of love;
We saw the last embers of daylight die,

And in the trembling blue-green of the sky
A moon, worn as if it had been a shell
Washed by time's waters as they rose and fell
About the stars and broke in days and years.

I had a thought for no one's but your ears:
That you were beautiful, and that I strove
To love you in the old high way of love;
That it had all seemed happy, and yet we'd grown
As weary-hearted as that hollow moon.

## 'Washed by time's waters'

In my first book, *A New Day Dawning: A Portrait of Ireland in 1900*, I described Yeats as 'Ireland's turn-of-the-century man', an exponent of an expansive nationalism, 'in tune with the national mood'. 'His politics had a foot in various nationalist camps ... Yet there were already omens of the difficulties that lay ahead for Yeats's ideas of Ireland's destiny.'[1]

Yes, the *fin de siècle* was a time when Yeats began to be washed by the salty waters of what turned out to be a formative era in Irish history. Those years were formative for Yeats too, for whom this was 'a period of unusual self-reflection and remaking'.[2] His engagement with nationalist Ireland reached its peak as the century turned, but he was already being ruffled by the rise of fresh strands of political activism that were more single-minded and thus less accommodating to his esoteric vision of Ireland's future.

Looking back, we can see that there were other contenders for the title of Ireland's 'turn-of-the-century man': Arthur Griffith, who founded Cumann na nGaedheal, a precursor to Sinn Féin, in 1900, edited a new nationalist paper, *The United Irishman*; future Easter Rising leader Patrick Pearse was a rising talent in the Gaelic League when in 1899 he dismissed Yeats as 'a mere English poet of the third or fourth rank', who, for having the cheek to set up an 'Irish' Literary Theatre, ought 'to be crushed';[3] future 1916 leader James Connolly was making headway as a trade union organiser and was active in the pro-Boer movement; and John Redmond was chosen, in 1900, to lead the reunited Irish Party, which finally delivered Home Rule in 1914, before war and insurrection blew it away. Still, despite the later achievements of that quartet, there is a case to be made for Yeats, who was approaching the peak of his powers at that time, as both a writer and a presence in Irish public life.

I am using 'Adam's Curse' from his 1904 collection *In the Seven Woods* to represent Yeats's life at this time because it incorporates two themes that preoccupied him: an emerging frustration with what he saw as 'the noisy set' who were gaining ascendancy in Ireland; and the profound disappointments of his private life. 'Adam's Curse' is a poem of temporal angst and love's longing. It's also a wondrous piece of writing, crammed with memorable lines.

In my opinion, it is the first of Yeats's poems that displays his mature twentieth-century voice. The language has an elegant, conversational tone not found in his nineteenth-century poems. Yeats later wrote that 1900 was the year when 'everybody got down off his stilts'.[4] That was certainly something that he resolved to do. As he told Lady Gregory in 1903, 'My work has got far more masculine. It has more salt in it.'[5] It was indeed a salty time, for Yeats and for Ireland.

In her autobiography Maud Gonne recalled the inspiration behind 'Adam's Curse', an evening Yeats spent with Gonne and her sister, Kathleen, who, in response to a compliment from Yeats, replied that it was hard work being beautiful. The following day Yeats made the latest of his many marriage proposals – 'O Maud, why don't you marry me and give up this tragic struggle and live a peaceful life?' Willie, she replied, 'I will not marry you. You would not be happy with me.'

When he protested, she insisted that he was happy 'because you make beautiful poetry out of what you call your unhappiness ... Poets should never marry. The world should thank me for not marrying you.'[6] Now that is a magnificent way to brush off a marriage proposal, and from the lips of someone who would marry another man just a year later! Yeats, in his thirty-seventh year when he wrote 'Adam's Curse', was exasperated by Maud's deepening commitment to the 'tragic struggle' for Irish freedom, to hurling 'the little streets upon the great' as he wrote in a 1908 poem, 'No Second Troy'.

The poet Padraic Colum has described meeting Yeats around that time. As Colum puts it, he was 'a man of the theatre':

> He had written *The Wind Amongst the Reeds*, and it was known that he was eager to pass from such tremulous kind of poetry to the more public kind that he would have to grapple with in the theatre ... He was preparing himself for a new career – indeed I might say for a new sort of being ... At this time, Yeats was still the

youngish man of the velvet jacket and the flowing tie. To the Catholic intelligentsia ... he was subversive. But that did not recommend him to the other side, the ascendancy side, the side of his father's friend, Professor Dowden ... But the fact that two sides of the Irish public were hostile to him made this thirty-year-old man interesting, and to be interesting, Yeats would probably have said, was the first duty of a public man. And Yeats wanted to be a public man.[7]

That astute assessment was made as Yeats immersed himself in 'theatre business' while also seeking a new literary voice through his plays. In Colum's eyes, Yeats was 'a marked man' in early twentieth-century Dublin.

The American author Horatio Sheafe Krans (1872–1952) wrote a profile on Yeats around the same time, which illustrates the international mark the Literary Revival had made. In Krans's view, Yeats was the 'representative man' of the Revival. As Yeats himself repeatedly did, Krans highlighted the dramatic impact of 'the break-up of Parnell's political ship' in steering that stream of political energy into another channel, where it could 'cultivate the finer elements of the national spirit' and hold fast to 'the noblest traits of Irish life and character'.[8] That is all pure Yeats!

## 'I bring you my passionate rhyme'

As I see it, Yeats's busy turn of the century actually began in 1896. I choose that date because of two women who came into his life, Olivia Shakespear and Augusta Gregory. At the ripe-enough age of thirty, Yeats finally established a home of his own at Woburn Buildings, a 'love-nest' in one cheeky description, to house what turned out to be a year-long relationship with Shakespear, 'a woman of great beauty' and 'incomparable distinction'.[9] Throughout his twenties he had lived with his family at Bedford Park after their return to London in 1887.

Yeats wrote some fine lines about Shakespear: 'She is as high as nature's skill can soar' and:

> You need but lift a pearl-pale hand,
> And bind up your long hair and sigh;
> And all men's hearts must burn and beat; ...

In 'The Lover Mourns for the Loss of Love' he provided an account of the affair's end as his enduring infatuation with the unattainable Maud won out:

> Pale brows, still hands and dim hair,
> I had a beautiful friend
> And dreamed that the old despair
> Would end in love in the end:
> She looked in my heart one day
> And saw your image was there;
> She has gone weeping away.

That reminds me of Paul Simon's song '50 Ways to Leave Your Lover' and, in Yeats's relationship with Shakespear ('white woman with numberless dreams' for whom the stars 'Live but to light your passing feet'), there was an element of the Stephen Stills lyrics in 'Love The One You're With'. Their relationship had staying power and Yeats continued to correspond with Shakespear until her death less than five months before his own.

## 'Traditional sanctity and loveliness'

In the summer of 1896 Yeats began what would become an immensely fruitful 35-year friendship with Lady Augusta Gregory. He was in the west of Ireland with the Symbolist poet Arthur Symons when they were invited to Gregory's home at Coole Park. While Symons took a sharp dislike to their host, Gregory soon became Yeats's most reliable collaborator and confidante. As Symons observed sourly: 'As soon as her terrible eye set upon him, I knew that she would keep him.'[10] But then, Yeats was probably ripe for being kept, and Gregory turned out to be immensely accomplished as a keeper, and was a folkloric finder for him too.

Gregory is up there with Maud Gonne and his wife George as a contender for the tag of the most important woman in Yeats's life (there were other contenders, of course, for Yeats was an amorous man). In a journal entry in 1909, when Gregory was seriously ill, Yeats provided the clearest statement of what she had come to mean to him:

> She has been to me mother, friend, sister and brother.
> I cannot realise the world without her – she brought
> to my wavering thought steadfast nobility. All day the
> thoughts of losing her is like a conflagration in the
> rafters. Friendship is all the house I have.[14]

When the two met, she was the 44-year-old widow of Sir William Gregory, the former colonial Governor of Ceylon, who Augusta Persse had married when her husband was thirty-five years her senior. In her younger years she had been a staunch Unionist, anonymous author of an anti-Home Rule pamphlet, *A Phantom's*

*Pilgrimage or Home Ruin*, but by the time Gregory met Yeats her politics were moving in a nationalist direction and continued to do so, even if she never fully shed her ascendancy values.

In his book about Gregory, novelist Colm Tóibín summed up her ambivalences beautifully: 'And slowly she began to love Ireland also, in the way other nationalists of her time loved Ireland, inventing and discovering a rich past for her, and imagining a great future, and managing to ignore the muddy and guilt-ridden history in between this ancient glory and the time to come.'[12] After her husband's death she devoted herself to the estate at Coole Park, where she lived with her son Robert, who would become the subject of two important Yeats poems, 'In Memory of Major Robert Gregory' and 'An Irish Airman Foresees his Death'. Until his marriage in 1917 Yeats spent long spells in residence at the Gregory home, where he enjoyed the run of the place and came to be seen as an interloper by Robert and his wife. What Yeats found at Coole Park was 'a life of order and of labour, where all outward things were the image of an inward life'.[13]

As one account puts it, at Coole Park Yeats had 'found a *home* for the first time', in which Gregory was some kind of 'surrogate mother' to him.[14] His host clearly doted on Yeats, who enjoyed being the object of her attention. There is no evidence of any sexual relationship between them, although Gregory was not immune to the pull of passion. She had a brief but intense affair with the Irish-American lawyer and patron of the arts John Quinn, and was evidently a compelling personality. The brilliant, hyperactive US President Theodore Roosevelt, not an easy man to win over, was an admirer of her work.

Gregory came into her own in the early twentieth century with two collections of Irish mythological tales, *Cuchulain of Muirthemne* (1902) and *Gods and Fighting Men* (1903), for which Yeats contributed glowing introductions. 'I think this book is the best that has come out of Ireland in my time ... for the stories which it tells are a chief part of Ireland's gift to the imagination of the world – and it tells them perfectly for the first time.'[15] Never one to skimp in praising his friends, he believed that Gregory's book could stand alongside *Morte d'Arthur* and the Welsh epic, the *Mabinogion*.[16]

As an Irish speaker, Gregory also helped Yeats get a better grip on the folklore of rural Ireland. He acknowledged that 'The Stories of Red Hanrahan' were rewritten with Gregory's support, as she had helped him put the 'artificial, elaborate English' he had used in the 1890s into 'that simple English she had learned from her Galway countrymen', so that the thought in his folkloric stories 'had come closer to the life of the people'.[17] Gregory's linguistic achievement became known (and mocked) as Kiltartanese after the district in which she lived ('my countrymen Kiltartan's poor' in 'An Irish Airman Foresees his Death').

## 'A woman Homer sung'

Ireland's political climate began to heat up in the late 1890s, a time when unionists rallied to mark 1897's diamond jubilee of Queen Victoria's coronation and nationalists predictably pushed back against a monarch who Maud Gonne dubbed 'the Famine Queen'. Yeats was present when Maud addressed an anti-Jubilee protest meeting on Dublin's College Green and later attended a rally organised by the future 1916 leader James Connolly.

It is difficult to conceive of the poet who wrote of 'the heavens' embroidered cloths' being in the thick of a demonstration that culminated in a police baton charge resulting in one death and 200 injuries. Yeats and Gonne took refuge in the National Club, where he wisely locked the doors to prevent a fired-up Maud from re-entering the fray. That experience unsettled Yeats, who understandably disliked that kind of situation but knew that Maud was 'the idol of the mob & deserves to be'.[18] The gulf between Gonne's urge towards radical action and Yeats's esoteric literary nationalism was becoming more and more apparent.

Remarkably, Yeats found himself installed as Chairman of the 1798 Centenary Committee, set up by the London branch of the Young Ireland Society, and was back and forth to Dublin trying to iron out differences between the London and Dublin committees. While he professed to finding the whole thing trivial and tiresome, he actually seems to have been excited by it all. George Moore may have been on the money when he suggested that Yeats thought of himself 'briefly, in the role of a leader'.[19]

At a 1798 memorial convention he proposed a resolution declaring, unsurprisingly, the group's 'belief in the right of Ireland to freedom'.[20] During 1898 he participated in various centenary events, delivering some strongly nationalistic speeches extolling that 'high and holy cause' and urging the 'Union of the Gael' based on the 'more intense national feeling' that had arisen in Ireland.[21] Yeats was present in August for the laying of the foundation stone for the Wolfe Tone memorial on St Stephen's Green, which drew a large and enthusiastic crowd, and where Yeats delivered another 'Fenian' speech.

All of this nationalist activity kept him close to Gonne, and she belatedly opened up to him about her relationship with the French nationalist Lucien Millevoye and the children she had with him. Those revelations, and Gonne's insistence that she could never marry him, left Yeats feeling 'like a very battered ship with the masts broken off at the stump'.[22]

Further burnishing his nationalist credentials, he attacked Professor Atkinson of Trinity College for describing all folklore 'as essentially abominable'. Yeats accused Atkinson and his peers of cultivating 'a chuckling cynicism', but predicted the eventual eclipse of their deadening influence and the ascent of those who, like himself, wanted 'to bind rich and poor into one brotherhood'.[23] Yeats had long been critical of Trinity College and its most distinguished academic, his father's friend Edward Dowden, who he saw as 'withering' on the 'barren soil' of Unionist Dublin.[24] Dowden, who was an arch Unionist, had been kind to the young Yeats, who, however, professed himself to have had 'a blind anger against Unionist Ireland' because of its opposition to the Irish literary movement.[25]

His political engagement brought him to the attention of officialdom, and a police report in 1899 described him as 'a literary enthusiast, more or less a revolutionary, and an associate of Dr Mark Ryan'.[26] This grossly underrated his literary prowess and significantly inflated his revolutionary involvement. Ryan, a London-based Irish doctor who was one of the leading Fenians in Britain and thus under perennial police scrutiny, knew Yeats through the Irish Literary Society, and probably swore him in as a member of the Irish Republican Brotherhood (IRB).

Maud Gonne involved Yeats in a madcap scheme to support the Boer cause, for which they received £2,000 from the South African Republics' representative in Brussels. The money was purloined by the eccentric nationalist Frank Hugh O'Donnell, and Yeats and Gonne had to entreat the IRB not to kill O'Donnell. That episode caused both to distance themselves from the IRB. Gonne shifted her allegiance to Arthur Griffith's movement, which later morphed into Sinn Féin. Yeats's political activities caused George Moore to urge Yeats to realise, as Wagner had, 'that his mission was not politics but art'.[27]

## 'Theatre business'

Although Yeats had written plays from early on (the first version of *The Countess Cathleen* was completed in 1892), the idea of establishing an Irish dramatic movement had its origins in a discussion in the summer of 1897 involving Edward Martyn and Gregory. Mayo-born George Moore, already a successful novelist, was recruited to back the new venture. Moore returned to Ireland seeking to kindle what turned out to be a quixotic commitment to his native land, and his main output was a comically mischievous account of his involvement in the Literary Revival in his memoir *Hail and Farewell*, containing unkind depictions of Yeats and Gregory.

The Irish Literary Theatre's aim was to show that 'Ireland is not the home of buffoonery and easy sentiment ... but the home of ancient idealism'.[28] The project,

[79]

which aspired to stand 'outside all the political questions' that divided Ireland, was, therefore, a continuation of Yeats's long-standing bid through literature to revive what he perceived as Ireland's ancient spirit.

The theatre's first season in 1899 featured Yeats's *The Countess Cathleen* and Martyn's Ibsenite play, *The Heather Field*. The project was bathed in controversy from the start. Even before it launched, Martyn, its principal financial backer, got cold feet about Yeats's play, fretting about passages he thought were 'of an uncatholic and heretical nature' destined to 'create scandal'. In the end, sufficient clerical reassurance was secured to mollify his anxious conscience. Martyn subsequently funded the publication of Arthur Griffith's influential tome *The Resurrection of Hungary* (1904) and became the first President of Griffith's Sinn Féin.

As before, Yeats continued to mull over what he saw as Ireland's stellar literary potential. Whereas other countries were moving from their 'moments of miracle', Ireland was just 'passing into hers'.[29] The Irish, he argued, had inherited 'the intellectual traditions of the race that give romance and the kingdom of faery to European literature'. Contrasting the realities of the present with the glories of the Gaelic past, he wrote that: 'Our daily life has fallen among prosaic things and ignoble things, but our dreams remembered the enchanted valleys.'[30] Wonderful stuff that!

His new theatre, he wrote in an American journal, was an elite literary movement that had captured 'a part of the thought of Ireland',[31] but it actually had the opposite effect by galvanising Yeats's opponents. The existence of the Irish Literary Theatre made Yeats's movement a target for those who found his views unorthodox and at variance with mainstream nationalist opinion as it evolved in the early twentieth century.

Yeats hoped the theatre would be 'a wise disturber of the peace', and insisted that 'literature is the principal voice of the conscience, and that it is its duty age after age to affirm its morality against the special moralities of clergymen and churches, and of kings and parliaments and peoples'.[32] It does not take much imagination to figure out how such an attitude would have gone down with more conventionally pious minds!

*The Countess Cathleen* was met with demonstrations on the part of James Joyce's contemporaries at university, in which Joyce, though later a critic of Yeats's 'peasant' plays, took no part. The idea of selling a soul to the devil for gold to fend off starvation offended Catholic sensibilities and was condemned by Cardinal Logue on the strength of a pamphlet written by Frank Hugh O'Donnell.

Lines like these were inevitably provocative to conventional souls:

> What is the good of praying? father says.
> God and the Mother of God have dropped asleep.
> What do they care, he says, though the whole land
> Squeal like a rabbit under a weasel's tooth?

Never one to dodge controversy, Yeats boldly hit back at the cardinal for his 'singular naiveté', which epitomised what Yeats saw as the 'carelessness and indifference' of the older generation in Ireland. Yeats believed that Logue did not represent 'the opinion of the younger and more intellectual Catholics'.[33] I would like to have been a fly on the wall at Ara Coeli in Armagh if and when the cardinal laid eyes on Yeats's broadside against him. It was probably unwise of Yeats to claim that he was better acquainted with the views of his flock than the cardinal was!

This was the first time that Yeats's code of literary nationalism met with real resistance. His contretemps with Gavan Duffy in the early 1890s was a dispute within the literary movement concerning its direction, but at the turn of the century there was real pushback from influential elements possessing different visions of Ireland's destiny.

## No 'daughter of Houlihan'

Queen Victoria's visit to Ireland in April 1900 gave Yeats a further opportunity to air his advanced nationalist views. In the *Freeman's Journal* he alleged that the 81-year-old queen had been sent to Ireland out of 'hatred of our individual national life'. Thus, it was the duty of Irishmen to protest against the visit 'with as much courtesy as is compatible with vigour'. He concluded that 'every Irishman who would not sell his country for an Imperialism that is but materialism, more painted and flaunting than of old, should speak his mind'.[34]

In the conservative *Dublin Daily Express*, he warned that those who cheered the queen would also be cheering an empire that was robbing the Boer Republics of their liberty, just as it had robbed Ireland of its freedom.[35] Pro-Boer views had by that time become a marker of advanced Irish nationalism. Yeats exulted in the fact that his views had made him popular in Ireland, especially with the younger generation.[36] It is no wonder that Douglas Hyde wrote to him a little later, agreeing with Yeats's view that they both had 'the extreme party behind us', by which was meant the Fenian strand in Irish nationalism.

As it turned out, Yeats's friends in 'the extreme party' were not terribly interested in his brand of literary nationalism, and tended to defer to the Church on perceived matters of morality. Religiously heterodox, Yeats, who was being accused of 'neo-paganism' and of 'trying to substitute Cuchullin for Christ',[37] was never going to win over the clergy. Yeats's stated ambition to build up 'a school of spiritual thought in Ireland' was bound to cut across Catholic preferences. Yeats also continued to harbour hopes of allying with Maud Gonne on a Celtic fraternity to be set on a lake island that would become 'the centre of our mystical and literary movement',[38] but, predictably, nothing came of that venture.

The popular songster Percy French, although comparatively apolitical himself, probably reflected Unionist opinion when he had a go at Yeats in a humorous ditty set in the Vice-Regal Lodge, where he has the Queen cut loose:

'And I think, there's a slate,' sez she,
'Off Willie Yeats,' sez she.
'He should be at home,' sez she,
'French polishin' a pome,' sez she
'An not writin' letters,' says she
'About his betters,' sez she,
'Paradin' me crimes,' sez she,
'In the "Irish Times",' sez she.[39]

Despite voicing consistently disloyal sentiments on platforms in Ireland, Yeats was regularly welcomed in the salons of the rich and privileged in London society, and in their country homes. They either didn't know about his political views or they didn't care.

## 'The golden apples of the sun'

In those years before and after the century turned, Yeats did indeed pluck many fine apples from the figurative tree of poetry with two significant collections, *The Wind Among the Reeds* (1899) and *In the Seven Woods* (1904). Those books confirmed his standing as a major poet. Irish mythology and folklore continued to be key reference points, and Sligo the setting in poems such as 'The Hosting of the Sidhe', where:

> The host is riding from Knocknarea
> And over the grave of Clooth-na-Bare;
> Caoilte tossing his burning hair,
> And Niamh calling *Away, come away:* ...

'The Song of Wandering Aengus', a magnificent poem written at Lady Gregory's home, represents in my opinion the peak of Yeats's achievement as a lyric poet of the Literary Revival:

> Though I am old with wandering
> Through hollow lands and hilly lands,
> I will find out where she has gone,
> And kiss her lips and take her hands;
> And walk among long dappled grass,
> And pluck till time and times are done
> The silver apples of the moon,
> The golden apples of the sun.

In 'The Secret Rose', Yeats combines his rose symbolism with Christian and Celtic imagery, and an account of Cuchulain's wife, Emer. And there is a stirring crescendo:

> ... I, too, await
> The hour of thy great wind of love and hate.
> When shall the stars be blown about the sky,
> Like the sparks blown out of a smithy, and die?
> Surely thine hour has come, thy great wind blows,
> Far-off, most secret, and inviolate Rose?

The title poem of *In the Seven Woods* (1904) evokes the woods around Lady Gregory's home at Coole Park, which became his preferred retreat and where he spent more and more time:

> I have heard the pigeons of the Seven Woods
> Make their faint thunder, and the garden bees
> Hum in the lime-tree flowers; and put away
> The unavailing outcries and the old bitterness
> That empty the heart.

That collection also contains the fiery 'Red Hanrahan's Song about Ireland', which was Maud Gonne's favourite of Yeats's poems, no doubt because she knew she was Yeats's model for Cathleen, the daughter of Houlihan, who personified Ireland:

> The wind has bundled up the clouds high over
> Knocknarea,
> And thrown the thunder on the stones for all that
> Maeve can say.

Angers that are like noisy clouds have set our hearts
   abeat;
But we have all bent low and low and kissed the quiet
   feet
Of Cathleen, the daughter of Houlihan.

You can see why Maud was pleased with that poetic, patriotic flourish, a poem that truly fulfilled Yeats's ambition
to sing to 'sweeten Ireland's wrong', but with lines of true
merit. Red Hanrahan, an eighteenth-century poet and
hedge-schoolmaster, was a character in Yeats's occult stories collected as *The Secret Rose* (1897), which he described
as an attempt at 'that aristocratic, esoteric literature,
which has been my chief ambition'.[40] Hanrahan, who
thinks 'but of Ireland and the weight of grief that is on
her', was conceived by Yeats as some combination of the
poet himself and the eighteenth-century Irish language
poet Eoghan Rua Ó Súilleabháin.

## 'Of bankers, schoolmasters and clergymen'

*Ideals in Ireland* (1901), a collection of essays edited by Lady
Gregory, captures the Irish cultural zeitgeist at the turn of
the century. Gregory intended her book to show 'in what
direction thought is moving in Ireland'.[41] Yes, 'thought'
was on the move, but it was setting off in diverse directions. In his essay Æ looked to a new national spirit that
would bring to life 'a thousand dormant energies', while
George Moore argued for the revival of the Irish language,
which he confessed he was too old to learn, and Douglas
Hyde let fly at his alma mater, Trinity College, 'that English
fort' blinded by politics and religious bigotry.

Yeats's contribution conjured up an image of Ireland 'as full of energy as a boiling pot' in which 'national life was finding a new utterance'.[42] Ireland could be in the arts, 'as she is in politics, a voice of the idealism of the common people'.[43] In a postscript to Gregory's book, he saw Ireland's cultural movements as part of 'the quarrel of two traditions of life, one old and noble, one new and ignoble'.[44] In this aversion to commercialism and its attendant vulgarity, he hoped that those with 'Gaelic habits of mind' might one day 'spread a tradition of life that makes neither great wealth nor great poverty, that makes the arts a natural expression of life'.[45]

In terms of the future direction of Irish thought, the most influential of these tracts was probably D.P. Moran's essay 'The Battle of Two Civilisations', a founding document of the Irish Ireland movement of the early twentieth century. When Yeats wrote about a 'noisy set', he may well have had the combative editor of *The Leader* in mind. Moran returned to Dublin from London in 1900 to set up his crusading journal.

Parnell's demise in 1891 had left Moran resentful of England, but also conscious of Ireland's failings, and of the country's seeming inability to do anything to improve its lot. Moran convinced himself that he had unwittingly been a 'West Briton' all his life, and now wanted to expunge that identity, not just for himself, but for Ireland too. The Irish language could be the X factor in reviving Ireland's fortunes, as it was a unique possession in which the Irish could not be overshadowed by their more powerful neighbour.

Moran possessed a suite of avid prejudices, among which was an animus towards the writers of the Literary

Revival, who, he believed, 'lacked every attribute of genius except perseverance'. He cast his brilliantly hostile eye on Yeats's idea of a national literature in English. It was, he wrote, one of 'the most glaring frauds that the credulous Irish people had ever swallowed'. Moran wanted Ireland to be 'original Irish, and not imitation English'.

In attracting Moran's scorn Yeats was in good company, for the pugnacious journalist also dismissed the architects of Grattan's Parliament in the 1780s (long revered by nationalist Ireland) as 'the English who happened to be born in Ireland'. Wolfe Tone, leader of the United Irishmen and lauded to this day as the father of Irish republicanism, was, according to Moran, 'not an Irishman'. Moran's conclusion was that, 'The foundation of Ireland is the Gael, and the Gael must be the element that absorbs.'[46] This was a definition of Irish identity that could not fit with Yeats's view of things.

Yeats tried to meet Moran's concerns halfway when he advocated turning 'from a purely political nationalism with the land question as its lever, to a partly intellectual and historical nationalism like that of Norway with the language question as its lever'.[47] Yeats was willing to accept the idea of the Irish language as a barrier against 'the growing vulgarity of England'.[48] But Moran had no interest in the kind of compromise Yeats envisaged, whereby the revival of the language would happen alongside continued Irish writing in the English language, which, Yeats insisted, must 'for a long time to come be the chief influence in shaping the opinions and the emotions of the leisured class in Ireland'.[49]

Moran continued to insist that no Anglo-Irish poet could speak to the heart of Ireland as Burns had done in

Scotland: 'Even Mr Yeats does not understand us, and he has yet to write even one line that will strike a chord of the Irish heart. He dreams dreams. They may be very beautiful and "Celtic", but they are not ours.'[50] Yeats's letters to Gregory show that he was bruised by these attacks, which he attributed to Moran being a self-taught man 'with no cultivated tradition behind him'.[51] I am not sure about that. Moran, though his views had an unpleasant air to them, was educated at Dublin's Castleknock College, which was probably up there with Yeats's education at London's Godolphin School or Dublin's High School.

George Russell led Yeats to believe that the Jesuits were hostile on account of his mysticism, and that they were behind Moran's repeated attacks on him.[52] *The Irish Independent*, now owned by prominent businessman William Martin Murphy, who would become a *bête noire* for Yeats in the decade that followed, also weighed in with criticism, to which Yeats responded acidly: 'I have listened of late to a kind of thought, to which it was customary to give the name "obscurantism," among some who fought hard for intellectual freedom when we were all a few years younger.' He raised the alarm about a hatred of ideas among 'the more ignorant sort of Gaelic propagandist' and 'the more ignorant sort of priest'.[53] It was now clearly a 'gloves off' moment for Yeats in his battle against his Irish foes.


## 'She had the walk of a queen'

Yeats's nationalism probably peaked in 1902 with the Dublin production of *Cathleen ni Houlihan*. Written in tandem with Lady Gregory, it was the most openly nationalistic work either writer ever produced. Set in 1798, the play depicts a visit to the Gillane family by an old woman on the eve of the wedding of their son, Michael. In an unmistakable allegory of Ireland's experience, she complains that strangers have come and taken her land. She has promises to make to those who join her in expelling the strangers:

> They shall be remembered for ever;
> They shall be alive for ever;
> They shall be speaking for ever;
> The people shall hear them forever.

Michael abandons his wedding plans to follow the old woman, Cathleen ni Houlihan, and join with the French who have landed in the west of Ireland. The old woman then becomes a young girl who 'had the walk of a queen'. The role of Cathleen was played by Maud Gonne. Yeats's father enthused about the play, which he saw as 'an appeal, a challenge, a rousing call to patriotism'.[54] Lady Gregory's one-time lover, the anti-Imperialist writer Wilfred Scawen Blunt, liked it best of all of Yeats's plays. He saw 'in it all the tragedy of Ireland'.[55] Yeats himself was pleased with its success. The hall was crowded for Yeats's play and Æ's *Deirdre*. Yeats gushed to Gregory about how their play had been 'most enthusiastically received' and at how Maud Gonne had played Cathleen 'magnificently and with weird power'.[56]

The writer and politician Stephen Gwynn, who attended the performance, praised Maud Gonne as 'a woman of superb stature and beauty', but 'went home asking myself if such plays should be produced unless one was prepared for people to go out to shoot and be shot'.[57] George Bernard Shaw thought it a play 'which might lead a man to do something foolish', while the Abbey's Lennox Robinson thought it had 'made more rebels in Ireland than a thousand political speeches or a hundred reasoned books'.[58]

In an interview with a London paper in April 1902, Yeats offered a tidy analysis of the Irish political scene. He saw Irish Party leader John Redmond as akin to Daniel O'Connell, while the Gaelic movement and those allied to it like himself were the equivalent of the Young Irelanders of the 1840s. For Yeats, 'the fading romance of parliamentary life' had liberated 'all the other pent-up forces of the nation'.[59] Asked about the aim of the Gaelic movement, he defined it as 'helping to preserve the national character of the people, and to prevent the country from becoming an imitation England',[60] a sentiment that could easily have come from the pen of D.P. Moran.

Yeats offered a measured assessment of Redmond, who, he said, had not touched the imagination of the younger generation but was able to take 'a larger view, a wider outlook'.[61] This proved prescient as, a decade later, Redmond's 'wider outlook' caused him to encourage enlistment for World War I, but he failed to persuade many of the younger Irish generation, who ignored his advice and some of them ended up fighting in the Easter Rising.

## 'For he gave all his heart and lost'
Yeats got the shock of his life in 1903 when Maud Gonne revealed that she was converting to Catholicism and planning to marry John MacBride, a celebrated figure

who had fought on the Boer side in the South African War (1899–1902). In a series of passionate letters, Yeats begged her not to proceed with what he rightly believed would be an unsuitable marriage. If she did so, she would 'fall into a lower order & do great injury to the religion of free souls that is growing up in Ireland' and that might enlighten the world.

Gonne, he insisted, possessed influence in Ireland because she came to the people from above: 'You represent a superior class, a class where people are more independent, have a more beautiful life, a more refined life.' In tune with the lofty attitudes of his later years, he urged her to come back to herself and 'take up again the proud solitary haughty life' that made her 'seem like one of the golden gods'.[62] He wrote that calling off her marriage was 'perhaps the last thing I shall ever ask of you'. It was not. There were subsequent marriage proposals and continued poetic tributes. On this occasion, the appeal not to betray her own soul fell on deaf ears and Gonne married MacBride in Paris on 21 February 1903.

Yeats was now more and more inclined to see himself as part of a 'small sect' of 'cultivated people' that would perennially struggle to be popular. Yet, he wanted Irish people 'to think of Ireland as a sacred land'.[63] It was, he believed, necessary 'in a country like Ireland to be continually asserting one's freedom if one is not to lose it altogether'.[64] Within a few months of her marriage Gonne was dining with Yeats in London, admitting that she had wed 'in a sudden impulse of anger'. When he asked her if she was happy, she replied that she was 'capable of neither happiness nor unhappiness',[65] which does not sound like a perfect state of mind for a newlywed!

## 'New commonness on the throne'

Yeats was no fan of royal visits, with 'their appeal to all that is superficial and trivial in society', calling them 'part of the hypnotic illusion by which England seeks to keep captive the imagination of this country'.[66] Just as he had done with Queen Victoria in 1900, he spoke out against the 1903 visit to Ireland of Edward VII. He co-signed a strident letter stating that no one who valued 'national dignity or honour' could participate in welcoming the King of England, representing as he did 'the power responsible for all our evils'.[67]

In reply to suggestions that the Wyndham Land Act had been passed to coincide with the royal visit, he insisted that it had been 'won by the long labours of our own people',[68] which was certainly a valid point. Unable to resist the opportunity, in a letter to Arthur Griffith's *United Irishman* he jibed at the Catholic hierarchy for decorating a reception room at Maynooth in the King's racing colours. With tongue firmly in cheek, he suggested that parishes hosting race meetings would henceforth be the most sought after by ambitious priests. He laid a sarcastic ambush for Ireland's two leading Catholic churchmen when he expressed the hope that Cardinal Logue would have 'something' on Sceptre and that Archbishop Walsh had 'a little bit of all right' for the Chester Cup. James Joyce took up this story in the 'Cyclops' episode of *Ulysses*, which makes me believe that he may have seen Yeats's 1903 broadside.[69] It was not just the king's Irish visit that irked Yeats. He had no time for the new occupants of Buckingham Palace, hence the reference in his verse to 'new commonness on the throne'.

## 'All that delirium of the brave'

Yeats was on a visit to the United States in 1904 when he delivered one of his most full-throated endorsements of Ireland's national cause. The occasion was a commemoration of the patriotic death of Robert Emmet, whose execution in 1803 following his failed rebellion gave him saint-like status among Irish nationalists, especially in America, where I know of three memorials devoted to his memory. Yeats spoke on 28 February 1904 at New York's Academy of Music, where an attendance reported to number 4,000 gathered to hear him laud the fallen Irish hero.

We know from a letter Yeats wrote to Lady Gregory that his heart was not wholly seized with patriotic fervour. He confessed that he had completely thought himself out 'of the whole stream of traditional Irish feelings on such subjects. I am just as strenuous a nationalist as ever, but I have got to express these things all differently.'[70] His audience would never have suspected that he had such hesitations as he treated them to a full fusillade of his strenuous nationalism. Ireland, he said, had placed Emmet 'foremost among her saints of nationality', because he had shown 'that there was something in Ireland which not all the wealth of the world could purchase'.[71]

Emmet, who had gone to his death 'in a kind of ecstasy of self-sacrifice', had hoped to give Ireland 'a victorious life', but he had given her instead 'what was almost as good – his heroic death'.[72] Patrick Pearse, speaking more than a decade later at the Dublin funeral of O'Donovan Rossa, where he made his name as an orator, would have been pleased to have come up with such a rhetorical crowd-pleaser. Yeats's Irish-American audience, 'the cream of the Irish race in New York', lapped up this patriotic feast. The welcome Yeats received would, it was predicted, 'tingle pleasantly in his ears as long as he lives'.[73]

Reflecting the Fenian disregard for constitutional politics, he observed that a successful politician, Daniel O'Connell, had secured a few laws, but that the 'unsuccessful' Emmet had given Ireland patriots. Even Parnell's achievements had, he said, come at 'a very great price' by 'putting aside everything to attain her one political end'.[74] The new spirit gripping the country, of which he was part, had made 'Irish intellect occupy itself with Ireland'.[75] The Gaelic League had become 'a great moral power'. This 'unconquerable energy' would ultimately prevail in Ireland, and 'its music will fill the world'.[76] Such buoyant sentiments must have pleased his Irish-American audience no end. Anyone listening to him, or reading what he had to say, would be justified in viewing him as a thoroughgoing Irish nationalist of the advanced, Fenian school.

## 'Where men plow and sow and reap'

Until about the middle of the twentieth century's first decade, Yeats maintained a classic late-romantic view of Ireland, seeing it as an oasis of traditional values in an increasingly materialistic world. As he put it in 1903:

> What is this nationality we are trying to preserve, this thing that we are fighting English influence to preserve? ... If you examine to the root a contest between two peoples, two nations, you will always find that it is really a war between two civilizations, two ideals of life. ... Ireland will always be in the main an agricultural country. Industries we may have, but

we will not have, as England has, a very rich class nor whole districts blackened with smoke ... I think that the best ideal for our people ... is that Ireland is going to become a country where, if there are few rich, there shall be nobody very poor ... Ireland will always be a country where men plow and sow and reap ... We wish to preserve an ancient ideal of life.[77]

That bucolic vision of Ireland bears considerable resemblance to the most famous piece of political rhetoric from post-independence Ireland, the then Taoiseach Éamon de Valera's oft-quoted speech delivered on St Patrick's Day 1943, in which he conjured up the:

Ireland which we dreamed of ... the home of a people who valued material wealth only as a basis for right living, of a people who were satisfied with frugal comfort and devoted their leisure to the things of the spirit; a land whose countryside would be bright with cosy homesteads ... the laughter of comely maidens; whose firesides would be the forums of the wisdom of serene old age.[78]

This comparison illustrates how deeply Yeats had imbibed a heady turn-of-the-century cocktail of late romanticism, Celtic mysticism and nationalist political idealism, which Éamon de Valera still embodied four decades later in a very different national and international context. The years between 1896 and 1904 were important ones for Yeats and for Ireland. The poet of the Literary Revival began to shift ground in order to become, in time, a potent twentieth-century poetic voice.

All the while, his view of Ireland was evolving, becoming more sceptical. Irish nationalism was on the move during these years, with new ideas emerging to contest the space that the Irish Party had hitherto monopolised. Maud Gonne parted company with Yeats's literary movement, explaining that she did not have time 'for purely literary & artistic movements unless they can be made to serve directly and immediately the National cause'.[79] Yeats could not meet that criterion and that was the nub of his dilemma. He was part of a struggle for what he saw as the soul of Ireland, a contest he was ill-placed to win, but it was important for him, and for Ireland, that he stayed on the field.

In May 1903 Yeats explained to John Quinn that he was now inclined to look upon the world with 'somewhat more defiant eyes'. His defiance would become ever more pronounced as the Ireland of his time became more resistant to his ambitions for it, leading Yeats, a decade later, to pronounce the demise of romantic Ireland. That strange death of the Ireland of his dreams is the next staging post on Yeats's contentious, circuitous Irish journey.

# 4

## 'For men were born to pray and save'

### The Strange Death of Romantic Ireland

## September 1913

What need you, being come to sense,
But fumble in a greasy till
And add the halfpence to the pence
And prayer to shivering prayer, until
You have dried the marrow from the bone;
For men were born to pray and save:
Romantic Ireland's dead and gone,
It's with O'Leary in the grave.

Yet they were of a different kind,
The names that stilled your childish play,
They have gone about the world like wind,
But little time had they to pray
For whom the hangman's rope was spun,
And what, God help us, could they save?
Romantic Ireland's dead and gone,
It's with O'Leary in the grave.

Was it for this the wild geese spread
The grey wing upon every tide;
For this that all that blood was shed,
For this Edward Fitzgerald died,
And Robert Emmet and Wolfe Tone,
All that delirium of the brave?
Romantic Ireland's dead and gone,
It's with O'Leary in the grave.

Yet could we turn the years again,
And call those exiles as they were
In all their loneliness and pain,
You'd cry, 'Some woman's yellow hair
Has maddened every mother's son':

They weighed so lightly what they gave.
But let them be, they're dead and gone,
They're with O'Leary in the grave.


## 'You are safer in the tomb'

Yeats's poem 'September 1913', in which he declared 'romantic Ireland' to be 'dead and gone', has always intrigued me on account of its acerbic view of early twen-tieth-century Ireland, a time in Irish history to which I have long been drawn.[1] When I was posted to Berlin in 2009 as Ireland's Ambassador to Germany, the death of 'Celtic Tiger' Ireland was being widely and loudly pro-claimed. At that time of strife for the Irish economy in the wake of the global financial crisis, the Embassy declared 'A Year of Yeats' in 2011, seeing this as a way of deploying the lure of Irish literature in order to push back against the bad economic news emanating from Ireland that was in danger of shifting German attitudes towards Ireland in a decidedly negative direction.

That year I travelled to a number of German univer-sities to speak about our premier national poet and took the liberty of comparing him with Germany's Goethe in terms of his national significance in an Irish context. One of the talks I gave that year, inspired by 'September 1913', was entitled 'The Strange Death of Romantic Ireland',[2] which recounted the poet's increasingly disillusioned engagement with Ireland between 1905 and 1913.

Yeats certainly believed that something had been irretrievably lost during those years. 'The seeming needs of my fool-driven land' came to feel increasingly burden-some to him. Ten years before he composed 'September

1913', Yeats was basking in the renown of having written an inspirational nationalist play, *Cathleen ni Houlihan*, and was in the thick of preparations for the founding of the Abbey Theatre, one of his most enduring contributions to his country's cultural life.

What had gone so badly wrong? How had this 'Romantic Ireland' come to grief? And what was responsible for its demise? These are questions that a reader of 'September 1913' might validly ask. In search of answers, we need to turn the clock back to the last days of 1904 and Yeats's deepening immersion in 'theatre business'.

## 'The fascination of what's difficult'

The key to the emergence of the Abbey Theatre had been the arrival of a benefactor in the person of Annie Horniman (1860–1937), who Yeats had met through his involvement in the Hermetic Order of the Golden Dawn. Horniman was the daughter of a leading tea merchant and was also close to the actress Florence Farr, who performed in Yeats's *The Countess Cathleen* in Dublin in 1899, besides being one of Yeats's 'muses'.[3] At a cost of £3,000, Horniman purchased and refurbished the Mechanics' Institute on Abbey Street to turn it into a theatre. She remained a supporter of the Abbey until 1910, by which time she had invested more than £10,000 in the project.

The new theatre opened on 27 December 1904 with a triple bill headed by Yeats's *On Baile's Strand*, a play about Cuchulainn and the King of Ulster, Conchobar mac Nessa, which sustains his obsession with mythological Ireland's champion slayer:

Cuchulain has killed kings,
Kings and the sons of kings,
Dragons out of the water,
And witches out of the air ...

Gregory's *Spreading the News* was also performed alongside that guaranteed crowd-pleaser, *Cathleen ni Houlihan*.
In the years that followed, the Abbey demanded such
enduring attention that Yeats had cause to express:

My curse on plays
That have to be set up in fifty ways,
On the day's war on every knave and dolt,
Theatre business, management of men.

Yeats's creative energies were now devoted more to play-
writing than to poetry, where his true genius lay. Indeed,
he appears to have written little verse in the early Abbey
years, when his many chores there preoccupied him.
Maud Gonne may have been right when she appealed to
him not to allow involvement with the Abbey to distract
him from poetry, which was of 'far more value to Ireland
than the theatre'.[4] That may be unfair to Yeats's plays,
but none of them is essential reading. Yeats without his
impressive output of writing for the stage would still be
Yeats – with a reputation undiminished by their absence
from his portfolio. On the other hand, it is clear that
his experiences at the Abbey affected the way he wrote
poetry, with the birth of a more robust, argumentative
style. As T.S. Eliot recognised: 'It is impossible to disen-
tangle what he did for the Irish theatre from what the
Irish theatre did for him.'[5] Looking back in 1939 at his

life as a playwright, Yeats insisted that he had wanted the stage 'to become still so that words might keep all their vividness – and I wanted vivid words'.[6] There were plenty of vivid words in his later works.

His theatrical commitments clearly frustrated him, but it seems that much of the problem stemmed from his own domineering personality and his desire to completely control the new venture. Influenced by his reading of Nietzsche, he believed that 'strength shapes about itself' and that 'compromise is weakness'.[7] While the Abbey's predecessor, the Irish National Theatre Society, was run as an amateur company, Yeats wanted a truly professional theatre.

As he saw it, this meant concentrating authority in the hands of himself, Gregory and John Millington Synge. That naturally offended those who were happy with the original arrangements, and meant that there were a number of contentious departures from the new company. Yeats was unpopular with those who worked at the Abbey. That obsessive Dublin theatregoer Joseph Holloway described him as an 'irritating' producer, forever 'flitting about', interrupting the actors and always 'on the fidgets'.[8] Even his sister, Lollie, complained that 'he could never see any side of anything but his own'.[9]

George Russell (Æ) was exasperated by Yeats's behaviour, warning him that 'you have few or no friends in Dublin'. Yeats knew that there was an atmosphere of 'intense hostility' towards him, but he seemed unbothered, even buoyed, by it.[10] 'Irish people,' Æ wrote, 'will only be led by their affections.' He advised Yeats that Gaelic Leaguers, who were growing in influence, had no time for him. Æ believed that Yeats aspired to be an 'autocrat in literary, dramatic and artistic matters', but would eventually learn that 'a man with no friends and many enemies may for all his genius have less influence on his time than some person of one half his abilities'.[11] That was undoubtedly wise counsel from a sympathetic if exasperated admirer of Yeats's work, who loved his poetry but was alienated by his antagonistic personality.

Yeats brushed off Æ's complaints, telling him with a show of blithe arrogance that, 'I desire the love of a very few people, my equals or superiors. The love of the rest of the world would be a bond and an intrusion ... It is a long fight but that is the sport of it.'[12] In such a truculent mood, he was disinclined to listen to anyone, especially someone with Æ's more democratic, collegial instincts in life and literature.

In Yeats's journal, Æ is described as 'a man of genius' who was crippled intellectually by his egalitarian ethos. Æ had 'all the fanaticism of the religious reformer' and was a purveyor of 'dreams for the future that perish in conversation'. In his circle, 'A luxurious dreaming kind of spiritual lubricity takes the place of logic and will'.[13] Thus speaks a Nietzschean Yeats!

Boosted by the successful launch of the Abbey, an optimistic Yeats believed that a 'great dramatic school' was in the making, as indeed it was. At the Abbey, Yeats believed that they had 'pleased and affronted all in succession',[14] and that was certainly true. The theatre survived, but controversy was never far from its door. As he had a habit of doing, he sensed that 'the country is in its first plastic state and takes the mark of every strong finger'.[15]

There may indeed have been an element of plasticity about early twentieth-century Ireland, but it would prove hard to shape and would need more than a strong poetic finger, or even a Nietzschean one, to do the job. Important elements in nationalist Ireland started to bare their teeth in opposition to Yeats's ambitions for the country's future, 'the dream of my early manhood', as he wrote in his *Autobiographies*, 'that a modern nation can return to Unity of Culture',[16] but that was not to be the direction of travel for Ireland in the opening half of the twentieth century.

## 'Between the proud and the proud'

As always in Yeats's life, Maud Gonne featured strongly in his decade of disenchantment. Maud's marriage to John MacBride, never in good shape, began to fall apart in 1905, just two years after the couple were wed. As nationalist Ireland, including Yeats's first political/literary mentor, John O'Leary, sided with her husband, Yeats became Maud's chief ally and adviser at a time of great adversity for her.

Gonne's sister, Kathleen, told Yeats of the very serious allegations Maud had made against her husband, who, in Yeats's biased estimation, was 'a half insane brute' and 'the essence of all the cads of all ages'. Yeats would have his say about MacBride in verse in 'Easter 1916', where that 'drunken vainglorious lout' was among those seen to be 'transformed utterly' by the 'terrible beauty' of the Easter Rising. Maud, Yeats reported to Lady Gregory, was 'utterly crushed and humiliated'[17] by what had happened to her.

Yeats was rightly appalled at the view of Parnell's biographer, Barry O'Brien, that Maud should, as might be said in today's parlance, 'take one for the team' so that the

MacBride legend in nationalist Ireland could 'keep its lustre'.[18] Arthur Griffith was another who, having been an ally
of Gonne's in the pro-Boer movement at the turn of the
century, now took the part of her husband. Griffith had
been jailed a few years earlier for horsewhipping a Dublin
society magazine editor who had attacked Gonne in print.

The couple's dispute went through the courts in
France and, after searing accusations against MacBride
of grossly improper conduct, the marriage ended in
August 1906 in a legal separation. Nationalist Ireland
was inclined to blame Maud, and she was hissed at in the
Abbey Theatre when she turned up there chaperoned
by Yeats. What Yeats saw as Gonne's harsh treatment by
Griffith and his allies furthered his estrangement from
advanced Irish nationalism in its early twentieth-century guise. In 'Against Unworthy Praise' he mused about
Gonne's fall from grace within nationalist Ireland, 'the
labyrinth of her days':

> And how what her dreaming gave
> Earned slander, ingratitude,
> From self-same dolt and knave;
> Aye, and worse wrong than these.
> Yet she, singing upon her road,
> Half lion, half child, is at peace.

### 'Because we have made our art out of common things'

Arthur Griffith's Sinn Féin, founded in 1905, brought a
new dimension to nationalist politics although prior to
1916 it posed no threat to the ascendancy of the Irish

Party, led by John Redmond. In *Ulysses* Leopold Bloom sees Griffith as a coming man, although his wife, Molly, is characteristically sceptical. Joyce has one of his characters cheekily suggest that his fictional Leopold Bloom had suggested to Griffith the idea behind *The Resurrection of Hungary* that gave birth to Sinn Féin. Like Bloom in Joyce's novel, Griffith favoured a pragmatic approach to Ireland's national struggle, urging Irish parliamentarians to withdraw from Westminster and establish a breakaway assembly in Ireland.

Griffith had defended Yeats in the controversy surrounding his play *The Countess Cathleen* when it was first performed in 1899, but criticised Synge's *In the Shadow of the Glen* in 1903, as did Maud Gonne, who thought it 'horrid' and resigned from the Irish National Theatre Society as a result.[19] Griffith was on the attack again when Synge's play was revived by the Abbey in 1905, a year that also saw the production of Synge's latest offering, *The Well of the Saints*.

In a move that would become a habit, Yeats sprang to Synge's defence. All great writers, Yeats wrote, deployed 'abundant, resonant, beautiful, laughing living speech'. Synge had in common with the great dramatists 'a delight in language, a preoccupation with individual life'.[20] He recalled meeting Synge in Paris and urging him to 'Go to the Aran Islands' and from living among the people 'express a life that has never found expression'.[21]

The trouble was that there were those like Griffith who did not recognise the west of Ireland life that Synge presented so vividly in his plays, and were hostile to its depiction on the Dublin stage. Griffith wanted literature to serve Ireland's core political objective, but Yeats could never countenance such a limited role for Irish writing.

The Abbey Theatre's premiere of Synge's *The Playboy of the Western World* on 26 January 1907 was marred by a riot when, in the words of a telegram Yeats received from Gregory the following morning, 'Audience broke up in disorder at the word shift', an undergarment whose use on the Abbey stage was seen, Yeats observed, as 'a slander upon Ireland's womanhood'.[22]

The idealisation of rural life is not unusual in nationalist ideologies. Think of America's cult of the hardy pioneers and cowboys who won the west as part of the country's 'manifest destiny', and of the post-Civil War idealisation of the rural life of the antebellum South as part of the 'Lost Cause' narrative. The reality was at odds with the myth, but such myths often gain a tenacious hold on the public mind.

Joseph Holloway probably captured the response of many middle-class Dubliners when he observed that *The Playboy* was 'not a truthful or just picture' of the people of rural Ireland, but he probably went a bit over the top in describing it as the product of a morbid mind 'seeking on the dunghill of life for the nastiness that lies concealed there'. Synge, he wrote, was 'the evil genius of the Abbey, and Yeats his able lieutenant'.[23]

For Griffith, *The Playboy* was simply a tale of 'unnatural murder and unnatural lust, told in foul language'.[24] Maud approved of the protestors, 'earnest young fellows' who 'feel proud that they have suffered for the national cause'. She thought their action in disrupting the performances of *The Playboy* 'a healthy thing'.[25]

Yeats was on a lecture tour of Scotland when Synge's play premiered, but rushed back to confront its detractors. He took to the Abbey stage brandishing his advanced nationalist credentials as the author of *Cathleen ni Houlihan* and president of the 1798 Centenary Committee, but his appeals fell on deaf ears. In a subsequent debate about *The Playboy*, he made the case for freedom of artistic expression, insisting that 'the moment a writer is forbidden to show the weed without the flower, his art loses energy and abundance'.

With a characteristic Yeatsian flourish, he proclaimed that: 'The quarrel of our Theatre today is the quarrel of the Theatre in many lands; for the old Puritanism, the old bourgeois dislike of power and reality have not changed, even when they are called by some Gaelic name.'[26] His father, John Butler Yeats, rallied to the cause in a scene his son later captured in verse:

> My father upon the Abbey stage, before him a raging
>    crowd:
> 'This Land of Saints,' and then as the applause died
>    out,
> 'Of plaster Saints'; his beautiful mischievous head
>    thrown back.

Stirring stuff, but not likely to win over any uncommitted Dubliners!

The future literary critic Mary Colum was in the audience for Yeats's defence of Synge. 'I never witnessed,' she wrote, 'a human being fight as Yeats fought that night, nor knew another with so many weapons in his armoury.'[27] But it was to no avail; the odds were stacked against him. Conor Cruise O'Brien, who saw it as 'an act of high courage' for Yeats to stage *The Playboy*, believed that D.P. Moran of *The Leader* had helped organise the demonstrations in the Abbey Theatre.

O'Brien's view was that Moran, a quintessential Catholic nationalist, had been lying in wait for Yeats for years and that *The Playboy* offered him an opportunity to go for the jugular.[28] Yeats probably shared that view. In his essay on 'Synge and the Ireland of his Time' he complained that 'patriotic journalism' had 'prepared for this hour'. The attacks on Synge were, he thought, hypocritical, a 'defence of virtue by those who have but little'.

As performances of *The Playboy* continued to be disrupted, Yeats called in the police to restore order and, predictably, was sharply criticised for using forces under the control of the British government to silence a supposedly nationalist protest. There is a sense in which Yeats relished the fight against Catholic nationalism, with its, as he saw it, unromantic vision of Ireland's future. He resented the fact that Ireland was now being asked 'to obey the demands of commonplace or ignorant people ... imposing some crude shibboleth'.[29]

It had, he wrote to John Quinn, been 'for some time inevitable that the intellectual element here in Dublin should fall out with the more brainless patriotic force', represented by 'obscure members of the Gaelic League'.[30] Those patriotic forces, and their 'obscure' foot soldiers, turned out to be stronger and more resilient than Yeats might have imagined.

Yeats was hit hard by the rejection of *The Playboy* and Synge's early death two years later. Synge was, in Yeats's view, 'a drifting silent man full of hidden passion' who loved wild islands because he saw there 'what lay hidden in himself'.[31] With great foresight, he correctly predicted that *The Playboy*, 'the strangest, the most beautiful expression in drama of ... the unbroken character of Irish genius', would come to be loved 'for holding so much of the mind of Ireland'. Yes, Synge's work is still part of the Irish dramatic repertoire. (Some years ago at the Edinburgh International Festival, I attended a performance of all of Synge's plays in the course of a memorable, if stamina-sapping, afternoon and evening.)

The controversy over *The Playboy* was an important turning point in Yeats's engagement with Ireland as 'that rooted man' with 'a deep grave face' entered his personal pantheon, even though the two had not always seen eye to eye. As Yeats wrote much later:

> John Synge, I and Augusta Gregory, thought
> All that we did, all that we said or sang
> Must come from contact with the soil, from that
> Contact everything Antaeus-like grew strong.
> We three alone in modern times had brought
> Everything down to that sole test again,
> Dream of the noble and the beggarman.

In the hostile response to Synge's work, Yeats saw 'the dissolution of a school of patriotism that held sway over my youth'[32] and thus an emblem of the demise of 'Romantic Ireland'. In his poem 'On those that hated The Playboy of the Western World, 1907', he compares Synge with 'the great Juan riding by' and his detractors to Eunuchs 'staring upon his sinewy thigh'.

## 'But here's a haughtier text'

Yeats's private 'journal' from around the time of Synge's death offers bleak, uncomfortable insights into his state of mind. Its editor has described many of its entries as 'tetchy', the day's events 'marked up for venom' by a poet who 'found it hard to be patient with Dublin'.[33] A lot of what's there prefigures the patrician attitudes of his later years, and is deeply condescending and even sectarian. The 'new class rising in Ireland' (essentially a Catholic middle class) was, he believed, 'ill-bred in manner' and exhibited 'ill-breeding of the mind'.[34]

This charge of ill-breeding runs through the journal alongside the notion that humanity's more admirable qualities are all inherited. Throughout this text his bogeyman is 'politics', which he sees as having cheapened everything touched by it. From believing in his younger years that writing of a high artistic standard could serve to 'sweeten Ireland's wrong', he now considered that 'even the highest political motives will not make an artist'.[35] Yet in the decade that followed he continued to engage himself in Irish politics, as scribe, senator and commentator.

Many of Yeats's journal entries exude a profound anti-Catholic bias. They reveal a particular animus towards Catholic education, which he blamed for the 'lack of the moral element in Irish public life'. All of those who had ennobled Irish politics – Grattan, Davis and Parnell – were from the Protestant community, while the one great Catholic figure, Daniel O'Connell, 'had the gifts of the market place, of the clown at the fair'.[36] Now that kind of thing, chest-deep in bigotry, is well-nigh unpardonable. Here's a final flourish from his journal:

> The whole system of Irish Catholicism pulls down the able and well-born if it pulls up the peasant, as I think

it does. A long continuity of culture like that at Coole (Lady Gregory's home) could not have arisen, and never has arisen, in a single Catholic family in Ireland since the Middle Ages.

I wonder why? An Irish nationalist would undoubtedly argue that the absence of a 'continuity of culture' in Catholic Ireland was due not to any innate incapacity but to an oppressive polity that made such achievements impossible.


### 'Pensioner Yeats'

His growing disenchantment notwithstanding, Yeats looked to protect his credibility in nationalist Ireland and was careful to avoid any public association with the British administration there. In 1909, after the damage done by the controversy over *The Playboy*, the Abbey took an opportunity to put itself back in nationalist Ireland's good books, defying the wishes of Dublin Castle by staging a Shaw play, *The Shewing-up of Blanco Posnet*, which had been banned from the London stage.

Yeats and Gregory explained their decision thus: 'we must not, by accepting the English Censor's ruling, give away anything of the liberty of the Irish theatre of the future'. If they were to grant the Lord Lieutenant of Ireland – 'a political personage' representing the British government – the right to censor the theatre, it would 'sooner or later grow into a political censorship' that could not 'be lightly accepted'.[37] Maud Gonne was among those who were pleased with Yeats's resolute stand against British interference.

In 1911, when Yeats was set to chair a celebrity dinner at London's Café Royal, he stepped down because it would require him to propose a toast to the king. Earlier, he had fretted about how receipt of a Civil List pension would affect his reputation in nationalist Ireland. After long hesitation, he accepted the grant of an annual sum of £150, but with the proviso that he would be free to adhere to his own political course in Ireland. Predictably, this led to D.P. Moran of *The Leader* dubbing him with relish as 'Pensioner Yeats'.

Yeats's life might at this time have taken a more conventional path, as his name was mentioned for literature chairs at the new University College Dublin (an unlikely option given the influence there of the Catholic Church coupled with Yeats's heterodox religious leanings) and Trinity College, where he expressed an interest in succeeding the distinguished literary critic, his father's old friend, Edward Dowden. Such an appointment and its attractive annual salary of £600 would have given Yeats a settled life as a Trinity don. One has to wonder if such a life would have been conducive to the 'old man's frenzy' that produced so much adventurous poetry in the decades that followed. In the event, when Dowden died in 1913 Trinity opted for a more conventional choice, Dr William Abraham Trench, described by Yeats with an air of icy condescension as 'a man of known sobriety of matter and of mind'.[38]

## 'But an heroic dream'

Yeats's relationship with Gonne warmed up when, according to Yeats's biographer, Roy Foster, nearly two decades after their first meeting, 'it seems that now they finally became lovers',[39] albeit briefly. Gonne's fixed preference, however, was for a spiritual rather than a physical liaison. A letter Gonne wrote in December 1908 confessed that 'Life is so good when we are together' and said that she was 'proud beyond measure of your love', but hoped that Yeats could 'accept the spiritual love & union I offer'. She expressed confidence that 'the spiritual union between us will outlive this life'.[40] And indeed it has, for Yeats's poems have permanently united them in the minds of subsequent generations.

Published in 1912, *The Green Helmet and Other Poems* has been described as a 'transitional' collection, with poems that are 'cold and simple in style'.[41] The book is sprinkled with lines that reflect his continuing obsession with Maud, warmed no doubt by the recent physical intensification of their liaison. Here she is presented as 'A Woman Homer Sung':

> For she had fiery blood
> When I was young,
> And trod so sweetly proud
> As 'twere upon a cloud,
> A woman Homer sung,
> That life and letters seem
> But an heroic dream.

In the brilliant 'No Second Troy', devotion to Gonne mingles with a growing disdain for the 'ignorant men' to whom she had taught 'most violent ways'. In contrast with those she sought to lead, Gonne had 'a mind':

> That nobleness made simple as a fire,
> With beauty like a tightened bow, a kind
> That is not natural in an age like this ...

And, recognising her intrinsic radicalism, he accepted that a humdrum life would not satisfy her:

> Why, what could she have done, being what she is?
> Was there another Troy for her to burn?

In a diary entry about his obsession with Gonne, Yeats wondered, 'How much of the best that I have done and still do is but the attempt to explain myself to her.'[42] Indeed.

## 'What the exultant heart calls good'

With a seemingly straightforward appeal – co-signed by, among others, Gregory, Æ and Douglas Hyde in January 1905 – for public support for the purchase of a collection of modern French paintings, Yeats became associated with an issue that would become a source of profound disenchantment for the next decade of his life and beyond. Hugh Lane, who was Lady Gregory's nephew and a leading London art dealer, proposed the setting up in Dublin of a Municipal Gallery of Modern Art and assembled a collection of paintings for the gallery, which opened in temporary premises in 1908. A squabble then developed about the location of a permanent gallery, which caused Lane to bequeath to the National Gallery in London paintings he had conditionally gifted to Dublin Corporation.

The dispute about the gallery produced some of the bitterest poems of Yeats's writing life. Five such works were included in a 1913 volume, *Poems written in discouragement, 1912–1913*, whose title just about summed up the poet's mood as he approached his fiftieth birthday. Writing the following year, Yeats explained the anger behind his poetic diatribes. 'One could respect the argument,' he wrote, 'that Dublin, with much poverty and many slums, could not afford the £22,000 the building was to cost the city, but not the minds that used it.'[43]

Religion and politics could not create minds wise and generous enough, in Yeats's view, to 'make a nation'. Ranged against those forces, Ireland had 'but a few educated men and the remnants of an old traditional culture among the poor'. This is another Yeatsian evocation of his dream of uniting the noble and the beggar-man. In Yeats's opinion, both were stronger before 'the rise of our new middle class which made its first public display during the nine years of the Parnellite split, showing how base at moments of excitement are minds without culture'.[44]

I confess to having an aversion to Yeats's writing at this time. Yes, the poems he wrote have a robustness that sets them apart from his earlier work, but they are unhappily replete with grievance. He was in danger of succumbing to a version of the bitterness he detected in others, and becoming a 'blind and bitter' poet. His poem 'To a Wealthy Man, who Promised a Second Subscription if it were Proved the People Wanted Pictures' (which, by the way, must be one of the longest titles in the annals of poetry; its original title was even longer!) is especially rancorous, unpleasantly so in my opinion. His target was Lord Ardilaun, a member of the Guinness family, who is urged to:

Look up in the sun's eye and give
What the exultant heart calls good
That some new day may breed the best
Because you gave, not what they would,
But the right twigs for an eagle's nest!

All well and good, but the poem's derogatory dismissal of 'Paudeen' ('Let Paudeens play at pitch and toss') and 'Biddy' is brazenly bigoted and, I think, offensive:

You gave, but will not give again
Until enough of Paudeen's pence
By Biddy's halfpennies have lain
To be 'some sort of evidence',
Before you'll put your guineas down,
That things it were a pride to give
Are what the blind and ignorant town
Imagines best to make it thrive.

The poem goes on to compare early twentieth-century Dublin with Renaissance Italy, to the former's inevitable disadvantage, but then what time and place would not fall short against that gargantuan yardstick?

The affray continues in his poem 'Paudeen':

Indignant at the fumbling wits, the obscure spite
Of our old Paudeen in his shop, I stumbled blind
Among the stones and thorn-trees, under morning
    light; ...

And it did not stop there. In 'To a Friend whose Work has Come to Nothing', he launched into an appeal to Maud Gonne to be 'secret and exult':

Now all the truth is out,
Be secret and take defeat
From any brazen throat,
For how can you compete,
Being honour bred, with one
Who, were it proved he lies,
Were neither shamed in his own
Nor in his neighbours' eyes.

The thesis here is objectionably elitist in its insinuation that only those of a certain class have the ability to behave honourably. There's some fine writing there, but I find that it is marred by the blustering derision aimed at what might be called ordinary Dublin folk.

The saga surrounding Hugh Lane's paintings turned out to be a long and contentious one. The facts of the case are not as disreputable as Yeats claimed. Dublin Corporation did set aside an annual subvention of £500 to support the proposed gallery and later committed a further £2,000 to the project. This was a substantial commitment, but it was not enough to satisfy Lane, who was high-handed in his insistence that the gallery be located on a bridge across the Liffey (which would have resulted in the removal of the Ha'penny Bridge, an iconic Dublin landmark), with the building to be designed by the leading British architect, Edwin Lutyens. Eventually, patience was exhausted and Yeats's *bête noire*, William Martin Murphy, declared that he 'would rather see in the City of Dublin one block of sanitary houses at low rents replacing a reeking slum than all the pictures Corot and Degas ever painted'.[45]

An unsigned codicil to Lane's will in which he left the paintings to Dublin was discovered after his death on the *Lusitania* in 1915, but the British authorities declined to recognise it. Yeats was still on manoeuvres about the Lane pictures when he was a senator in the 1920s. The controversy dragged on until 1959, when it was agreed to alternate the disputed works between Dublin and London.

## 'Was it for this the wild geese spread the grey wing upon every tide'

The poem in which Yeats reported the demise of 'Romantic Ireland' was first published in *The Irish Times* on 8 September 1913. It was originally entitled 'Romance in Ireland', then 'Romantic Ireland' and ultimately 'September 1913'. It is a public poem where Yeats speaks with unfettered self-confidence about the Ireland of his time. His sharp rhetoric leaves no room for doubt as to the depth of his conviction that something vitally important had ceased to be. Those he sees as the guilty parties are savagely derided. They 'fumble in a greasy till' and 'add prayer to shivering prayer' until they have 'dried the marrow from the bone'.

Where Yeats saw decline and decay on account of the burgeoning influence of clerks and shopkeepers, others would have seen something quite different taking place. After all, Ireland's Home Rule movement appeared in 1913 to be on the verge of accomplishing its hitherto-elusive goal. The Irish Party now held the balance of power at Westminster and the Third Home Rule Bill was introduced in 1912. With the removal of the House of Lords' veto, Home Rule seemed destined, despite dogged opposition from Ulster Unionists and British Conservatives, to finally be granted to Ireland. Home Rule would have given Ireland a native parliament, albeit with limited powers, for the first time since 1800, thus realising a long-held nationalist ambition. When the Home Rule Act passed in the summer of 1914, it was widely celebrated in nationalist Ireland and, but for the outbreak of World War I, would likely have been implemented in some form or other before the end of that year.

The year 1913 was a time when members of the Gaelic League felt part of an exciting national movement aimed at reviving the Irish language. Founded in 1893, the League became something of a consuming passion for middle-class nationalists. Many of those who participated in Ireland's struggle for independence were drawn into political activity by their enthusiasm for the language revival. Advocates of what was called an Irish Ireland aimed to promote a self-reliant, self-sufficient Ireland, thoroughly Gaelic and Catholic in character.

D.P. Moran cajoled his readers to eschew what he called 'West Britonism' and to embrace the idea of an Irish Ireland. Many of his critics would have suspected Yeats, who had called nationalist attacks on him 'the work of ignorant men', of being a West Briton, although that charge seems to me to be well wide of the mark.[46]

As Yeats put pen to paper on 'September 1913', nationalist Ireland was astir. The establishment of the Ulster Volunteers in January 1913 to resist Home Rule had set in train a nationalist response that culminated in November of that year with the creation of the Irish Volunteers under the leadership of the scholar and co-founder of the Gaelic League, Eoin MacNeill. Volunteering generated immense enthusiasm and the numbers involved quickly multiplied.

The oath-bound Irish Republican Brotherhood was busy seeking to influence the Volunteers and, although the organisation was brought under the control of the Irish Party, its radical potential never evaporated. It asserted itself again when the Volunteers split at the outbreak of war in 1914.

The Irish labour movement was coming into its own in the second decade of the twentieth century, and it was the Dublin Lockout that inspired Yeats to write 'September 1913', even though he was not an instinctive ally of the labour movement. The poem was more a reflection of his hostility to those who were ranged against the workers, Dublin business figures who had refused to back Hugh Lane's gallery and Catholic groups who tried to prevent Dublin workers' children from being shipped out to fraternal families in Liverpool.

During the 1913 lock-out, Yeats vented his spleen against 'Dublin fanaticism', charging nationalist papers 'with deliberately arousing religious passion' and 'appealing to mob law day after day' to defeat the city's workers: 'Intriguers have met together somewhere behind the scenes that they might turn the religion of Him who thought it hard for a rich man to enter into the Kingdom of Heaven into an oppression of the poor.'[47] Finally, those who first read the poem in the Unionist *Irish Times* probably revelled in this report of Romantic Ireland's decline and fall!

## 'Yet could we turn the years again'

If Yeats had put down his poetic pen after writing 'September 1913' and the splenetic poems that accompanied it in *Responsibilities*, I do not think his reputation would have flourished to the degree that it has in Ireland or in the wider world. Bitter disenchantment is not an attractive quality, in life or in writing.

In Yeats's defence, setting up a full-time theatre was a major task, and no one involved had any experience of such a venture. There were tensions and rivalries aplenty. Frank and William Fay were significant figures in Dublin dramatic circles, and they were embittered by what they saw as shoddy treatment at Yeats's hands. Frank Fay described Yeats as 'an impossible person to head a theatre' on account of his lack of knowledge of acting and 'his impish faculty for making mischief'.[48]

Yeats also had the unenviable task of navigating Miss Horniman's tempestuous, intemperate demands and obsessions. She had insisted that the cheapest seats in the Abbey should cost one shilling, which inevitably trimmed audience numbers, allowing *The Leader* to crow that the sixty-two people in the audience for one performance 'do not make a nation'.[49] Horniman appears to have been, at a minimum, and to put it gently, unstable, and she clearly had what we might call 'a soft spot' for Yeats. Prudishly, she took exception to the boisterousness of the Abbey troupe when it toured Britain!

Lady Gregory had no time for Horniman, who in turn resented Gregory's close relationship with Yeats. Gregory compared Horniman to 'a shilling in a tub of electrified water – everybody tries to get the shilling out'.[50] But Horniman's money was needed to keep the Abbey afloat and Yeats was prepared to do what was necessary to keep her onside. She was deeply suspicious of Irish nationalism and was always on the lookout for slights and transgressions. As Yeats put it, Horniman 'never felt any interest in the Irish side of our work' but wanted productions of 'universal artistic interest',[51] which, of course, would always have been Yeats's goal too, except that he tended to converge on the universal via an Irish national route.

There were fiery exchanges between Yeats and Horniman in 1910 when the Abbey inadvertently neglected to close its doors as a mark of respect to the deceased King Edward VII. By then, Horniman had stepped back from involvement with the Abbey and tried to recruit Yeats for a theatre venture she had planned in Britain. Yeats's reply to her gives a telling insight into his inveterate Irishness despite the disappointments that had beset him and the bigoted views he had developed. To accept Horniman's proposal would, he believed, require him to write for an English audience, an effort in which he might fail for lack of understanding and sympathy. 'I understand my own race & in all my work, lyric or dramatic I have thought of it ... I shall write for my own people – whether in love or hate of them matters little – probably I shall not know which it is.'[52] Indomitable Irishness on display there.

## 'With O'Leary in the grave'

What did Yeats mean when he wrote of 'Romantic Ireland'? John O'Leary represented for him the last expression of 'All that delirium of the brave.' When O'Leary died in 1907 Yeats did not attend the funeral of his first literary/political mentor. As he explained in a subsequent essay:

When O'Leary died I could not bring myself to go to
his funeral, though I had been once his close fellow-
worker, for I shrank from seeing about his grave so
many whose Nationalism was different from anything
he had taught or I could share.

In Yeats's view O'Leary – and John F. Taylor, the orator
with whom Yeats had tangled in the 1880s and 1890s –
belonged 'to the romantic conception of Irish nationality'.
'They were the last to speak an understanding of life and
Nationality, built up by the generation of Grattan [who
is not normally included in that category], which read
Homer and Vergil, and the generation of Davis, which
had been pierced through by the idealism of Mazzini,
and of the European revolutionists of the mid-century.'[53]
That's as good an explanation as I have seen of Yeats's
conception of romantic nationalism. In 'September 1913'
he compiled a roll of honour of 'Romantic Ireland', 'the
wild geese' who left Ireland after the Battle of Aughrim
and the Treaty of Limerick in 1691, as well as Lord Edward
Fitzgerald, Robert Emmet and Wolfe Tone. This is a classic nineteenth-century nationalist choir of martyrs. Those
who were preparing for Ireland's revolutionary surge as
Yeats composed his dirge had those self-same figures as
their cherished antecedents.

Yes, a certain brand of Irish nationalism did come to
grief in the first decade of the twentieth century, specifically Yeats's eclectic version. The culprit in Yeats's mind
was Catholic nationalism. What Yeats did not appreciate
was that, as he wrote repeated laments for the Ireland
of his youthful dreams, the sound of a new dispensation
could be heard by those with their ears to the ground.

A book by the British constitutional historian Vernon Bogdanor, *The Strange Survival of Liberal England*, pushes back against the influential thesis advanced in George Dangerfield's classic *The Strange Death of Liberal England* (1935). Dangerfield painted a picture of a Liberal England that had flared brightly in the opening years of the century but had 'by the end of 1913 been reduced to ashes'.[54] Nationalist Ireland was a place apart. It profited from the early twentieth-century flowering of 'Liberal England', which had been an equivocal ally of the Irish Party since the 1880s. This alliance had taken the Home Rule movement to the verge of triumph in 1913.

What occurred in Ireland between 1916 and 1918 was the strange death of Home Rule Ireland, as the party that had dominated the Irish political landscape for four decades now found itself 'with O'Leary in the grave'. Yeats's literary movement had played a part in that demise by helping shift some of the focus of public life from political calculation to cultural expression. Tellingly, there are no Yeats poems about the Irish Party titans of his time, John Redmond and John Dillon. The legendary Cuchulain of Yeats's poems and plays was no pragmatic, incremental parliamentarian!

Behind what Yeats perceived as the decay of Romantic Ireland lurked a more adamantine strain of separatist nationalism peopled historically by United Irishmen, Young Irelanders, Fenian plotters and, for a time, cultural nationalists like Yeats and the members of the Gaelic League. In 1913 the smart money would have been on the triumph of Home Rule Ireland and the parliamentary nationalism it embodied. But events in the world intervened and ushered in a new era for Ireland, one that blended the idealism of the late nineteenth-century Irish revival with the hard-nosed ethos of the Fenian movement.

For Yeats, 'Ireland's great moment had passed' and artists who ought to be the servants of 'life in its nobler forms ... became as elsewhere in Europe protesting individual voices'.[55] As it turned out, Ireland's 'great moment' had yet to come, and it would be a winner – including for Yeats, as it helped energise his writing. Notwithstanding what Yeats memorably announced in 'September 1913', that year did not deliver a death certificate for 'Romantic Ireland', but it did, I think, mark the end of romantic Yeats. Ezra Pound wrote of Yeats in 1914 that the sad 'minor note ... was going out of his poetry', which was 'becoming gaunter, seeking greater hardness of outline'.[59] From the 'vague enchanted beauty'[57] of his earlier work would emerge the 'terrible beauty' of his later poetry.

# 5

# 'A terrible beauty'

## Yeats's Easter Rising

## The Wild Swans at Coole

The trees are in their autumn beauty,
The woodland paths are dry,
Under the October twilight the water
Mirrors a still sky;
Upon the brimming water among the stones
Are nine-and-fifty swans.

The nineteenth autumn has come upon me
Since I first made my count;
I saw, before I had well finished,
All suddenly mount
And scatter wheeling in great broken rings
Upon their clamorous wings.

I have looked upon those brilliant creatures,
And now my heart is sore.
All's changed since I, hearing at twilight,
The first time on this shore,
The bell-beat of their wings above my head,
Trod with a lighter tread.

Unwearied still, lover by lover,
They paddle in the cold
Companionable streams or climb the air;
Their hearts have not grown old;
Passion or conquest, wander where they will,
Attend upon them still.

But now they drift on the still water,
Mysterious, beautiful;
Among what rushes will they build,
By what lake's edge or pool

Delight men's eyes when I awake some day
To find they have flown away?


## 'Nine-and-fifty swans'

While the main focus of this chapter is Yeats's towering history poem 'Easter 1916', which was completed in
September of that year, I could not resist prefacing these
pages with the text of 'The Wild Swans at Coole', once
described as a poem of 'primal simplicity'[1] and which was
also written in the autumn of 1916.

'The Wild Swans at Coole' is not just a fine poem. It also
seems to me to be instructive about Yeats's state of mind
now that he had passed his fiftieth year, had published
the first volume of his *Autobiographies* and was gripped by
a renewed urge to make sense of his life, and to put it in
order. Part of the disorder he experienced stemmed, as
always, from his unfinished dealings with Maud Gonne,
for whom he retained a seemingly unquenchable desire.
With the death of her estranged husband in 1916, she was
free again to marry Yeats, whose heart remained 'sore'
on account of his unrequited passion. With a consciousness of encroaching age he felt that he no longer 'trod
with a lighter tread'. In the poem, the wild swans seem
to be egging him on to 'passion and conquest', and, in
a way, that's what he did, writing passionate poems and
conquering the modernist literary era that was about to
dawn as he wrote about 'those brilliant creatures' gracing
'the brimming water' at Coole Park.

Nothing is permanent. Yeats accepts he may wake
one day to find that those 'mysterious, beautiful' swans
have departed, just as his own youth already had. To my

ear this is a mature elegy, 'almost Wordsworthian', in one estimation.[2] It harks back to the still-youthful Yeats of the late nineteenth century, author of 'The Lake Isle of Innisfree' and other such late-romantic poems. But things have changed. The writing is different. While the 'Lake Isle' and the 'Wild Swans' are both nature poems, the thoughts that skim across the lake at Coole are weightier, more heavily burdened with life's experience than those that inhabited the 'bee-loud glade' of Innisfree. The later poem exhibits some of the meditative qualities of Yeats's fully mature work, but is without the haughty rage and the eclectic compendium of ideas that would find expression in his poetry during the 1920s and 30s. The 'Wild Swans' even contains an echo of 'Easter 1916' in the words 'All's changed' in its third stanza.

I would probably not be writing this book about W.B. Yeats had it not been for what happened in 1916. That is because the events of 1916 changed Ireland, and they also altered the tenor of Yeats's interaction with the land of his birth. Yeats's life changed too in the years following the Easter Rising as he married and started a family. If Yeats's writing had not shifted gears in the wake of the Easter Rising, I doubt that he would be seen, as he now is, as an indispensable Irish writer. Without the transformation of Ireland's standing in the eyes of the world that occurred after 1916, it is entirely possible that Yeats would not have been awarded the Nobel Prize in 1923, for it was clearly a recognition of the poet and also of the country whose achievements he was seen to personify.

There is a sense in which the Easter Rising helped rescue Yeats from the slough of disenchantment into which he had descended on the back of the disappointments that had beset him during the previous decade. After 1916 he entered again into a more productive, if always somewhat fraught, engagement with Ireland; one that produced some of his finest poems, the works on which his reputation ultimately hinges. With his keen political antennae, Yeats knew that he was living in a transformed Ireland. As he wrote in July 1916, '"Romantic Ireland's dead and gone" sounds old-fashioned now. It seemed true in 1913, but I did not foresee 1916. The late Dublin Rebellion, whatever one can say of its wisdom, will long be remembered for its heroism.'[3] Yeats was invariably in thrall to the heroic, be it the heroism of Cuchulain or of his own inner circle. The events of 1916 appealed to him at that level.

### 'For a barren passion's sake'

Let us begin this interconnected tale of Ireland's transformation and Yeats's poetic renewal in 1914 with the publication of *Responsibilities: Poems and a Play*, the central text of Yeats's middle period. The American critic Harold Bloom has described much of this collection as 'abortive work', eclipsed by the events of 1916/17, which, he argues, 'seem more and more fortunate, whenever the interrelation between Yeats's life and poetry is considered'.[4] Yes, that's spot on. It squares with my view of Yeats's evolution as a writer. He found new vigour and inspiration during the years following the Rising from engaging with and reflecting on the dramatic march of events in Ireland.

The year 1914 witnessed the outbreak of World War I, an event that ultimately caused Ireland to ignite, albeit on a far smaller scale and at a completely different level of intensity from the conflagration on Europe's blood-soaked battlefields. In *Responsibilities* Yeats continued to explore the theme of disenchantment that had preoccupied him during the previous decade, and in 'To a Shade' he warns the ghost of Parnell not to return to contemporary Dublin because:

> The time for you to taste of that salt breath
> And listen at the corners has not come;
> You had enough of sorrow before death –
> Away, away! You are safer in the tomb.

In *Responsibilities*, autobiography becomes part of Yeats's poetic province as his own life and his family background assume a greater role in his writing. Ancestral pardon is sought from his 'old fathers':

> *Pardon that for a barren passion's sake,*
> *Although I have come close on forty-nine,*
> *I have no child, I have nothing but a book,*
> *Nothing but that to prove your blood and mine.*

Those introductory lines in *Responsibilities*, in which he insists that his blood had not passed 'through any huckster's loin', were written in response to George Moore, who in *Vale*, the third volume of his impish account of Dublin literary life, *Hail and Farewell*, lampooned Yeats for thundering 'against the middle classes, stamping his feet, working himself into a great temper, and all because the middle classes did not dip their hands into their pockets and give Lane the money he wanted for his exhibition'.

Moore mocked Yeats for his 'strange belief that none but titled and carriage-folk could appreciate pictures'. In Moore's assessment, Yeats, descended from millers and 'a portrait painter of distinction', was himself middle class.[5]

The extent to which Moore's mockery rankled Yeats is clear from his *Autobiographies* ('It was Moore's own fault that everyone hated him except a few London painters'[6]) and in the closing rhymes of *Responsibilities*, where he describes himself as having, because of 'undreamt accidents', become:

> *Notorious, till all my priceless things*
> *Are but a post the passing dogs defile.*

Maud Gonne continues to be a major presence in these poems. In 'The Grey Rock' (a rare Yeats poem set in England), in which he pays tribute to his Rhymers' Club companions at the Cheshire Cheese pub in London, Maud appears as 'a woman none could please'. In a nod to her legendary status in Yeats's imagination, she is compared with 'rock-nurtured Aoife', mother of Cuchulainn's son. Even when he writes about deceased friends, poets Lionel Johnson and Ernest Dowson, Maud and his Irish critics remain in his thoughts:

> *And I am in no good repute*
> *With the loud host before the sea,*
> *That think sword-strokes were better meant*
> *Than lover's music – let that be,*
> *So that the wandering foot's content.*

'Fallen Majesty' broods on Maud's now-faded prominence. With a big dollop of poetic licence, he wrote that:

> ... A crowd
> Will gather, and not know it walks the very street
> Whereon a thing once walked that seemed a burning
>     cloud.

Yeats once described how Maud had power over crowds and could persuade people to do her bidding 'not only because she was beautiful, but because that beauty suggested joy and freedom'.[7]

In 'Friends', he praises Olivia Shakespear (no thought 'Could ever come between / Mind and delighted mind'), Lady Gregory (who 'Had strength that could unbind / What none can understand') and of course to Maud ('that took / All till my youth was gone / With scarce a pitying look').

In 'A Coat', which comes at the end of this collection, a disgruntled Yeats looks back over his writing career and seems to want to chart a new path:

> I made my song a coat
> Covered with embroideries
> Out of old mythologies
> From heel to throat;
> But the fools caught it,
> Wore it in the world's eyes
> As though they'd wrought it.
> Song, let them take it,
> For there's more enterprise
> In walking naked.

This suggests that in 1914 Yeats was thoroughly out of sorts with the Ireland of that time and may well have been tempted to distance himself from its affairs. He would have been welcomed with open arms in England, where a knighthood and a poet laureateship would have been in prospect had he been willing to discard his Irish obsessions, but that was not to be his choice.

## 'In a dragon-guarded land'

The Home Rule movement never made its way into Yeats's poetry, even as that venerable political project approached its zenith in 1912–14. The introduction of the Third Home Rule Bill in May 1912 spurred a furious response among Ulster Unionists, resulting in the mass signing of a Solemn League and Covenant, whose supporters declared their undying opposition to Home Rule. It was not long before a paramilitary body, the Ulster Volunteers, emerged with the aim of resisting Home Rule, if necessary by force of arms.

Ulster Unionists had support from the British Conservative party, which viewed Home Rule as an illegitimate move on the part of Asquith's Liberal government, whose hold on power depended (quite legitimately, of course) on the votes of the Irish Party's MPs. Irish nationalists followed the Ulster Unionist example and by the beginning of 1914 there were two rival militias, the Ulster Volunteers and the Irish Volunteers, ranged against each other on opposing sides of the Home Rule divide. Then, in March 1914, British forces stationed at the Curragh made it plain that they would not enforce Home Rule on Ulster. Civil war in Ireland seemed a real possibility.

Yeats was a supporter of Home Rule, though perhaps not a very vocal or passionate one, and he made an effort to assuage the fears of the Protestant community about the retention of their freedoms in a self-governed Ireland. He conceded that Ulster Protestants had reason to fear intolerant attitudes among nationalists but thought that these could be successfully countered once Home Rule became a reality. Optimistically, he claimed that 'the responsibilities of self-government and the growth of political freedom are the most powerful solvents for sectarian animosities'.[8] Protestants would, he thought, be well able to fight their corner in a Home Rule Ireland. It is certainly true that island-wide self-rule would have needed to take a different course from the one followed by the Irish Free State in the 1920s and beyond, but Unionists were unwilling to take that chance.

As crisis fomented in Ireland, in January 1914 Yeats set off for America for what would be another lucrative tour, one that enabled him to purchase and restore Thoor Ballylee near Lady Gregory's home in County Galway. When asked about the worsening situation at home, his response was cautiously optimistic: 'I have no idea what sort of compromise can be arranged, but I believe that one will be worked out.'[9]

## 'No gift to set a statesman right'

When war came in August 1914, the leaders of nationalist Ireland, John Redmond and his colleagues in the Irish Party, committed themselves to the war effort and urged their supporters to enlist for service in defence of Catholic Belgium. In all, some 210,000 Irishmen volunteered to fight, 57 per cent of whom were Catholics,[10] and perhaps as many as 50,000 lost their lives during the conflict. Advanced nationalists opposed enlistment and were accused of being pro-German. At a public event in November 1914 that commemorated the centenary of the birth of Thomas Davis, and in which Patrick Pearse, an opponent of enlistment, also participated, Yeats made his position plain when he said that, 'I am not more vehemently opposed to the unionism of Professor Mahaffy than I am to the pro-Germanism of Mr Pearse.'[11]

Mahaffy was the Unionist Provost of Trinity College, who had banned Pearse from speaking at the College and suppressed its Gaelic Society. Yeats's speech was notable for its praise for Davis as 'the foremost moral influence on our politics' and his criticism of Daniel O'Connell, whose personal influence he viewed as 'almost entirely evil' as he appealed to 'the commonest ear'. He did, however, acknowledge that O'Connell possessed a 'deep affection-ate heart'.[12] It is telling to find Yeats in 1914, with Home Rule already granted but not implemented, preferring the romantic revolutionary (Davis) to the parliamentary reformer (O'Connell).

Considering that he lived in England for most of the war, it is remarkable how little attention Yeats paid to that unprecedented, existential conflict. Writing to his father in September 1914, he maintained that inept young British officers had 'died with useless heroism when the moment came'. The war, he supposed, would end in a draw and with 'everybody too poor to fight for another hundred years'.[13] With a peculiar air of detach-ment, he described the war as a 'bloody frivolity' and 'the most expensive outbreak of insolence and stupidity the world has ever seen'. He proudly declared that he gave the war 'as little of my thought as I can',[14] and wondered 'if history will ever know at what man's door to lay the crime of this inexplicable war?' Like most wars, it was, he thought, 'a sacrifice of the best for the worst'.[15] When, reluctantly, he agreed to write for a wartime anthology, his contribution took an offhand approach, of which his Irish-American friend, John Quinn, a strong supporter of the war even before America joined in 1917, was quite critical. Yeats wrote:

> I think it better that in times like these
> A poet's mouth be silent, for in truth
> We have no gift to set a statesman right;
> He has had enough of meddling who can please
> A young girl in the indolence of her youth,
> Or an old man upon a winter's night.

This was a strange display of insouciance from a poet who was by now embedded in the British establishment and in receipt of a government pension. While he may have thought of himself as having no political 'gift' in a British context, he never lacked an ambition to contribute to public life in Ireland. His casual approach to the war certainly contrasts with how deeply the Easter Rising moved him.

During the winters of 1914 and 1915, Yeats retreated to the Stone Cottage at Ashdown Forest in Sussex with American Ezra Pound and his wife, Dorothy Shakespear, daughter of Yeats's former lover, Olivia. Pound worked with Yeats on his poetry, helping him 'to get back to the definite and concrete'.[16] Pound was by then an enthusiastic advocate of James Joyce's work. When Yeats learned of Joyce's financial circumstances in wartime Zurich, where he had fled from Trieste in 1915, egged on by Pound he generously wrote to his friend Edmund Gosse about a subvention for Joyce from the Royal Literary Fund. In his submission, he described Joyce as 'a man of genius'.[17]

Writing with foresight, and before *Ulysses* had even begun to appear in print, Yeats argued that Joyce had the promise of 'a great novelist of a new kind'.[18] When questioned about Joyce's politics, he assured Gosse that Joyce 'never had anything to do with Irish politics, extreme or otherwise', and added, perceptively, that for men such as Joyce 'the Irish atmosphere brings isolation, not anti-English feeling'.[19] On the back of Yeats's efforts, Joyce was awarded £75, which, in his biographer's words, helped influence 'the more relaxed tone of the Bloom episodes of *Ulysses*, to which he now bent his mind'.[20]

In the first days of 1916 Yeats told Joseph Hone, author of *William Butler Yeats: The Poet in Contemporary Ireland*, that his biography contained exactly what he wanted 'some young men in Dublin to know', namely that his work had been done 'in every detail with a deliberate Irish aim'.[21] That was a fair assessment, but there were those who actively doubted Yeats's Irishness because his political identity was complex and nuanced in an environment in which more trenchant forms of politics had steadily prevailed.

As a reflection of his literary and social prominence, Yeats was approached about a knighthood, but turned it down as he did not want 'anyone to say of me "only for a ribbon he left us"'.[22] In what turned out to be an accurate assessment, he compared his life to a house 'still unfinished, there are so many rooms and corridors that I am still building upon foundations laid long ago'.[23] He would build that house, literally and metaphorically, at Thoor Ballylee.

## 'Wherever green is worn'

The roots of the Easter Rising go back to the nineteenth century, to the Fenian movement of the 1860s, which survived largely through Irish-American fealty to the cause of Irish freedom. The Fenian spirit was rekindled by a new generation in the early twentieth century and with continued support from American Fenians, who in 1908 sent Tom Clarke to Dublin, where his tobacconist shop became a hub of separatist activity. The opportunity Fenians had been waiting for came when the Home Rule crisis gave birth in 1913 to the Irish Volunteers.

By the time war broke out the following August the Volunteers numbered 160,000, and they succeeded in importing weapons and recruiting and exercising openly, preparing to defend Home Rule from the opposition mounted by the Ulster Volunteers. Such a public display of nationalist military muscle would have been unthinkable in the nineteenth century, but in the wake of the Ulster crisis all bets were off and the authorities were forced to acquiesce to a nationalist paramilitary force openly training its burgeoning ranks. In Berlin, the kaiser savoured the prospect that a civil war in Ireland could divert British attention from the budding crisis on the continent as tensions grew between Britain, France and Germany.

The outbreak of war split the Volunteers, with a majority accepting Redmond's advice that they should support the war effort. Others in the Volunteers, perhaps 10,000 in all, resolved to defend Ireland on home soil. The Easter Rising was engineered by those within the Irish Volunteers who decided to await a wartime opportunity to rise against British rule in Ireland. The Volunteers – steered surreptitiously by members of the

Irish Republican Brotherhood – after a false start the previous day, mobilised on Easter Monday 1916, capturing prominent buildings including the General Post Office, which became the rebels' headquarters, and declared an independent Irish Republic. Perhaps 1,500 individuals were involved in the Rising, and around 450 people were killed during the fighting in Dublin. The insurgents held out for six days before surrendering in the face of the British military's vastly superior firepower.

Fifteen individuals seen, in some cases inaccurately, as leading figures in the Rising were executed in the first half of May. (Roger Casement suffered a similar fate in London later in the year.) Many other Volunteers, and even people with no direct involvement in the Rising, were sent to prison or were interned in Britain. The Rising changed the Irish political landscape, and this led eventually to the eclipse of the Irish Party, which had been politically dominant in Ireland for decades.

## 'A terrible beauty'

The Rising energised Yeats, and, in 'Easter 1916', drew from him what I regard as one of the English language's finest twentieth-century history poems. The events of 1916 became a source of enduring fascination for him, and he continued to think and write about it long afterwards, for example in 'Man and Echo', one of the poems written during the final months of his life, and in his last play, *The Death of Cuchulain*. Like almost everyone else, Yeats was taken aback by what happened during Easter week 1916. When he first heard the news, he was in Gloucestershire staying with the painter William

Rothenstein. The dramatic events in Dublin affected him more profoundly than he would have imagined. 'I had no idea,' Yeats wrote, 'that any public event could so deeply move me.'

On 11 May, while the execution of the Rising's leaders was still ongoing, he wrote to Lady Gregory about 'the Dublin tragedy' and of his 'great sorrow and anxiety'.[24] At that early stage he was already trying to write about the executed men: 'terrible beauty has been born again'. He thought the Rising could have been avoided had the British Conservative Party committed itself not to rescind the Home Rule Bill that had become law in 1914, but I doubt that. Those behind the Rising wanted to go well beyond the limited framework offered by Home Rule. The actual implementation of Home Rule in 1914 might have made a difference, but that was not to be.

In his letters Yeats fretted that 'all the work of years' had been overturned, 'all the bringing together of classes, all the freeing of literature and criticism from politics'.[25] As always, Maud Gonne was on his mind. She was heartened to see that 'tragic dignity' had returned to Ireland and believed that: 'Those who die for Ireland are sacred'. That included even her estranged husband, who had left her son, Seán, 'a name to be proud of'.[26] Seán MacBride went on to become Ireland's Foreign Minister in the late 1940s and won the Nobel Peace Prize in 1974.

Within weeks of the Rising Yeats told John Quinn that: 'We have lost the ablest and most fine-natured of our young men.' Echoing sentiments that many people across Europe must have had about the impact of World War I, he commented that: 'A whole world seems to have been swept away.' Weighing up his own responsibility, he wondered if he could have done anything 'to turn those young men in some other direction'.[27] Although he professed to dread being embroiled in controversy, he wanted to return to Dublin 'to live, to begin building again'.[28]

It is worth recalling that although Yeats had always been a frequent visitor, he had not lived in Dublin since the family decamped and moved to London in 1887. In June 1916 he told the poet Robert Bridges that: 'All my habits of thought are upset by this tragic Irish rebellion which has swept away friends and fellow workers.' He remarked astutely that 'one knows nothing of the future except that it must be very unlike the past'. That was a canny observation, easy to make in hindsight, but not completely evident in the immediate aftermath of the Rising.

## 'We know their dream'

'Easter 1916' was completed in the months after the Rising and published privately the following year. It was not made more widely available until 1920, evidently because Yeats did not want it to stir further an already troubled pot, although publishing in the thick of the War of Independence also entailed an element of risk-taking on his part, publicly nailing his colours to the green mast of nationalist Ireland, 'now and in time to be'.

'Easter 1916' is, in my opinion, the first great poem of Yeats's full literary maturity. It is a complex, evocative piece of writing. Harold Bloom calls it 'a model of sanity and proportion'[29] and so it is – and much more besides. The poem begins in a conversational tone:

> I have met them at close of day
> Coming with vivid faces
> From counter or desk among grey
> Eighteenth-century houses.

This tells us that Yeats was acquainted with many of the 'vivid faces'[30] who participated in the Rising. As he told Gregory in May, 'Cosgrave, who I saw a few months ago in connection with the Municipal Gallery project and found our best supporter, has got many years' imprisonment.'[31] Yes, William T. Cosgrave (1880–1965) fought in the Rising at the South Dublin Union under the command of Éamonn Ceannt, one of the seven signatories of the Proclamation of the Irish Republic. In the end, Cosgrave spent just under a year in prison in England before being elected as an MP in a by-election in May 1917, one of Sinn Féin's earliest electoral breakthroughs. Cosgrave went on to head up the first government of the Irish Free State from 1922 until he lost out to Éamon de Valera in 1932.

Yeats also thought it strange that 'old Count Plunkett' and his family should be 'drawn in to the net'. Plunkett's son, Joseph Mary, a poet, was one of the Rising's executed leaders. The Count, holder of a Papal title, had a brief moment of political prominence in 1917 as father of a martyred hero before he was shuffled aside by younger, hardier souls more suited to the cut and thrust of political and revolutionary activity.

In the years before the Rising, Yeats had fallen foul of the new breed of advanced nationalists. In the opening verse of 'Easter 1916' he admits he had thought they were merely posturing. They lived 'where motley is worn' and were the butt of clever jokes:

Of a mocking tale or a gibe
To please a companion
Around the fire at the club ...

'Easter 1916' goes on to describe four of the more prominent insurgents. First, Constance Markievicz:

What voice more sweet than hers
When, young and beautiful,
She rode to harriers?

Born Constance Gore-Booth in Sligo in 1868, she was one
of the 'dear memories' of his youth as a regular visitor to
Sligo. He would later build a beautiful, if ill-directed, poem
around the memory of Constance and her sister Eva, a pacifist, suffragist, trade unionist and social worker. Shedding
the influences of her privileged upbringing, Constance
married a Polish count and became thoroughly radicalised.
She was part of the Theatre of Ireland, which was set up as
an amateur and more unambiguously nationalistic rival to
the Abbey. In 1918 Constance Markievicz became the first
woman ever to be elected to the Westminster Parliament,
although she did not take her seat. She was also the first
woman to serve in an Irish Cabinet, a feat not matched until
the 1980s.

Patrick Pearse – 'This man kept a school and rode our
wingèd horse' – a poet and educationalist, was well known
to Yeats. As a precocious young Gaelic League activist writing in 1899 in the League's journal *An Claidheamh
Soluis* (The Sword of Light), Pearse had dismissed the Irish
Literary Theatre as 'anti-national'.[32] Pearse was critical
too of the Celtic Twilight, with which Yeats was strongly

identified, insisting that 'The Twilight People will pass with the Anglo-Irish Twilight.'[33] Pearse came to regret his youthful intemperance and softened his view of Yeats, who was later invited to speak at St Enda's, Pearse's school in Rathfarnham, where Yeats gave permission for his plays to be performed. Privately, Yeats had a dim enough view of Pearse, seeing him as someone who had been 'made dangerous by the Vertigo of Self-Sacrifice'.[34]

Thomas MacDonagh, who 'might have won fame in the end, / So sensitive his nature seemed, / So daring and sweet his thought', had once consulted Yeats about his poetry. Yeats saw him as 'a man with some literary faculty which will probably come to nothing through lack of culture and encouragement'. In Yeats's account, MacDonagh, then assistant headmaster at Pearse's school, was (in 1909) 'very low-spirited about Ireland' and losing faith in the Gaelic League.[35] By that time MacDonagh was an Abbey playwright, his play *When the Dawn is Come* having been staged there in 1908. Later, MacDonagh was involved in *The Irish Review* and in the Theatre of Ireland, which performed his play *Metempsychosis*, a satire on the esoteric religious movements that Yeats found so appealing. In the words of MacDonagh's entry in the *Dictionary of Irish Biography*, his play contained 'a wickedly accurate caricature' of Yeats. Appointed as a lecturer at University College Dublin in 1911, MacDonagh became prominent in the Irish Volunteers when it was set up in 1913 and, having at a late stage taken the oath and become a member of the Irish Republican Brotherhood, he was one of the seven signatories of the 1916 Proclamation. His posthumously published collection of literary criticism,

*Literature in Ireland: Studies in Irish and Anglo-Irish* (1916), with its concept of an 'Irish mode' in writing, expressed a view of Irish literature not far removed from Yeats's own.

Yeats's 'drunken vainglorious lout' who 'had done most bitter wrong / To some who are near my heart' was John MacBride, Maud Gonne's former husband. Given the circumstances of the MacBrides' marriage and subsequent separation, it was generous of Yeats to acknowledge that he, too, had been 'transformed utterly' by his involvement in the Rising. That second stanza illustrates the intimate nature of the Rising. Where else would a prominent poet have known personally so many members of a revolutionary group?

Another 1916 leader, James Connolly, is included in Yeats's closing paean of praise, from which Markievicz is omitted, presumably on the poetic ground that her name would not have scanned well! Also, unlike 'MacDonagh and MacBride, Connolly and Pearse', she was not among the executed dead, having been spared the firing squad on the grounds of her sex. Connolly, an Edinburgh-born trade unionist and socialist, commanded the Irish Citizen Army, which had been set up as a workers' militia after the Dublin Lockout of 1913.

In his poem about the Easter Rising, the left-leaning George Russell (Æ) referred to Connolly as 'my man'. That would not have applied to the more conservative Yeats, who, however, did recognise that Connolly was 'an able man'. Yeats had known Connolly from the nationalist demonstrations that had taken place in 1897 in opposition to Queen Victoria's Diamond Jubilee, to which he had accompanied Gonne. Connolly had also teamed with Gonne in pro-Boer activities at the turn of the century, which Yeats, then at the height of his nationalist engagement, had supported.

## 'Too long a sacrifice'

There is a sense in which 'Easter 1916' consists of two poems woven into one compelling ensemble. Had he put his pen down after the first two stanzas, it would' have been an interesting poem with a memorable, final refrain:

> Yet I number him in the song;
> He, too, has resigned his part
> In the casual comedy;
> He, too, has been changed in his turn,
> Transformed utterly:
> A terrible beauty is born.

Such a poem would have commemorated those 'vivid faces' who had fought and died in the Rising. But Yeats did not stop there. Instead, he embarks on an extended meditation about:

> Hearts with one purpose alone
> Through summer and winter seem
> Enchanted to a stone
> To trouble the living stream.

There's a beautiful image of:

> ... the birds that range
> From cloud to tumbling cloud,
> Minute by minute they change;
> A shadow of cloud on the stream
> Changes minute by minute; ...

[150]

Amidst the relentless tide of change, 'The stone's in the midst of all,' representing the element of permanence in life, that which does not yield to temporal forces. This shift of gear turns 'Easter 1916' into a major poem. Then comes the sentiment that, in my reading, lies at the heart of the poem, with the warning that:

> Too long a sacrifice
> Can make a stone of the heart.

Here we have Yeats meditating on the revolutionary ethos and fretting that it may lead to excessive single-mindedness. He worries that a willingness to make sacrifices in pursuit of noble goals can inadvertently turn hearts to stone.

Maud did not like Yeats's poem, which she thought was not worthy of him, nor of his subject. She took particular exception to his hearts of stone image, and claimed that he knew quite well 'that sacrifice has never turned a heart to stone though it has immortalised many & through it alone mankind can rise to God'.[36] I have seen one authority argue that Gonne is actually 'the presiding spirit' behind the poem,[37] but I find that a bit of a stretch. Yeats's nationalism was often routed through Gonne, yes, but she was not its totality.

Yeats then asks a question that would, decades later, become a kernel of revisionist history and is something that is debated to this day.

> Was it needless death after all?
> For England may keep faith
> For all that is done and said.

Would Home Rule have been granted as promised after World War I? Would that have resolved Ireland's divisions without recourse to violence? And would that have softened the stand-off between North and South? Those who challenge the revisionist thesis that the Rising caused 'needless death' point to the changing character of the British government, in which, by 1918, Conservatives sympathetic to Ulster unionism were in the ascendant.

After the thread of ambivalence that runs through the poem, Yeats concludes with a resounding chorus that makes the poem seem like a cheerleader for the Rising, which it is not:

> MacDonagh and MacBride
> And Connolly and Pearse
> Now and in time to be,
> Wherever green is worn,
> Are changed, changed utterly:
> A terrible beauty is born.

It is as if Yeats, within months of the Rising, was trying to write an agenda for future assessments of the events of 1916. As Yeats worked on his poem, there was no guarantee that the Rising had changed everything.

Not everyone saw the young revolutionaries who wanted to build on the Rising's legacy as the way of the future. Yeats's old verbal sparring partner, D.P. Moran, initially expected that the Sinn Féin leadership would need to stand aside and let the old heads in the Irish Party take matters forward. With those ambivalent words 'a terrible beauty', Yeats captured the complex character of the Rising: the terrible nature of the violence set against the dignity of the aspirations being pursued, and the personal heroism of those who sacrificed themselves in support of a seemingly hopeless cause.

One literary scholar has argued that Yeats's 'modernist ascent' began with 'Easter 1916' in an era when writers like him 'were responding to the challenges of the contemporary moment in aesthetically experimental ways'.[38] After completing 'Easter 1916' Yeats continued to reflect on the Rising. In 'Sixteen Dead Men', written in December 1916 but also held back from publication until 1920, he recognises the capacity of the executed leaders 'to stir the boiling pot':

> You say that we should still the land
> Till Germany's overcome;
> But who is there to argue that
> Now Pearse is deaf and dumb?
> And is their logic to outweigh
> MacDonagh's bony thumb?

This records the manner in which the sacrifice of the Rising's leaders weighed heavily on Ireland in the years that followed, as those who survived were determined to vindicate their slain heroes.

In 'The Rose Tree', written in April 1917, Yeats has Patrick Pearse and James Connolly discuss the watering of the tree:

> 'To make the green come out again
> And spread on every side,
> And shake the blossom from the bud
> To be the garden's pride.'

'But where can we draw water,'
Said Pearse to Connolly,
'When all the wells are parched away?
O plain as plain can be
There's nothing but our own red blood
Can make a right Rose Tree.'

Here we have Yeats exploring, and appearing to authenticate, the idea of blood sacrifice that has come to be associated with Patrick Pearse. Thus, within a year of the Easter Rising, Yeats had in his poetry rolled out all the themes that I recall being featured during the Rising's fiftieth anniversary commemoration in 1966, and in the years that followed – the Rising's role as an agent of change, the sanctification of its leaders, the impact of their sacrifice and the spectre of historical revisionism.

In his play *The Dreaming of the Bones*, which is set in 1916, Yeats imagines an encounter between a ghostly Diarmuid (McMurrough) and Dervorgilla, 'for seven hundred years our lips have not met' and a young man 'who was in the Post Office' and, if captured, would be 'put up against a wall and shot'. The couple seeks forgiveness for the fact that Diarmuid, the twelfth-century King of Leinster, 'being blind and bitter and bitterly in love', brought 'a foreign army from across the sea', a reference to Diarmuid, faced with the vengeance of Dervogilla's wronged husband, inviting the Anglo-Normans to Ireland to help restore him to his kingdom. The young veteran of the Easter Rising insists that: 'never, never shall Diarmuid and Dervorgilla be forgiven'. At the time Yeats considered this strange little play one of his 'best things', but accepted that its link to 1916 meant that it might be thought 'dangerous'.

Yeats became involved in the effort to secure clemency for Roger Casement, the sixteenth person to be executed for participating in the Rising. A former British consular official who had been knighted for his efforts in exposing abuse of native populations in South America and the Congo, in retirement Casement became a fervent Irish nationalist. He went to Germany to seek support for the Rising and was arrested when he landed in Ireland accompanying a seized arms shipment. When Casement was convicted of treason, a campaign was launched to have him spared. Casement's death affected Yeats and well into the 1930s he was writing about the Casement Diaries that were leaked to the press in 1916 in order to discredit him on grounds of his homosexual activities. Like most Irish nationalists of his day, and since, Yeats believed the diaries to be forgeries:

> I say that Roger Casement
> Did what he had to do,
> He died upon the gallows
> But that is nothing new.
>
> Afraid they might be beaten
> Before the bench of Time
> They turned a trick by forgery
> And blackened his good name.

## 'To stir the boiling pot'

How did Yeats's writing respond so impressively to the

Rising when we know that privately he was in two minds about it? Throughout his life, Yeats was torn in different directions when it came to Irish affairs. He was at different times a Parnellite, an advanced nationalist, a social conservative, an advocate of the Anglo-Irish tradition and, latterly, an admirer of authoritarian politics. At heart, however, he was a romantic nationalist who convinced himself as a young man that there was something special about Ireland and its Celtic traditions. The events of 1916 renewed this belief and helped him sort out his life.

In the wake of the Easter Rising, Yeats began the final stage of his Irish journey, which would take him through the Irish revolution to a renewed disenchantment during the 1920s and on to his brush with Irish-style fascism in the 1930s. The Rising triggered a rebirth of his belief in the heroic possibilities of the Ireland of his time.

Over the course of 1917, Yeats's life assumed a more settled mode. In March he paid £35 to purchase a fourteenth-century Hiberno-Norman tower house at Ballylee, which he renamed Thoor Ballylee. It became a potent symbol in the poetry he wrote during the 1920s that appeared in *The Tower* (1928) and *The Winding Stair* (1933).


## 'The living beauty is for younger men'

On a visit to France in August 1917, Yeats made his final marriage proposal to Maud, which was rejected. Strangely, he then turned his attentions to Gonne's 22-year-old daughter, Iseult, whom he had known all of her life, and who was the subject of a beautiful poem entitled 'To a Child Dancing in the Wind', written in 1912. At that time,

Iseult, offspring of her mother's relationship with the French politician Lucien Millevoye, was eighteen years old. In his poem, Yeats urges Iseult to 'Dance there upon the shore' and reflects on the implications of her youth:

> Being young you have not known
> The fool's triumph, nor yet
> Love lost as soon as won,
> Nor the best labourer dead
> And all the sheaves to bind.
> What need have you to dread
> The monstrous crying of wind?

The 'love lost' is that of her mother and 'the best labourer' refers to Synge.

Yeats's romantic interest in this young woman is an uncomfortable aspect of his life story. I had a Twitter exchange some time back with someone who viewed Yeats's behaviour at this time as 'creepy' and hoped that Ireland would find a more savoury poetic voice to champion. In 1917, when he proposed to her, Iseult was not exactly 'a child dancing in the wind'. She was twenty-three years old and Yeats was fifty-two. Thus, the age gap between them was large but hardly unprecedented, then or now.

When T.S. Eliot married his second wife, Valerie, in 1957, there was an age gap of thirty-eight years between them. Lady Gregory, who was keen that Yeats should marry and settle down, was part of a marriage similar to the one Yeats considered contracting with Iseult. When she married Sir William Gregory in 1880, he was thirty-five years her senior and became a social and political mentor to her, as well as the father of her only child.

The awkwardness about the Yeats–Iseult Gonne liaison lies in the suspicion that, in his eyes, she was a substitute for her mother, who had repeatedly rejected him while nonetheless remaining extraordinarily close to him to the point where Yeats even sought her approval for his proposal to her daughter. Furthermore, Yeats had been a mentor and even a kind of substitute father figure to Iseult during the previous ten years. Indeed, Iseult had once proposed to Yeats, but that was presumably part of a girlish infatuation. In any case, Iseult eventually turned him down, but the two remained on good terms.

Iseult's rebuff caused Yeats's personal life to accelerate as he took up with 24-year-old Georgie Hyde-Lees, who was just two years older than Iseult. He had known her for some years as she was active in London's literary and spiritualist circles. In 1914 Yeats had sponsored her when she was initiated into the Hermetic Order of the Golden Dawn. He confessed to her mother that interest in occult matters was 'a very flirtatious business'.[39]

Georgie's mother, Nelly, remarried in 1911 and as a result Olivia Shakespear's brother, Henry Tucker, became Georgie's stepfather, which meant that her family was drawn into Yeats's circle. Dorothy Shakespear, Olivia's daughter, was Georgie's best friend and thought of her as 'awfully intelligent' and 'alarmingly intuitive', qualities that stood to her in managing her new husband's literary feints and romantic foibles. Yeats moved rapidly and proposed marriage on 26 September. Their nuptials took place on 20 October at Harrow Road Registry Office in London.

The Yeats marriage, which turned out to be a successful one, although not exactly conventional, got off to a remarkable start. Just weeks after his wedding Yeats wrote Lady Gregory what I think is, by any standard, an extraordinarily confessional letter. It begins with the kind of sentiment that millions of newlyweds have felt over the years: 'The last two days Georgie and I have been very happy.' But this was not an ordinary newly-wed experience, for he admitted that 'two days ago I was in great gloom'. That all changed when his new wife 'got a piece of paper, and talking to me all the while so that her thoughts would not affect what she wrote, wrote these words ...'[40]

This is his description of his wife's automatic writing, which would be a feature of their lives together for years to come. Although Yeats believed that his wife knew noth-ing of his great gloom, it seems to me that her automatic writing was, at least at one level, a knowing effort on her part to make good her marriage or, to put it another way, 'one of the most ingenious wifely stratagems ever tried to take a husband's mind off another woman'.[41] In his letter to Gregory, Yeats went on: 'From being more miserable than I remember being since Maud Gonne's marriage I became extremely happy. That sense of happiness has lasted ever since.'[42]

By December, he could report to Gregory that Georgie, or George as she became known, and Iseult were becoming great friends, 'first for my sake but now it is for each other's, and as both according to the new fashion for young girls are full of serious studies (both work at Sanskrit), it should ripen'. The recently anguished poet was now indubitably a happy man. 'My wife is a perfect wife, kind, wise, and unselfish ... She has made my life serene and full of order.'[43] Whatever its ulterior motives, his wife's labour, which produced 3,600 pages of automatic script, put him in contact with figures from the spirit world, who told him, among many other things, that 'we have come to give you metaphors for poetry'.[44] And so they did.


## 'Changed utterly'

Yeats's response to the Easter Rising changed his life. His renewed engagement with Irish affairs plucked him out from the personal and political dishevelment produced by the death of 'Romantic Ireland'. A revolution and a wife had come to his rescue. For the rest of his life, the Rising continued to fascinate him. In the late 1930s he asked:

> When Pearse summoned Cuchulain to his side,
> What stalked through the Post Office? What intellect,
> What calculation, number, measurement, replied?

Considering that Yeats had made Cuchulain a major figure in his own writing, Pearse's appropriation of the ancient Gaelic hero establishes a kind of spiritual kinship between the poet and the revolutionary. And Yeats could not shake off the idea that he might have borne some responsibility for the 'terrible beauty' of 1916, which I have seen dismissed as a vainglorious overreach on Yeats's part:[45]

> All that I have said and done,
> Now that I am old and ill,
> Turns into a question till
> I lie awake night after night
> And never get the answers right.

W.B. Yeats (1865–1939): 'That sang, to sweeten Ireland's wrong.'
(Library of Congress)

John O'Leary (1830–1907), who encouraged Yeats to become an Irish writer. 'Romantic Ireland's dead and gone, / It's with O'Leary in the grave.' (Library of Congress)

Maud Gonne (1866–1953), with whom Yeats had a lifelong romantic fascination. 'But one man loved the pilgrim soul in you.' (Library of Congress)

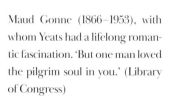

Charles Stewart Parnell (1846–1891), Ireland's 'uncrowned King'. 'Come gather round me, Parnellites / And praise our chosen man'. (Library of Congress)

Douglas Hyde (1869–1949), founder of the Gaelic League in 1893 and first President of Ireland, 'most popular of men' in Yeats's mind. (National Library of Ireland)

Lady Augusta Gregory (1852–1932), Yeats's closest literary ally. 'We were the last romantics.' (Library of Congress)

John Millington Synge (1871–1909), 'And here's John Synge himself, that rooted man.' (Alamy)

John Butler Yeats (1839–1922), 'My father upon the Abbey stage, before him a raging crowd.' (Library of Congress)

Arthur Griffith (1871–1922), described by Yeats as 'staring with hysterical pride'. The two had a chequered relationship stretching back to the 1890s. (National Library of Ireland)

Roger Casement (1864–1916), 'The ghost of Roger Casement / Is beating at the door.' (Library of Congress)

We know their dream; enough
To know they dreamed & died;
And what if excess of love
Bewildered them till they died?
I write it out in a verse
MacDonagh & MacBride
And Connolly & Pearse
Now & in time to be
Where ever green is worn
are changed, changed utterly;
A terrible beauty is born.

Sept 25. 1916

Written during the summer of 1916, 'Easter 1916' expressed Yeats's firm conviction that Ireland had been 'changed utterly' by the Easter Rising. (United Agents and Caitríona Yeats)

Yeats at the funeral of Kevin O'Higgins (1892–1927), the Irish Free State's 'sole statesman ... a soul incapable of remorse or rest'. (National Library of Ireland)

W.B. Yeats in 1923, the year of his Nobel Prize, which he described as 'part of Europe's welcome to the Free State'. (National Library of Ireland)

Did that play of mine send out
Certain men the English shot?

In 1915, when Yeats published the first volume of his *Autobiographies*, which he called *Reveries over Childhood and Youth*, he confessed to being 'sorrowful and disturbed' and concluded with the brooding thought that 'all life weighed in the scales of my own life seems to me a preparation for something that never happens'.[46] Things did happen in the two decades that followed, and they sealed Yeats's standing as a modern mage. Although he could never be viewed as an unambiguous admirer of the Easter Rising, it drew from him a poem that set a pattern for his later work, a great meditative poem inspired by events in Ireland. There is a book from the 1970s about the literary inspiration behind the Easter Rising – *The Imagination of an Insurrection*.[47] In Yeats's case, there was in 1916, I would say, the resurrection of an imagination.

# 6

# 'We had fed the heart on fantasies'

## Yeats on the Irish War of Independence and Civil War, 1918–23

## The Stare's Nest by My Window

The bees build in the crevices
Of loosening masonry, and there
The mother birds bring grubs and flies.
My wall is loosening; honey-bees,
Come build in the empty house of the stare.

We are closed in, and the key is turned
On our uncertainty; somewhere
A man is killed, or a house burned,
Yet no clear fact to be discerned:
Come build in the empty house of the stare.

A barricade of stone or of wood;
Some fourteen days of civil war;
Last night they trundled down the road
That dead young soldier in his blood:
Come build in the empty house of the stare.

We had fed the heart on fantasies,
The heart's grown brutal from the fare;
More substance in our enmities
Than in our love; O honey-bees,
Come build in the empty house of the stare.

## 'The heart's grown brutal'

'The Stare's Nest by My Window' is part of a magnificent, seven-part sequence of poems, 'Meditations in Time of Civil War', which amply illustrates Yeats's strengths as a mature writer, one who was able to handle big themes in longer poems that reveal a wisdom drawn from his personal experience and packaged in powerful, memorable lines of lasting resonance. Yeats's experience was anchored in the Ireland of his time. The years between 1918 and 1922 were Ireland's years, when the country's political fortunes were transformed, albeit at the cost of partition and civil war. Yeats was intensely interested in that story, which became part of his story – and of his poetry.

In 2020, at the height of the Covid-19 pandemic, my friend, the lawyer and literary scholar Joseph Hassett, pointed out to me the relevance of Yeats's lines to the conundrums posed by the pandemic and the lockdown it necessitated:

> We are closed in, and the key is turned
> On our uncertainty ...

In his poem Yeats appeared to be speaking to us across the span of a century, from the aftermath of one pandemic to the teeth of another one. Hassett has written that:

> The wisdom Yeats distilled from the Irish experience applies around the world and seems never to lose its pertinence. Early in his life Yeats had foreseen that his local experience would have global resonance, an idea memorably expressed in his pronouncement, 'One can only reach out to the universe with a gloved hand – that glove is one's nation, the only thing one knows even a little of.'[1]

Yeats had come to know a lot about Ireland and had a great deal to say in the poems he wrote during the 1920s. To understand how he acquired the capacity to write poems like those published in *The Tower* (1928), we need to turn the clock back to 1918, with a newly married poet setting out on a new phase of his life.

## 'A measureless consummation'

In a 1968 obituary for Yeats's wife, George, the critic Richard Ellmann observed that, had her husband died in 1917 instead of marrying, he would have been remembered as 'a remarkable minor poet' with a great lyric gift, 'but who, except in a handful of poems, did not have much to say with it'. In Ellmann's view, Yeats's marriage to George 'released his energies like a spring'.[2] This is based on the notion that, while Yeats's early work was memorable, it was not all that weighty. The poems he wrote in the last two decades of his life were nothing if not weighty. Part of that weightiness was absorbed from the exhilarating and unsettling developments unfolding in Ireland.

Yeats's general demeanour also underwent a significant change at this time. The bitter, disenchanted poet of the first decade of the century was no more. The caustic anger of those years gave way to a more generalised anxiety about the drift of events in Ireland and beyond. At the same time you get the impression of a happier individual, enjoying married life, drawing contentment from the completion of Thoor Ballylee and deriving comfort and enlightenment from his wife's automatic writing.

With an evident recognition of the shared character of this esoteric venture with his new wife, he wrote that: 'A very profound, very exciting mystical philosophy – which seems the fulfilment of many dreams and prophecies – is coming in strange ways to George and myself.'[3] Remarkably, considering his age and long intellectual formation, he felt that 'for the first time I understand human life' and confessed that he lived 'with a strange sense of revelation and never know what the day will bring'.[4] Even his health was suddenly better.

## 'All life's epitome'

The year 1918 began tragically for Lady Gregory when her only son, Robert, a World War I pilot, was killed in action in Italy, where his plane may have been shot down mistakenly by his own side. Although the two were not always on the best of terms, and Robert Gregory distinguished himself chiefly at cricket, shooting and horsemanship, Yeats presents him as someone who had 'genius' as a landscape painter – although there is little enough evidence to support that thesis.

While Yeats may privately have seen Robert Gregory as a dilettante, his death drew from him a major poem, 'In Memory of Major Robert Gregory', which is an example of how Yeats can brilliantly universalise incidents from within his own circle. The poem also remembers Lionel Johnson, Synge and his uncle, George Pollexfen ('In muscular youth well known to Mayo men for horsemanship'). Yeats learned a lot about horses from his uncle, and later deeply impressed English author G.K. Chesterton with his equine knowledge.[5] Those departed friends were now joined by Robert Gregory 'in the discourtesy of death'.

Yeats surely exaggerates Gregory's virtues ('our perfect man') out of respect for his mother, but his tribute is a sustained and powerful one:

> Some burn damp faggots, others may consume
> The entire combustible world in one small room
> As though dried straw, and if we turn about
> The bare chimney is gone black out
> Because the work had finished in that flare.
> Soldier, scholar, horseman, he,
> As 'twere all life's epitome.
> What made us dream that he could comb grey hair?

Robert Gregory was also the subject of another poem that has become one of Yeats's more popular works: 'An Irish Airman Foresees his Death', a war poem that could easily serve as a pacifist manifesto, with its claim that:

> Those that I fight I do not hate,
> Those that I guard I do not love;
> My country is Kiltartan Cross,
> My countrymen Kiltartan's poor ...

There is an echo here of Tom Kettle's explanation to his daughter Betty that his service on the battlefields of the Western Front, which subsequently led to his death at Ginchy during the Battle of the Somme in 1916, was driven not by loyalty to king or emperor:

> But for a dream, born in a herdsman's shed,
> And for the secret Scripture of the poor.[6]

Yeats's poem comes to a crescendo with the airman's assertion that:

> A lonely impulse of delight
> Drove to this tumult in the clouds;
> I balanced all, brought all to mind,
> The years to come seemed waste of breath,
> A waste of breath the years behind
> In balance with this life, this death.

It's a fine poem, but I am not sure it provides much in the way of comfort to the bereaved.

While Lady Gregory clearly had a deep interest in the people of Kiltartan, from whom she collected folklore, her son lived mainly in London, even after he became the owner of the family estate on his twenty-first birthday in 1902. It seems to me that Yeats's poems about Robert Gregory have his mother as both their inspiration and their chief audience. It is to his credit that those poems of that particular moment, that of Robert Gregory's death, and written almost to order, are such fine compositions with a universal appeal.

## 'Pull down established honour'

The established order was being pulled down in Ireland in 1918. The political atmosphere was heating up as a groundbreaking General Election loomed, the first with women's suffrage. Sinn Féin, a rising force with a young and energetic membership, sought to capitalise on the burgeoning legacy of the Easter Rising and thus overturn the Irish Party's long-held political ascendancy in Ireland.

Sinn Féin won four by-elections during 1917 and, by October of that year, had shed its original aim of securing a dual monarchy for Ireland and had become a republican party under the leadership of Éamon de Valera, for whom Griffith, the party's founder more than a decade earlier, had agreed to step aside. The Irish Party enjoyed some renewed success in 1918 but was undone by the British government's plan to introduce conscription in Ireland. This caused a major political crisis and resulted in the Irish Party withdrawing its MPs from Westminster and joining a national movement opposed to compulsory military service.

As ever, Yeats had his finely tuned ear to the ground and spotted the grave risks associated with the British government's effort to extend conscription to Ireland. If conscription were to be imposed on Ireland (and it never was), Yeats feared that 'disastrous outbreaks' of violence would take place across nationalist Ireland. 'I doubt,' he wrote, 'the priests and the leaders being able to keep the wild bloods to passive resistance.'

Ireland was in 'a dangerous condition' and 'the old historical passion' was 'at its greatest intensity'. Young men, he said, were 'mad jealous of their leaders for being shot'![7] He joined with Gregory, Æ, Hyde and others in writing to the *Nation* newspaper, protesting that the imposition of conscription would end 'all hope of peace in Ireland and goodwill towards England in our lifetime'.[8]

Yeats spent much of 1918 in Ireland, staying at Ballinamantane near Coole Park, where his marriage 'settled into a happy pattern'.[9] Much time was spent supervising the rebuilding work at nearby Thoor Ballylee, which gave him bounteous satisfaction. Writing to his father, he said that he was 'making a setting for his old age, a place to influence lawless youth, with its severity and antiquity'.[10] According to Yeats's first biographer, his fifty-third birthday was marked in the unusual environs of Gloucester Jail, where Arthur Griffith and Desmond FitzGerald (later a Free State Minister and father of a future Taoiseach, Garret FitzGerald) got permission from the prison governor to arrange a celebration of Ireland's national poet.

Yeats would surely have been astonished had he known that Griffith, with whom he had a tetchy history, had proclaimed him the greatest poet to have come out of Ireland.[11] Yeats's own tribute to a republican felon,

Constance Markievicz, is a fine poem, but hardly a rousing tribute to her political creed:

> Did she in touching that lone wing
> Recall the years before her mind
> Became a bitter, an abstract thing,
> Her thought some popular enmity:
> Blind and leader of the blind
> Drinking the foul ditch where they lie?

The Yeatses ended their first full year of married life renting Maud Gonne's home on St Stephen's Green, where they spent some months during the Spanish flu pandemic. Dublin had often irritated Yeats, but he now thought it 'a more amusing place than it used to be'.[12] While Yeats himself escaped the deadly virus, his family had two potentially fatal brushes with it. In late 1918 his New York-based, 79-year-old father, John Butler Yeats, became dangerously ill, but eventually pulled through with the help of New York lawyer and patron of Joyce and Yeats, John Quinn.

Not long after news of his father's illness reached Yeats in Dublin, the flu posed a more direct threat to his family when his pregnant, 27-year-old wife, George, was struck down. It was an alarming time for the Yeats family, as that strain of flu took a surprisingly heavy toll on people between the ages of fifteen and forty, who accounted for almost half of the total deaths recorded.

Yeats thought for a time that his wife was in danger of dying, but by mid-December she was on the mend and gave birth to their daughter, Anne, two months later. At the height of George's illness, Maud Gonne turned up unexpectedly at Yeats's door. As she was the subject of an exclusion order, Maud had come to Ireland illegally and, fearing a police raid that could put at further risk his seriously ill wife, Yeats turned Gonne away, which caused a predictable clash between the two. Word was put around Dublin maliciously that Yeats had tried to keep Gonne locked up in London so that he could have her Dublin home. Inevitably, their relationship suffered a serious setback, but they were again writing regularly to each other in 1920, with Maud seeking his advice and sympathy with respect to Iseult's difficult marriage with Francis Stuart. And, of course, Maud continued to feature in his writings for the rest of his days.

If the world had been shaken up by the impact of war, revolution and a pandemic, James Joyce was doing his best to shake up the literary scene. Although Joyce was a writer of a very different kind, Yeats expressed appreciation of *Ulysses* when it was serialised in *The Little Review*, beginning in the summer of 1918, and thought that Joyce had 'certainly surpassed in intensity any novelist of our time'.[13]

When *Ulysses* finally appeared in book form in Paris, Yeats commented positively on it, even though he had only read its first thirty pages. 'It has,' he wrote, 'our Irish cruelty and also our kind of strength and the Martello Tower pages are full of beauty.'[14] As those pages are ones that even the casual reader of *Ulysses* has probably managed to get through, one wonders if Yeats ever read the novel in its entirety. And indeed, in planning to meet Joyce during the summer of 1923, more than a year after its publication, Yeats expected to have to use 'the utmost ingenuity to hide the fact that I have never finished *Ulysses*'.[15] Whether he ever read it fully or not, he became one of the book's early champions.

## 'The nineteenth autumn has come upon me'

The twentieth century's nineteenth year saw the publication of *The Wild Swans at Coole* (an earlier edition had been published by his sisters' Cuala Press in 1917). The collection does not include his Easter Rising poems, 'Easter 1916', 'Sixteen Dead Men' or 'The Rose Tree', all of which were written in 1916 or 1917. He clearly thought that it was still too early to go public on the Easter Rising and its consequences.

Personal relationships are at the heart of this volume, those with Maud, Iseult and his wife George, who is Sheba in 'Solomon to Sheba':

> Sang Solomon to Sheba,
> And kissed her dusky face,
> 'All day long from mid-day
> We have talked in the one place,
> All day long from shadowless noon
> We have gone round and round
> In the narrow theme of love
> Like an old horse in a pound.'

I am not sure that 27-year-old George would necessarily have been flattered by the image of 'an old horse' being applied to her even obliquely, but she must have been pleased with the poem's last verse and its expression of her husband's satisfaction with the fruits of married life:

Said Solomon to Sheba,
And kissed her Arab eyes,
'There's not a man or woman
Born under the skies
Dare match in learning with us two,
And all day long we have found
There's not a thing but love can make
The world a narrow pound.'

Considering the number of poems in this volume about Iseult Gonne, it must have been important to George that she had, by the time these works appeared, befriended Iseult. And, of course, poems like 'To a Young Girl' were written before their marriage:

My dear, my dear, I know
More than another
What makes your heart beat so;
Not even your own mother
Can know it as I know,
Who broke my heart for her
When the wild thought,
That she denies
And has forgot,
Set all her blood astir
And glittered in her eyes.

At fifty, when he wrote that poem, Yeats had not lost the gift for love poetry!

## 'A man who is but a dream'

'The Fisherman' is one of the best-known poems in *The Wild Swans at Coole*. It was composed in 1915 and thus reflects Yeats's disappointments at that time, but it does so in a gentler, more considered fashion than do the raging verses in *Responsibilities*. Here Yeats reflects on the ideal Irishman of his dreams during his Celtic Twilight phase:

> The freckled man who goes
> To a grey place on a hill
> In grey Connemara clothes
> At dawn to cast his flies,
> ...
> This wise and simple man.

This was the kind of person who had spurred Yeats's desire:

> To write for my own race
> And the reality;

But other realities had intervened to wreck the poet's best-laid plans. Instead, he had come a cropper at the hands of:

> The craven man in his seat,
> The insolent unreproved,
> And no knave brought to book
> Who has won a drunken cheer,
> The witty man and his joke
> Aimed at the commonest ear,
> The clever man who cries

The catch-cries of the clown,
The beating down of the wise
And great Art beaten down.

Although there are echoes here of 'September 1913' and his other poems of disenchantment, this is a subtler offering that does not seem dead set on giving offence. And the poem refuses to submit to despair. Instead, he sallies forth 'In scorn of this audience' and:

Imagining a man,
And his sun-freckled face,
And grey Connemara cloth...

A man who does not exist,
A man who is but a dream;
And cried, 'Before I am old
I shall have written him one
Poem maybe as cold
And passionate as the dawn.'

And that's what Yeats did. Instead of bowing to the numbness of despair, he fought back with fine-tuned weapons, a sophisticated pen dipped in an eclectic wisdom in preference to the blunt cudgel he had employed in some of his earlier public poems.

## 'The centre cannot hold'

First published in January 1919, 'The Second Coming' is perhaps Yeats's most oft-quoted work. It is shaped by insights gleaned from his wife's automatic writing, which

Yeats said had given him 'a strange sense of revelation'.[16] With George's help, he was able to concoct a belief system that brilliantly served his needs, even if others have struggled to make sense of it. Yeats eventually pulled it all together in a bewilderingly difficult book, *A Vision*, described as 'Yeats's attempt to understand the calamitous events of that time, and also to predict the future.'[17] It is given over 'to locating types of human personality and historical ages between the poles of extreme subjectivity and extreme objectivity, according to their place in a scheme of intersecting gyres which corresponds to the phases of the moon'.[18] For most readers, *A Vision* is Yeats's exercise in incomprehensibility equivalent to Joyce's *Finnegans Wake*.

George Yeats's effort was phenomenal. Over a seven-year period she undertook 450 sessions of automatic writing, which produced 3,627 pages of script.[19] This psychic activity understandably became a burden to her, but her husband was fully hooked on what she was able to reveal to him, and she was willing, at times wearily, to fulfil his needs.

It is unnecessary to get into the intricacies of the psychic liaison between the newly married couple, but you have to be impressed with George Yeats's ingenuity and with her husband's willingness to buy into it all. Yeats absorbed from his wife's 'instructors' the idea of history unfolding in 2,000-year cycles and of twenty-eight human types matching the phases of the moon. This meant that when the poem was composed the Christian epoch was into its final century.

This is how Yeats explained his idea of what lay in store for humanity:

> At the present moment the life gyre is sweeping outward, unlike that before the birth of Christ which was narrowing, and has reached its expansion. The revelation which approaches will however take its character from the interior gyre. All our scientific, democratic, fact-accumulating, heterogeneous civilisation belongs to the outward gyre and prepared not the continuance of itself but the revelation as in a lightning flash ...[20]

That's why Yeats believed that things were about to fall apart and that something new and very different was on the way.

As the poem's enduring appeal demonstrates, its power does not depend on knowledge of the esoteric thinking behind it. 'The Second Coming' is one of those poems of the last two decades of Yeats's life in which he wrote with depth of vision and authority of expression. What I call Yeats's 'history poems' are usually rooted in specific Irish events, but 'The Second Coming' has a wider, more general reference. Its mystical provenance notwithstanding, it is a poem of its time, reflecting Yeats's deepening anxiety about the state of the world around him.

Over the years 'The Second Coming' has shown a remarkable capacity to relate to the preoccupations of other times, including our own. During the coronavirus pandemic I tweeted a few lines from the poem, which attracted a hugely enthusiastic response. Many of my Twitter followers saw it as creatively addressing the world's many predicaments in 2020. It's not that the poem has a consoling tone, but readers seem, nonetheless, to be buoyed by its diamond-like lucidity.

The poem's historical hinterland was a deeply troubled one. I doubt that there was a more dramatic three months in twentieth-century history, outside of wartime, than those between November 1918 and January 1919, from which 'The Second Coming' emerged. As we have seen, Yeats had paid astonishingly little attention to World War I, a conflict that had taken the lives of 8.5 million combatants and even more civilians.[21] To make matters worse, the Spanish flu had rampaged through Europe in the closing months of the war. By the time the pandemic had run its course it had killed far more people than the four-year war that had just ended.[22]

I am not saying that the pandemic shaped his poem, but it must have deepened Yeats's sense of foreboding about the state of the world around him. The war's aftermath became a major revolutionary moment. In Berlin on 6 January 1919, revolutionary Spartacists occupied a number of public buildings and proclaimed a German Soviet Republic. This uprising was short-lived and was put down ruthlessly, resulting in the deaths of 1,200 insurgents.

By now a man of conservative mind, Yeats feared that change would more likely be for the worse than for the better, that 'things fall apart' more readily than they stay together. There was ample reason to be uneasy about the state of the world as he sat down to write this great poem. War had savagely shattered the old certainties of the *belle époque.* New states were being born – Hungary, Poland, the Kingdom of Serbs, Croats and Slovenes and the Czechoslovak Republic – rising from the ruins of defeated empires. The map of Europe that he and his contemporaries had known for so long was being dramatically redrawn.

In Ireland, the march towards independence was gaining pace. In December 1918 Sinn Féin triumphed in the post-war General Election, with a demand for outright independence. The composition of 'The Second Coming' roughly coincided with the meeting of the First Dáil, attended solely by Sinn Féin MPs, and the issuing of a Declaration of Independence on 21 January. That was also the day when, in effect, Ireland's War of Independence began, with an ambush at Soloheadbeg in County Tipperary in which two members of the Royal Irish Constabulary were killed.

A few months later, Yeats was still full of apprehension about the course of events in Ireland, where he feared that 'wild bloods' were in the ascendant. 'What I want,' he wrote, 'is that Ireland be kept from giving itself (under the influence of its lunatic faculty of going against everything which it believes England to affirm) to Marxian revolution or Marxian definitions of value in any form.' He considered Marxist values to be 'the spear-head of materialism and leading to inevitable murder'. He believed that Ireland's instinctive Anglophobia, a semblance of which he shared, 'kills all thought and encourages the most miserable kind of mob rhetoric'.[23]

Despite his alarm about Ireland's future, he appeared to relish being in the midst of the country's upheavals. As he told John Quinn, 'It looks as if I may have a spirited old age.' It would, he thought, be pleasant to leave Ireland 'until the tumult of war had died down', but 'would one ever come back?' His tower in Galway was assuming ever richer significance for him 'as a fitting monument and symbol', 'a place full of mystery and romance with plenty to do every day'.[24]

In 'The Second Coming' things are seen to be spiralling out of control to the point where 'the falcon cannot hear the falconer' and 'mere anarchy is loosed upon the world'. His language is apocalyptic: 'the blood-dimmed tide is loosed' and 'the ceremony of innocence is drowned'. His prediction is that 'the centre cannot hold'. At the time, there were real fears that Soviet-style regimes might emerge in different parts of a turmoil-ridden continent, mirroring what had happened in Russia in 1917.

The poem's most powerful lines come at the end of the first verse, which came to be seen as a premonition of the disasters of the authoritarian 1930s:

> The best lack all conviction, while the worst
> Are full of passionate intensity.

This is the mature Yeats at his best – a master oracle, sallying forth with seemingly unbounded faith in the validity of his insights.

The poem's second stanza owes much to the vision of history emerging from his wife's visions, with a 'rough beast, its hour come round at last' that 'slouches towards Bethlehem to be born'. This prophetic image is compelling, as is the language in which it is couched – 'the indignant desert birds' and 'twenty centuries of stony sleep' being 'vexed to nightmare by a rocking cradle'.

Like all great poems, 'The Second Coming' gives us lots to mull over. Had Yeats been clearer about what he had in mind with the 'rough beast' that slouches towards Bethlehem, the poem would have been anchored in the moment and lacked the ability to appeal to later generations of readers. Writing on the centenary of Yeats's birth in 1965, the literary critic Edward Engelberg observed that Yeats had 'once seemed remote, old-fashioned, reactionary ... his warnings in poems like "The Second Coming" or "The Gyres" offensive and hysterical. We have had to witness too much to think such things today.'[25] Viewed from the perspective of the 1960s, Yeats's vision was seen to have gained relevance with the passage of time. It has continued to speak to subsequent generations.

Yeats came to recognise the poem's success as a prophetic tool. Writing to his friend Ethel Mannin in 1936, he expressed his 'horror at the cruelty of governments', be they 'Communist, Fascist, nationalist, clerical, anti-clerical.' He insisted that he had not been silent, but had used 'the only vehicle I possess – verse. If you have my poems by you, look up a poem called "The Second Coming". It was written sixteen or seventeen years ago and foretold what is happening.' He concluded that 'it takes fifty years for a poet's weapons to influence the issue'.[26]

## 'Days are dragon-ridden'

The War of Independence left Yeats with no scope for sitting on the fence, and he duly weighed in with criticism of the notorious Black and Tans, a poorly disciplined police force recruited from among demobilised war veterans. The shift in his position towards alignment with Sinn Féin, who were not his natural allies, reflects the broader evolution of national opinion at that time. Yeats's sister Lily, who thought of herself as 'just a mild nationalist', found herself being drawn towards Sinn Féin as a reaction to Black and Tan atrocities.[27] Yeats's reputation as a supposed Sinn Féin supporter landed him in trouble in

Scotland in November 1921 when a lecture he had been set to give in Aberdeen was cancelled and he was deemed by one protestor to be 'an enemy of the Nation'. With his battles at the Abbey Theatre behind him, Yeats found the prospect of interruptions from the audience 'rather pleasantly exciting'.[28]

In 'Reprisals', a poem devoted to Robert Gregory's memory but not published at the time because of Lady Gregory's objections to it, he rages against murdering soldiers and seeks to summon Robert Gregory back to Kiltartan, where:

> Half-drunk or whole-mad soldiery
> Are murdering your tenants there.
> Men that revere your father yet
> Are shot at on the open plain.

On account of those Black and Tan atrocities

> ... certain second thoughts have come
> Upon the cause you served, that we
> Imagined such a fine affair.

Yeats's argument was that the sacrifices made by Irishmen like Gregory during World War I were being mocked by the brutal deeds perpetrated in Ireland in Britain's name. It should be noted that Robert Gregory, unlike his mother, remained a staunch Unionist and imperialist, and might thus not have fully disapproved of tough medicine being meted out to unruly elements in the locality.

During his time living in Oxford in 1920/21 Yeats appeared at the Oxford Union, where he vehemently condemned the British government's actions in Ireland. He alleged that Britain had done in Ireland what Germany had done to Belgium, which, in the wake of World War I, was a pretty savage comparison.[29] For her part, Lady Gregory wrote a number of anonymous pieces for an English liberal paper condemning the British military's actions in Ireland.

In April 1921, with the War of Independence in full flow, Yeats told Olivia Shakespear that he and George were 'nerving' themselves to go to Ireland and mentioned that he was working on 'thoughts suggested by the present state of the world'.[30] This became 'Nineteen Hundred and Nineteen', which he saw as 'simple and passionate, a lamentation over lost peace and lost hope'. It is one of Yeats's more challenging poems, but it is full of arresting images. Who can resist the pull of such phrases as 'wax in the sun's rays', 'no cannon had been turned into a ploughshare', 'the barbarous clamour of a gong' and 'man is in love and loves what vanishes'? Yeats begins with an elegy for all that has been lost:

> Many ingenious lovely things are gone
> That seemed sheer miracle to the multitude,
> Protected from the circle of the moon
> That pitches common things about.

And he mulls over the world's lost innocence:

> O what fine thought we had because we thought
> That the worst rogues and rascals had died out.

Yeats's extended meditation on the state of the world was set off by some murders perpetrated in the Gort area by the

Black and Tans. As is invariably the case with Yeats's work, these incidents are melded with other elements, in this case snatches of ancient literature and philosophy, to produce potent verses whose appeal transcends their Irish setting:

> Now days are dragon-ridden, the nightmare
> Rides upon sleep: a drunken soldiery
> Can leave the mother, murdered at her door,
> To crawl in her own blood, and go scot-free;
> The night can sweat with terror as before
> We pieced our thoughts into philosophy,
> And planned to bring the world under a rule,
> Who are but weasels fighting in a hole.

And the poem goes on in this vein:

> Violence upon the roads: violence of horses;
> Some few have handsome riders, are garlanded
> On delicate sensitive ear or tossing mane,
> But wearied running round and round in their courses
> All break and vanish, and evil gathers head: ...

As he often does in his later poetry, Yeats adds a broader reflection.

> But is there any comfort to be found?
> Man is in love and loves what vanishes,
> What more is there to say?

With lines like those, Yeats reveals himself to be a writer of true weight and deep insight whose work speaks to us across the generations and will likely continue to do so in the time to come.

## 'The spreading laurel tree'

When Anne Butler Yeats was born in Dublin on 26 February 1919 she drew from her father a powerful elegy, 'A Prayer for my Daughter'. In this poem, however, the satisfaction brought by the birth of his first-born child is overshadowed by 'the great gloom' that is in his mind. We find him:

> Imagining in excited reverie
> That the future years had come,
> Dancing to a frenzied drum,
> Out of the murderous innocence of the sea.

He wants his daughter to have 'natural kindness' and to learn 'courtesy' and cultivate 'heart-revealing intimacy'. His model for what to avoid is clearly Maud Gonne, who through 'intellectual hatred' and 'her opinionated mind' had become 'an old bellows full of angry wind'.

The poem's parting advice is for his daughter to have a house 'Where all's accustomed, ceremonious':

> For arrogance and hatred are the wares
> Peddled in the thoroughfares.
> How but in custom and in ceremony
> Are innocence and beauty born?
> Ceremony's a name for the rich horn,
> And custom for the spreading laurel tree.

Leaving their daughter behind in the care of his sisters, Yeats spent several months in 1920 touring the United States accompanied by George, who met his New York-based father for the first time. The two liked each other.

There was considerable American interest in Yeats's take on developments in Ireland. Although his lecture topics studiously avoided current Irish issues, in his response to questions he tended to be markedly nationalistic. On one occasion he described Ireland as 'a country of oppression' and expressed his desire for some form of self-government for his strife-torn country. While he acknowledged Sinn Féin's mandate, he decried political fanaticism as 'a bitter acid that destroyed the soul'.

John Quinn brought him to a rally at which de Valera spoke. He was not an admirer, viewing de Valera as 'A living argument rather than a living man. All propaganda, no human life, but not bitter or hysterical or unjust.'[31] He thought de Valera would fail and be pushed aside by others. How wrong Yeats was with that assessment, as de Valera went on to serve as Taoiseach for twenty-one years, followed by two terms as President of Ireland.

In the closing months of 1920 Yeats finally published 'Easter 1916', which he had kept in limited circulation since its composition more than four years before. Not only that, he also put into print his three other 1916 poems, 'Sixteen Dead Men', 'The Rose Tree ', and 'On a Political Prisoner' (Constance Markievicz). Conor Cruise O'Brien credited him with great political courage: 'The Black-and-Tan terror was now at its height throughout Ireland. To publish these poems in this context was a political act, and a bold one: probably the boldest of Yeats's career.'[32]

December 1921 was perhaps the most dramatic month in modern Irish history. Negotiations between a Sinn Féin delegation led by Arthur Griffith and Michael Collins, and the British government under the leadership of Prime Minister David Lloyd George concluded on 6 December with agreement on a treaty granting dominion status to the twenty-six Irish counties that in 1922 became the

Irish Free State. Then, as Dáil Éireann debated the treaty in an increasingly bitter atmosphere, the Sinn Féin movement split between supporters and opponents of the treaty.

Yeats was troubled by these developments, and confessed that he was 'in great gloom about Ireland'. He saw 'no hope of escape from bitterness' and feared that 'the extreme party' might carry the country: 'When men are very bitter, death and ruin draw them on as a rabbit is supposed to be drawn on by the dancing of the fox.' He feared that he might have to abandon both Ireland and England, and did not want his children to 'inherit bitterness' in Ireland or to have them grow up in England, where 'being Irish by tradition, and family and fame, they would be in an unnatural condition of mind and grow, as so many Irishmen who live here do, sour and argumentative'.[33] Yet it was not long before he decided that Ireland should become his family's base, as by now he was 'not much disturbed about the state of Ireland – it will come right in three or four months I think'.[34] That assessment turned out to be unduly optimistic.

In January 1922 Yeats accepted Arthur Griffith's invitation to attend the Irish Race Conference in Paris as a representative of the Dáil government, which ruled the country in an acting capacity until the Irish Free State was formally established in December 1922. At the conference, where the Irish political divide was fully in evidence, Yeats showed his support for the provisional government and told Lady Gregory that he was willing 'partly to identify the Abbey with government propaganda'.[35] The role he played as a supporter for the new regime caused a further rift with Maud. His brother, Jack B. Yeats, supported the anti-treaty side, while Lady Gregory too was sympathetic to de Valera's anti-treaty Republicans.

John Butler Yeats died in New York in February 1922, having spent the last fourteen years of his life there. His correspondence with his son is a gem, well worth dipping into. Yeats marvelled at his father's ability, 'more than any man I have ever known', to live 'in the happiness of the passing moment'.[36]


## 'Caught in the cold snows of a dream'

Yeats was living at Thoor Ballylee by April 1922, and before long a civil war was being fought all around him. In his letters he gave nonchalant reactions to the disturbances in his vicinity. Fretfully, he wondered if literature would be changed 'by that most momentous of events, the return of evil'. His attention was roused by the fact 'that everybody speaks with caution as no-one knows who will be master to-morrow'.[37] He was aware of 'the murders of protestants in Cork', which did not surprise him. He knew that 'when there were so many fire-arms in wild hands an attempt to reply in that way to Belfast must come', which was a reference to violence against Catholics there.

His analysis of the political situation was deft and accurate: 'We have popular leaders representing a minority but a considerable one, who mock the appeal to the vote and may be able for a time to prevent it.'[38] Already showing signs of a preference for strong government, he predicted that the result of Ireland's upheavals would be 'not a demagogic but an authoritative government'.[39] Later, he reported to Olivia

Shakespear that 'everywhere one notices a drift towards Conservatism, perhaps towards Autocracy'. He added that 'there is nothing so dangerous to a modern state, when politics take the place of theology, as a bunch of martyrs. A bunch of martyrs (1916) were the bomb and we are living in the explosion.'[40]

Yeats watched the Collins–de Valera pact of 1922, designed to stave off civil war, and believed that it was prompted by a fear of social revolution and a response to a reported plot by army chiefs in Ulster to reconquer Ireland. The violent upheavals in the surrounding countryside seemed strangely to excite him. Here's a sample of his almost whimsical commentary on the Civil War: 'Life here is interesting, but restless and unsafe – I have two bullet holes through my windows – as it must always be when the sheep endeavour to control the goats who are by nature so much the more enterprising race.'[41]

This period of turmoil he lived through brought forth one of his greatest works, 'Meditations in Time of Civil War'. In a note on this poem, Yeats explained that before it was finished 'the Republicans blew up our "ancient bridge" one midnight. They forbade us to leave the house, but were otherwise polite, even saying at last "Good night, thank you", as though we had given them the bridge.'[42] With roads being blocked near Thoor Ballylee:

> For the first week there were no newspapers, no reliable news, we did not know who had won, who had lost, and even after newspapers came, one never knew what was happening on the other side of the hill or of the line of trees. Ford cars passed the house from time to time with

coffins standing upon end between the seats ... One felt an overmastering desire not to grow unhappy or embittered, not to lose all sense of the beauty of nature.[43]

The poem begins with a meditation on 'Ancestral Houses', 'among a rich man's flowering lawns':

> Amid the rustle of his planted hills,
> Life overflows without ambitious pains;

His apprehension about the demise of 'the inherited glory of the rich' was founded on the destruction of many of the great houses of the Anglo-Irish during the violence of the War of Independence and the Civil War. He worried that the greatness he attributed to the Anglo-Irish tradition was in jeopardy, that violence and bitterness might eclipse life's nobler instincts:

> O what if levelled lawns and gravelled ways
> Where slippered Contemplation finds his ease
> And Childhood a delight for every sense,
> But take our greatness with our violence?
> ...
> What if those things the greatest of mankind
> Consider most to magnify, or to bless,
> But take our greatness with our bitterness?

The poem's second section, 'My House', expresses his deep satisfaction with Thoor Ballylee:

> A farmhouse that is sheltered by its wall,
> An acre of stony ground,
> Where the symbolic rose can break in flower,

Old ragged elms, old thorns innumerable,
The sound of the rain or sound
Of every wind that blows; ... .

Later in this sequence of poems, he worries about his descendants losing 'the flower':

Through natural declension of the soul,
Through too much business with the passing hour,
Through too much play, or marriage with a fool?

'Meditations' contains some truly great Yeats lines:

I count those feathered balls of soot
The moor-hen guides upon the stream,
To silence the envy in my thought;
And turn towards my chamber, caught
In the cold snows of a dream.

The poem reveals Yeats's skill at focusing on the particular, 'an affable Irregular' and 'a brown Lieutenant and his men / Half dressed in national uniform' and drawing imperious, luminously worded conclusions from his observations:

We had fed the heart on fantasies,
The heart's grown brutal from the fare;
More substance in our enmities
Than in our love; ...

The poem ends with Yeats wondering if he could have proved his worth 'In something that all others understand or share':

But O! ambitious heart, had such a proof drawn forth
A company of friends, a conscience set at ease,
It had but made us pine the more. The abstract joy,
The half-read wisdom of daemonic images,
Suffice the ageing man as once the growing boy.


## 'I must nourish dreams'

Yes, Yeats had nourished himself on dreams of Ireland's future. During the revolutionary era he saw at close quarters the dream of independence being realised and also witnessed the dimming of that dream under the strains of civil war. When Yeats's friend Oliver St John Gogarty, now best known as the inspiration for the character of Buck Mulligan in *Ulysses*, paid tribute to Yeats in the Senate he indulged in more than a little hyperbole when he commented that: 'If it had not been for Yeats there would be no Irish Free State.' Yet there was more than a grain of reality in Gogarty's assertion. Yeats had certainly thrown his lot in with this emerging political entity, and with an intense engagement that would persist for most of the rest of his life and bring forth continued poetic riches.

Looking back over his life in poetry, in 1936 he wrote that he was 'a man of my time, through my poetical faculty living its history'.[44] At no other period of his life was that assertion as true as it was when Ireland's history was most vibrant, between 1918 and 1922. Yeats's commitment to revolutionary Ireland was exceptional. After all, despite the 'violence upon the roads' and 'that dead young soldier in his blood', he moved his English wife and young family back to Ireland, which became his main abode for most of the rest of his life. He sought to build a

nest for himself and his family not in 'the empty house of the
stare' (an old west of Ireland word for starling) but in a new
state, an Ireland that would 'suffice the ageing man as once
the growing boy'.

# 7

## 'We the great gazebo built'

### The Anglo-Irish Yeats

## In Memory of Eva Gore-Booth and Con Markievicz

The light of evening, Lissadell,
Great windows open to the south,
Two girls in silk kimonos, both
Beautiful, one a gazelle.
But a raving autumn shears
Blossom from the summer's wreath;
The older is condemned to death,
Pardoned, drags out lonely years
Conspiring among the ignorant.
I know not what the younger dreams –
Some vague Utopia – and she seems,
When withered old and skeleton-gaunt,
An image of such politics.
Many a time I think to seek
One or the other out and speak
Of that old Georgian mansion, mix
Pictures of the mind, recall
That table and the talk of youth,
Two girls in silk kimonos, both
Beautiful, one a gazelle.

Dear shadows, now you know it all,
All the folly of a fight
With a common wrong or right.
The innocent and the beautiful
Have no enemy but time;
Arise and bid me strike a match
And strike another till time catch;
Should the conflagration climb,
Run till all the sages know.
We the great gazebo built,

They convicted us of guilt;
Bid me strike a match and blow.


## 'An image of such politics'

The 1920s was the decade when Yeats's commitment to Irish public life was at its deepest. Those years, when he spent more time in Ireland than ever before, also produced his best work, notably in *The Tower* (1928), with its slew of magnificent poems. Against the odds in a wickedly turbulent world, he managed to weave poetry and public life into a glorious tapestry that he hung against the encroachments of age and ill health. While he may ultimately have concluded that Ireland in the 1920s was 'no country for old men', he made every attempt to make it his country, and that effort yielded a rich poetic harvest.

There's a well-known adage often applied to US presidential politics to the effect that 'you campaign in poetry and you govern in prose'. The same could be said of independence movements. As one source puts it, 'the dissipation of revolutionary aspiration in post-revolutionary disillusionment is by now a commonplace of modern political history'.[1]

In the Irish case, there was a lot of poetry in the air in the latter stages of the struggle for freedom. After all, three of the seven signatories of the 1916 Proclamation, Patrick Pearse, Thomas MacDonagh and Joseph Plunkett, were published poets, while the cultural and intellectual movements of the preceding quarter of a century, led by Yeats and Douglas Hyde, had aided and arguably front-ended the political transformation that took place between 1916 and 1921. Indeed, Hyde's Gaelic League has been described as 'the nursery for the revolutionary generation of 1916'.[2]

And there was much that was ploddingly prosaic about the Ireland of the 1920s in which Yeats sought to play a public role. One historian has described Ireland in the twenty years after independence as 'the history of a disappointment ... a flat, narrow place that lost the courage of its own revolution's convictions, a cruel, timid place that was hard on its weakest and too much in thrall to those who preached right from wrong ... it was an Eden smashed into the tiniest bits in the bitter knowledge that we had done it to ourselves'.[3] Perhaps inevitably, given its confessional composition and 'the role played by Catholicism in confirming a sense of national identity'[4] in Ireland, the new state was heavily influenced by a Catholic ethos, but that was a source of deep dismay and frustration to many less pious souls.

In the early years of its independence Ireland was a country where the realities of managing the affairs of a new state during and after a damaging civil war squeezed out the idealism that had driven the country's freedom struggle in the preceding decade. I happen to think that the Irish Free State did respectably well in navigating its way through the shoals of economic depression and the extreme ideologies that wrecked polities elsewhere in Europe. I have no doubt, however, that the government that held power throughout the 1920s was hidebound, and sorely lacking in imagination and compassion. The politicians had good cause to be daunted by the challenges facing them, but a more expansive and energetic response might reasonably have been expected of them.

Indeed, they appeared to pride themselves on a stolid conservatism and behaved with excessive brutality during the Civil War in crushing their opponents by means of extrajudicial actions. Largely accepting the need for the prose of responsible government, Yeats supported the government's draconian policies, which strained his ties with Maud Gonne, 'protesting in sibylline old age … against what seems to her a tyranny'.[5] The unlawful execution of seventy-seven Republicans during the Civil War embittered Irish politics for generations. There is no doubt that, after the excitement of the decade of revolution, the 1920s were a big let-down for many who had given broad backing to the independence movement, including Yeats and some of the other leading Irish writers of that era.

## 'Two girls in silk kimonos'

With its evocation of the 'great windows' of 'that old Georgian mansion', 'In Memory of Eva Gore-Booth and Con Markievicz' is my favourite among the many poems that express Yeats's growing enthusiasm for the Anglo-Irish tradition. As Yeats's disappointment with the prosaic realities of independent Ireland deepened, he took refuge in the – by then – faded glories of Anglo-Ireland, which he thought could yet have value for Ireland and for the troubled world into which the Irish Free State emerged in 1922.

Written in 1927, this poem does something of a disservice to the two women it seeks to memorialise, the Sligo-born sisters Eva Gore-Booth and Constance Markievicz. Brought up as part of a privileged, landowning family in the west of Ireland, the two women had broken with the conservative traditions of their caste and taken radical paths of their own making. For Yeats, as one scholar puts it, with their addiction to abstract political slogans, the sisters had 'forfeited their birthright of natural beauty and traditional wisdom for mere golden dreams'.[6]

While Constance Markievicz was not to everyone's taste, she did have the distinction of being the first woman ever to be elected to the Westminster Parliament. In 1927 she was elected to Dáil Éireann for de Valera's Fianna Fáil party, but died before she could take her seat. I am not sure that Yeats's depiction of her 'conspiring among the ignorant' does justice to her courageous willingness to discard the values of her family and social class in favour of a life of unrelenting activism in support of workers' rights, suffragism and the cause of Irish independence.

The dismissal of Eva Gore-Booth as an advocate of 'some vague Utopia' does an even greater injustice to her life as a poet, labour activist, pacifist and suffragist. Eva's poetry has not attracted the appreciation it deserves. Her best-known poem, 'The Little Waves of Breffny', which I once read at a function at her graveside in Hampstead while serving as Ambassador in London, is not her best work:[7]

> The great waves of the Atlantic sweep storming on
>     their way,
> Shining green and silver with the hidden herring
>     shoal,
> But the Little Waves of Breffny have drenched my
>     heart in spray,
> And the Little Waves of Breffny go stumbling through
>     my soul.

[200]

I prefer the poem she wrote about her imprisoned sister in the wake of the Easter Rising:

> The wind is our confederate
> The night has left her doors ajar,
> We meet beyond earth's barred gate,
> Where all the world's wild Rebels are.[8]

Even though he was out of sync with the sisters' politics, Yeats nonetheless declares his desire to rally with them, drawing on the 'talk of youth' and a shared Anglo-Irish heritage, on which the sisters had turned their backs. In the poem, he wants to 'strike a match and blow', which seems to me to evoke a form of aristocratic nationalism founded, perhaps, on the legacy of Edmund Burke; a brand of politics, which, of course, would not have appealed to either of those 'two girls in silk kimonos'. In any case, that was never a runner in a country with such a huge Catholic, nationalist majority who would naturally have been loath to cede their hard-won ascendancy after centuries of painful subordination.

## 'I choose upstanding men'

When we talk about the Anglo-Irish tradition, Ireland's contested eighteenth century quickly comes into focus. The historian J.C. Beckett once explained why it is so difficult to make a measured assessment of that tradition:

> For many Irishmen, perhaps for most, the eighteenth century is a kind of hiatus in the life of the nation, a valley of humiliation between the failure of national aspirations in the Jacobite war and their revival more than a hundred years later.[9]

For Yeats, the eighteenth century ultimately became 'that one Irish century that escaped from darkness and confusion',[10] but he did not always see things that way. His progressive enchantment with the great Anglo-Irish figures of that era, Berkeley, Burke and Swift, reflects a parallel disenchantment with the Ireland of Yeats's own time.

In the 1880s and 90s Yeats had scorned the Anglo-Irish tradition, whose output simply did not fit with his focus on Irish mythology, the Gaelic past and the country's rich folklore. At that time, Yeats was disinclined to regard Jonathan Swift's work as Irish, although he acknowledged the Dean's genius.[11] Neither Swift nor the other eighteenth-century writers he grew to admire made it into a list of best Irish books Yeats compiled in 1895.[12] Instead, he chose to name as national writers 'only those who have written under Irish influence and of Irish subjects'.[13]

In Yeats's view, Swift was someone 'with a more living temperament' than any of his contemporaries: 'He was as near a supreme man as that fallen age could produce.' For the young Yeats, the eighteenth century 'had set chop-logic in the place of the mysterious power'.[14] Yeats was always in thrall to mysterious powers, which he often tracked to Ireland, and the eighteenth century had little appeal to the young poet from that point of view.

By the 1920s Yeats was in open revolt against what he saw as a betrayal by narrower minds of Ireland's glorious potential. The Anglo-Irish writers of the eighteenth century became intellectual cudgels in Yeats's argument with Ireland, which provided the backdrop for some of his greatest poetry. In his play *The Words upon the Window-Pane* (1930), Yeats had one of its characters observe that:

in Swift's day men of intellect reached the height of their power – the greatest position they ever attained in society ... everything great in Ireland and in our character, in what remains of our architecture, comes from that day.[15]

## 'Bound neither to Cause nor to State'

Yeats's infatuation with eighteenth-century Ireland was not widely shared. In the collective memory of nationalist Ireland, that was the era of the Penal Laws, which institution-alised discrimination on religious grounds. As the popular nationalist historian Dorothy Macardle wrote in 1937:

The Penal Laws were devised with coherence and consistency to deprive Catholics of property, of education, and of the franchise, of the guardianship of children, of the control of land, and to exclude them from every professional employment save that of medicine, and from every position of influence in the State.[16]

The Cork-born writer Daniel Corkery (1878–1964) was an influential voice in Ireland during the 1920s and 30s, helping to set the cultural parameters of the new state during its formative years. A man with a strong Irish Ireland outlook, Corkery was perhaps the pre-eminent intellectual critic of the Anglo-Irish tradition that Yeats was busy lionising. In his influential book *The Hidden Ireland*, Corkery conjured up an image of eighteenth-century Ireland, a country 'speckled with ruins – broken abbeys, roofless churches, battered castles, burnt houses, deserted villages, from which the inhabitants were being cleared to make room for beasts'.[17] His work focused on the lives and writing of those eighteenth-century poets who kept alive a Gaelic literary tradition against a backdrop of military defeat, political enfeeblement and economic decline.

Corkery was a regular contributor to *The Leader*, where, in less combative terms than its editor, D.P. Moran, he argued that Irishness was necessarily a compound of nationalism, attachment to the land and adherence to the Catholic faith. In his study *Synge and Anglo-Irish Literature*, described as 'perhaps the most sustained attack on the whole concept of Anglo-Irish culture ever written',[18] Corkery argued that Anglo-Irish literature was incapable of expressing 'the genius of Ireland in the English language'.[19]

Genuine Anglo-Irish literature would, he insisted, express on every page 'the spirit of Irish nationalism' and could not be 'alien-minded'.[20] Corkery thought it impossible for the work of Yeats and his peers to be 'the foundation of a school of poetry in which those three great forces, Religion, Nationalism, the Land, will find intense yet chastened expression'.[21] By Corkery's reckoning, Yeats, although he refrained from assailing him directly, had no place in the new Irish cultural dispensation, but the poet stood his ground, insisting on the value and validity of Anglo-Ireland. By the 1920s Yeats had developed sharp elbows to defend his positions. He insisted that, 'Anglo-Ireland is already Ireland. You may revive the Gaelic language but you cannot revive Gaelic civilization.' While accepting that there might be 'pure Gaels' on the Blasket Islands, he was sure that there were none at the heart of government or in the judiciary and the universities: 'We have not only English but European thoughts and customs in our heads and in our habits. We could not, if we would, give them up.' Although he had long championed Anglo-Ireland, he professed to hate all hyphenated words.[22] Yeats was no slouch in waging his own culture war in defence of his image of Ireland's destiny!

In 'Meditations in Time of Civil War', Yeats set out his stall with regard to Anglo-Ireland:

Surely among a rich man's flowering lawns,
Amid the rustle of his planted hills,
Life overflows without ambitious pains;
...
And never stoop to a mechanical
Or servile shape, at others' beck and call.

The poem goes on to conjure up images of 'gardens where the peacock strays', of 'levelled lawns and gravelled ways', of 'slippered contemplation' and of 'buildings that a haughtier age designed'. All told, this is an idealised, idyllic view of things, which, of course, could not always square with reality. Thus, while nationalist Ireland was strengthening its cultural defences and boosting Gaelic Ireland, Yeats was doubling down on his commitment to Anglo-Ireland, a bastion of 'the inherited glory of the rich'.

## The Bounty of Sweden

When news of Yeats's Nobel Prize broke in November 1923, Oliver St John Gogarty proposed a Senate motion of congratulations to the body's most illustrious member. Gogarty described the award as 'the most significant thing that has befallen this country', which was saying a lot considering that it had just attained its independence!

Historically, Ireland had not been accepted 'into the comity of nations', but the Swedish Academy's decision had changed all of that, and Ireland's civilisation would in future be judged by Yeats's achievements.[23]

Yeats must have been gratified by the handsome tribute paid to him by Senate Chairman Lord Glenavy, who said that the Senate took pride in Yeats's accomplishment 'on account of the courage and patriotism which induced him twelve months ago to cast in his lot with his own people here at home, under conditions which were very critical and called for the exercise of great moral courage'.[24] Yeats generously recognised that the prize had been awarded to him 'as a representative of a literary movement and a nation'.[25] The novelist Joseph Conrad, who must have harboured hopes of being recognised for his own work, also saw Yeats's Nobel Prize as 'a literary recognition of the new Irish Free State'.[26]

Although the Swedish Academy had offered to send his medal and prize to him through the Swedish Embassy in Dublin, Yeats and George set out for Stockholm in early December 1923 to accept his Nobel Prize in person. In making this journey, he would be the last Irish writer to appear in person at a Nobel Prize ceremony until Seamus Heaney collected his prize in 1995. The other Irish recipients were honoured in absentia. George Bernard Shaw's award was picked up for him by the British Ambassador and Samuel Beckett's by the French envoy.

When quizzed about Ireland while transiting through Copenhagen, Yeats said that 'if the British Empire becomes a voluntary Federation of Free Nations, all will be well, but if it remains as in the past, a domination of one, the Irish question is not settled'. He resolved to talk about 'the work of my generation in Ireland, the creation of a literature to express national character and feeling but with no deliberate political aim'.[27]

Yeats was charmed by the Swedish royal family, describing the king as 'intelligent and friendly' and Princess Margaretha as 'full of subtle beauty, emotional and precise, and impassive with a still intensity suggesting that consummate strength which rounds the spiral of a shell'.[28] The Free State poet evidently had an eye for a princess! The Swedish Royal Theatre's production of *Cathleen ni Houlihan* was, he thought, a match for 'an exceedingly good Abbey performance', although he understood the need for 'differences of interpretation', as aspects of the play that would rouse 'an Irish audience powerfully for historical reasons' would not resonate with a Swedish one.[29] Admiration for its royal family made him compare Sweden favourably with countries where 'every democratic dream had been fulfilled' and where 'all men would display to others' envy the trophies won in their life of struggle',[30] an observation that reflected Yeats's scepticism about popular democracy.

The theme for his speech, 'The Irish Dramatic Movement', was chosen in the belief that his involvement with the Irish theatre was responsible 'for whatever fame in the world I may possess'. Strangely, he was inclined to talk down the reputational glitter of his gift as a lyric poet, which is where his popular reputation squarely rests, although, for me, his greatest work was produced in the decade and a half after he collected his Nobel Prize and the £7,000 cheque that went with it. Part of the money he received was used to bail out Cuala Press, his sisters' business, and to pay for expensive private medical treatment for Lily.

Together with his co-workers in the Abbey Theatre, Gregory and Synge, he had, he believed, 'gone below all that is modern and restless, seeking foundations for an Ireland that can only come into existence in a Europe that is still but a dream'.[31] This makes me wonder what Yeats would have made of twentieth-century Ireland, anchored as it is in the reality of a union of sovereign European nations, but that would definitely be a digression!

Yeats's Nobel Prize sealed his international fame. A.C. Benson, author of the English patriotic panegyric 'Land of Hope and Glory', was one of the many prominent individuals who wrote to Yeats, praising him for his 'detachment from the urgent *present*', which brought him into line 'with the great spirits of the past and future'.[32] As it happens, Yeats's achievement actually derived from his ability to attach himself to 'the urgent present' while at the same time communing with the past and looking to the future.

## 'A sixty-year-old smiling public man'

On 11 December 1922 Yeats became a member of the new state's Senate. Being a senator put him at some risk during Ireland's Civil War, which lasted into the summer of 1923. It meant that Yeats had an armed guard to protect him. Worried by the violence around him, he hoped to be 'of some use' to Ireland 'now that order is the conspiracy of a few'.[33] A newly energised Yeats derived satisfaction from 'the slow exciting work of creating the institutions of a new nation – all coral insects but with some design in our heads of the ultimate island'.[34]

In a nod to Mussolini's seizure of power in Italy, Yeats expressed the view that Ireland, reacting from 'the present disorder is turning its eyes towards individualist Italy'.[35] It is important to note that admiration for Mussolini was more common in the 1920s than later, when he became an acolyte of Hitler's. At a gala dinner held during the 1924 Tailteann Games, Yeats quoted Mussolini, 'a great popular leader', about trampling on 'the decomposing body of the Goddess of Liberty', and suggested that future generations would have as their task 'not the widening of liberty but recovery from its errors'.

He looked to 'the building of authority, the restoration of discipline, the discovery of a life sufficiently heroic to live without opium dreams'.[36] That rhetorical flourish caused Governor General Tim Healy, Parnell's nemesis in 1890, to joke that 'our Bard' had ignored his own advice (in 'Down by the Sally Gardens') to 'take life easy'![37] Yet Yeats also wrote about wanting Ireland to become 'a modern, tolerant, liberal nation'.[38] His persistent concern for minority rights was not in tune with the priorities of authoritarian regimes, and he seemed blind to the fact that, should a force for authoritarian order have emerged in Ireland in the 1920s, it was quite likely to have been ultra-Catholic and dismissive of Anglo-Irish concerns.

In that era of upheaval, Yeats yearned for conservative rule. Writing from Dublin, he asserted that: 'We are preparing here behind our screen of bombs and smoke a return to conservative politics as elsewhere in Europe.'[39] The Senate was, Yeats thought, 'a fairly distinguished body, much more so than the lower house, and should get much government into our hands'.[40] Thus, he thought he could 'intrigue a great deal' and get his way against the younger, less able members of the new Cumann na nGaedheal government, but that was not to be. The emerging rulers of the new state proved themselves to be more adept than Yeats might have predicted. There was no way they were going to be shuffled aside, their democratic mandate ignored in favour of the rule of Yeats's fellow 'able men' from the Senate. In any case, convocations of 'able men' have a habit of being less than the sum of their parts.

I recently came across a yellowed clipping from a 1982 Irish newspaper that has survived the passage of four decades and the multiple moves I made around the world as part of my diplomatic career. It marked the sixtieth anniversary of the first Irish Senate through the memories of its last surviving member, Edward MacLysaght (1887–1986), who told of its 'pleasant, non-party, club-like atmosphere'. MacLysaght, who served under Yeats's chairmanship on the Committee of Irish Manuscripts, noted that, in its first three-year session, the Seanad passed 534 amendments to 130 bills sent to it by the Dáil. He described Yeats as 'one of the more prominent and helpful Senators', in contrast with Oliver St John Gogarty, whom MacLysaght saw as one of the chamber's 'twisters'.[41] James Joyce would probably have agreed with that dim assessment of his 'Buck Mulligan'.

Yeats was among those senators, half of the total, who were appointed by government, mainly to give representation to former Unionists who might otherwise have felt ill at ease in the new state. In the Senate he aligned himself with the group of independent senators composed of landed individuals and senior business figures, almost all Protestant in religion and traditionally Unionist in politics. Yeats took his responsibilities seriously – excessively so in the view of his wife, who felt that it interfered with his writing. It has been calculated that he was present for more than 60 per cent of the body's meetings during his six years as a senator.[42]

Although he professed to have interested himself solely in cultural matters, in fact he intervened on the inspection of prisons, on the independence of judges and on the position of women in the civil service when he opposed discrimination against married women who, until the 1970s, were required to resign from their jobs once they were married.

While serving in the Senate Yeats spent more time in Dublin than at any other time since his childhood. From their fashionable home on Merrion Square, the Yeatses became part of Dublin society and mixed socially with government ministers and their wives. The fledgling state's political leadership impressed him as 'able and courageous', and as 'honest modern-minded men swimming still in seas of conspiracy of others' making', even if they were without what he called 'play of mind',[43] by which he probably meant that they were not intellectuals. Of course, but that was not their role. They were steering a leaky ship of state in precarious waters in the tense aftermath of a damaging civil war.

In his first Senate speech, Yeats argued that, 'the past is dead not only for us but for this country ... I suggest that we are assembled here no longer in a Nationalist or Unionist sense, but merely as members of the Seanad.'[44] In reality, the backdrop to the Senate's opening months was a fraught one. Senators were potential targets for anti-Treaty republicans, and some of those representing the landlord class became victims of attacks on their properties during the War of Independence and the Civil War. Life in Dublin at the beginning of 1923 was 'restless and unsafe' – a window in Yeats's home on Merrion Square sported two bullet holes.[45] He was anxious about his family's security and wanted to move them temporarily to Wales, but a valiant George felt that leaving would be 'a bitter mistake' and resolved to 'stick it out'.[46]

Early in his senatorial term, it fell to him to pay tribute to Arthur Griffith, who had died the previous summer, depriving the emerging Free State of one of its most experienced figures. Yeats had frequently crossed swords with Griffith, whose hard-edged brand of nationalism was unpalatable to his poetic sensibility. In his Senate tribute, he acknowledged that Griffith had been of 'particular value to his country' because 'he gave his faith not to an abstract theory, but to a conception of this historic nation'.[47]

This critique of 'abstract theory' was aimed at anti-Treaty republicans who, in Yeats's mind, maintained a blind devotion to the idea of a republic. His support for the government during the Civil War, even when it took draconian actions, caused him to be further estranged from Maud Gonne, who threatened to end their friendship, 'to renounce my society forever',[48] if he did not denounce the government's treatment of republican prisoners – Gonne herself and her son, Seán, being among them. The prisoners issue had Yeats in a bind. While he was concerned about the conditions in which republican prisoners were being kept and joined other senators in making representations to government on their behalf, he considered that many critics' complaints were not well founded and besides, he did not want to 'embarrass the government'.[49] Yeats did intervene successfully with Cosgrave on Maud Gonne's behalf and his efforts contributed to her release in April 1923.[50]

## 'Excited, passionate, fantastical'

Yeats made unsuccessful overtures in London about the idea of dropping the oath of allegiance, which was offensive to republicans. On international issues, he opposed Ireland's membership of the League of Nations, which, he thought, risked dragging Ireland into foreign wars. That was a mistake, as the Irish Free State managed to play an honourable role at the League.

He also tried to use his position in the Senate to press for the return of the Lane pictures, on which he lobbied influential figures in London. At his behest, the Senate debated the issue, with Yeats setting out the case for the pictures coming to Dublin like a barrister in full command of his brief. The Senate duly passed a motion asking the government to press the British government for the return of the pictures to Dublin. Yeats told the Senate that: 'In fighting to recover these pictures you are fighting for a unique possession which will always remain unique and always give prestige to the Gallery that contains it.'[51] Many years would elapse before a settlement was reached between London and Dublin about ownership of the Lane pictures.

Ever eager for controversy, Yeats was excited by the emergence of a new publication, *Tomorrow*, 'a wild paper of the young', set up by Cecil Salkeld, F.R. Higgins and Iseult Gonne's husband, Francis Stuart.[52] Scenting 'a most admirable row' he wrote its editorial, although, prudently in light of his position as a senator, it was signed by Stuart and Salkeld. This manifesto pulled no punches in its assertion that 'we count among atheists bad writers and bishops of all denominations'.[53] Yeats had his way; the publication did stir controversy and attract sharp condemnation. It was duly suppressed after its second issue.

In his work on the Committee of Irish Manuscripts, Yeats was in his element. The Committee's report, written by Yeats and the scholar Alice Stopford Green, tugged at the heartstrings of nationalist Ireland, pointing out that centuries of British rule had made a 'wreckage of Irish learning and language'. Now that Ireland was independent it had an obligation to preserve for future generations the ancient learning of Ireland's 'full national tradition'.[54] In an effort to drive home the relevance of cultural investment, he observed that: 'Already the traditional imagination in these old books has had a powerful effect upon the life, and I may say upon the politics of Ireland.'[55]

In this, Yeats was surely thinking of the manner in which Irish mythology had fired his own imagination in the 1880s and 1890s. With his customary insistence on Irish literature's wider resonance, he argued that Irish manuscripts 'possess first of all their value to this country; then they possess their value to the world'.[56] The report made imaginative and practical suggestions, making a cogent case for the preservation of Ireland's Gaelic past through an annual subvention of £5,000. While the Committee's work was unanimously endorsed by the Senate, the report fell on deaf ears at a time of meagre public finances.

Yeats's attitude to the Irish language was a complex one. While he never managed to learn it, nor any language other than English, he drew considerable inspiration from translations of Irish-language texts. The work of his chief collaborators, Gregory and Synge, benefited from their knowledge of Irish. In the Senate, he spoke out against what he saw as tokenism with respect to the language. Oddly, he opposed the innocuous practice of dual-language signage, which he believed to be 'a form of insincerity'. In viewing it as 'injurious to the general intellect and thought of the country', he was clearly overstating his case. Irish-language scholarship was something to be fully supported, but not the 'pretence of people knowing a language that they do not know'. As he later wrote, 'Gaelic is my national language but it is not my mother tongue.'[57]

In a dialogue published in the *Irish Statesman* in 1924, he set out both sides of the argument. On one side, he presents the view of the language's enthusiasts, that 'If Ireland gives up Gaelic, it will soon be a suburb of New York,', but this is countered by the argument that: 'The Irish language can never again be the language of the whole people ... Because the Irish people will not consent that it should, having set their hearts on Glasgow and New York.'[58]

Looking back, we can see that compulsory Irish was not a success. Yeats was right to point out the level of hypocrisy involved in pushing the language in schools and on signage without any corresponding effort at making it a language of everyday life. On the other hand, it is doubtful if any policy could have succeeded in restoring Irish as the country's principal language, since that position was lost some time in the nineteenth century – or even earlier, by some calculations. What seems clear, however, is that a better job could, and should, have been done with the revival of the language.

## 'And add the halfpence to the pence'

For a man who in 'September 1913' had derided those who fumbled 'in a greasy till' and who were 'born to pray and save', arguably his most enduring contribution in the Senate was his chairmanship of the Coinage Commission, whose report has been described as 'a model of lucidity and freshness'.[59] Viewing stamps and coins as 'the silent Ambassadors of national taste', Yeats relished the work of selecting artists and fixing on a theme for the coinage's design. Steering clear of patriotic symbols, the choice fell on images of animals, suitable in Yeats's opinion for 'this horse-riding, salmon-fishing, cattle-raising country'.[60]

The committee selected designs submitted by the English sculptor Percy Metcalfe ahead of Irish artists, namely Jerome Connor, whose sculpture of Robert Emmet is in Dublin's St Stephen's Green and in Washington DC near the residence of the Irish Ambassador there; Oliver Sheppard, Yeats's contemporary at art school in the 1880s, who later designed the 1916 memorial at the General Post Office; and Albert Power, who had sculpted a bust of Yeats in 1918. In Yeats's view, Metcalfe's design far exceeded his rivals' offerings.

Yeats's work on this front had a lasting impact. Introduced in 1928, the Free State's coinage remained in circulation until the introduction of euro coins in 2002.

## 'I walk through the long schoolroom questioning'

As a senator, Yeats became interested in education and began to tour schools. His friend Joseph O'Neill, Secretary of the Department of Education, received a report detailing what teachers had told him, that 'young people are anarchic and violent and that we have to show them what the state is and what they owe to it'.[61] The condition of school buildings depressed him and he suggested putting their care into the hands of local committees, but that would, no doubt, have been seen as a threat to the Catholic Church's control of schools.

Yeats expressed admiration for the educational reforms introduced by Italian Education Minister Giovanni Gentile (who was described by Mussolini as the 'philosopher of fascism') and spoke in favour of a child-centred approach to education akin to that adopted by Patrick Pearse at his school at St Enda's in Rathfarnham. As a matter of principle, Yeats wanted to give the child of the poor as good an education as the child of the rich. His conclusion was that 'we should always see that the child is the object and not any of our special purposes'.[62] As he put it, 'I am convinced that as much wealth can come from the intellect of Ireland as will come from the soil and that the one will repay cultivation as much as the other.'[63] That far-sighted aim took decades to come to pass with the introduction of free secondary education in the late 1960s from which my generation drew immense benefit. It is difficult to square such egalitarian views with the politically reactionary sentiments Yeats expressed elsewhere.

In a series of Senate speeches, he criticised the poor condition of schools and proposed floating a national loan so that school buildings could be made fit places for the state's children. Around the country, he had found many schools to be 'filthy' and with insufficient space for the numbers being taught.[64] But he did have praise for some of what he had seen, notably a school in the south of Ireland managed by the Sisters of Mercy that was 'a model to all schools'.[65]

This may well be the setting for one of his most powerful poems, 'Among School Children', although while visiting schools in Waterford a few years ago, I came across competing claims between the Ursuline and Mercy Convents in Waterford. Wherever that school was, it did a good job of inspiring its visiting 'smiling public man':

> I walk through the long schoolroom questioning;
> A kind old nun in a white hood replies;
> The children learn to cipher and to sing,
> To study reading-books and history,
> To cut and sew, be neat in everything
> In the best modern way – the children's eyes
> In momentary wonder stare upon
> A sixty-year-old smiling public man.

The poem goes on to reflect on Maud Gonne, 'hollow of cheek as though it drank the wind' and on the poet's own position as 'a comfortable kind of old scarecrow'. There are asides too on motherhood and on Plato, Aristotle and Pythagoras, who:

> Fingered upon a fiddle-stick or strings
> What a star sang and careless Muses heard:
> Old clothes upon old sticks to scare a bird.

Yeats wraps up this meditation with some of the finest lines he ever wrote:

> Labour is blossoming or dancing where
> The body is not bruised to pleasure soul,
> Nor beauty born out of its own despair,
> Nor blear-eyed wisdom out of midnight oil.

O chestnut tree, great rooted blossomer,
Are you the leaf, the blossom or the bole?
O body swayed to music, O brightening glance,
How can we know the dancer from the dance?


## 'No petty people'

Yeats's Senate speech against the prohibition of divorce set down in belligerent terms his opposition to the policy of the new state being shaped by an exclusively Catholic ethos. His remarks were far from tactful and he clearly did not expect to win the day. His speech was directed more at the gallery of history than at his contemporaries.

The disappointed poet did not pull any punches as he set out the likely impact of Catholic-inspired policies on the prospects for Irish unity. 'If,' he said, 'you show that this country, Southern Ireland, is going to be governed by Catholic ideas and by Catholic ideas alone, you will never get the North ... You will put a wedge into the midst of this nation.'[66] While this was a valid point, it is also true that no amount of ecumenical gestures or inter-denominational outreach would have diluted the deep Unionist hostility to the Free State, though it might have been worth giving them a try.

Evidently on a rhetorical roll (and by all accounts Yeats was a powerful speaker), he fired broadsides at Archbishop O'Donnell and at Fr Peter Finlay (whom he had suspected of working against him two decades before when he was under attack from D.P. Moran of *The Leader*). He then launched into a paean of praise for the Anglo-Irish tradition, resurrecting the ghosts of his eighteenth-century heroes and warning the Irish majority not to underestimate Anglo-Ireland:

We against whom you have done this thing are no petty people. We are one of the great stocks of Europe. We are the people of Burke; we are the people of Grattan; we are the people of Swift, the people of Emmet, the people of Parnell. We have created most of the modern literature of this country. We have created the best of its political intelligence ... You have defined our position and given us a popular following. If we have not lost our stamina then your victory will be brief, and your defeat final, and when it comes this nation may be transformed.[67]

Now, I doubt that there was much support for Yeats's remarks, which his fellow Protestants in the Chamber almost certainly would have thought went too far. They, after all, were seeking to establish a position for themselves within Ireland's new political environment and were probably not keen to berate the Catholic majority with polemical broadsides. There is a sense in which Yeats, at this time, saw himself as a lone warrior, valiantly opposing the prevailing consensus in the new state.

On account of Fianna Fáil's abstention policies until 1927, there was no significant opposition in parliament (not that de Valera's party would have taken a different line on divorce from that of Cosgrave's government), and Yeats seemed to relish ploughing this lonely, invincibly unproductive furrow in opposition to the state's Catholic ethos.

In verse, Yeats repeated the ideas expressed in his speech. In 'The Tower', he echoed 'The Fisherman', when he declared that:

I choose upstanding men
That climb the streams until
The fountain leap, and at dawn
Drop their cast at the side
Of dripping stone; I declare
They shall inherit my pride,
The pride of people that were
Bound neither to Cause nor to State,
Neither to slaves that were spat on,
Nor to the tyrants that spat,
The people of Burke and of Grattan
That gave, though free to refuse –
Pride, like that of the morn,
When the headlong light is loose ...

Yeats believed that: 'The modern Irish intellect was born more than two hundred years ago when Berkeley defined in three or four sentences the mechanical philosophy of Newton, Locke and Hobbes, the philosophy of England in his day, and I think of Ireland up to our day, and wrote after each, "We Irish do not hold with this", or some like sentence.'[68]

In 'Blood and the Moon', he wrote of:

Swift beating on his breast in sibylline frenzy blind
Because the heart in his blood-sodden breast had
    dragged him
down into mankind,
Goldsmith deliberately sipping at the honey-pot of his
    mind,

And haughtier-headed Burke that proved the state a
    tree ...
And God-appointed Berkeley that proved all things a
    dream,

That this pragmatical, preposterous pig of a world, its
    farrow that so solid seem,
Must vanish on the instant if the mind but change its
    theme; ...

Trinity College Dublin's decision in April 2023 to 'dename' its Berkeley Library has brought the philosopher's reputation into focus. His *alma mater* became uncomfortable about Berkeley's position as a slaveholder during his time in America. The ensuing controversy has also drawn attention to his views about what he perceived as the racial inferiority of the native Irish.[69] On the other hand, his entry in the *Dictionary of Irish Biography* lauds his social activism during his time as Bishop of Cloyne and notes that his ideas 'on national identity and self-sufficiency' struck a chord with Éamon de Valera. History has many arcane and crooked byways that lie in wait to catch us off guard!

In his final Senate speech, as his collapsing health excluded him from seeking a further three-year term, Yeats expressed the view that it was more important to have 'able men' than 'representative men' in the Senate.[70] For six years he had been one of the Senate's able men and, as he departed, the Senate's Chairman generously assured him that he could be reappointed at any time, which was, of course, an unlikely proposition.

## 'You've disgraced yourselves again'

Sean O'Casey wrote three great plays between 1922 and 1926. His first two productions, *The Shadow of a Gunman* and *Juno and the Paycock*, which dealt with the War of Independence and the Civil War, went off without a hitch. They contained a distinctive working-class view of those events, but did not offend popular sensibilities. *The Plough and the Stars* was a different matter.

Set in 1916, the play's irreverent account of the Easter Rising pointed to an indifference, and even a hostility, on the part of working-class Dubliners. It irked those for whom the Rising had acquired hallowed status. Chief among the play's detractors were Hanna Sheehy-Skeffington, whose husband, Frank, was summarily executed by a deranged British officer during Easter week, and, almost inevitably, Maud Gonne. By now Yeats had accepted that he and Gonne 'will never change each other's politics. They are too deeply rooted in our characters.'[71]

From the Abbey stage, Yeats denounced those who opposed O'Casey's play: 'You have disgraced yourselves again. Is this to be an ever-recurring celebration of the arrival of an Irish genius? Once more you have rocked the cradle of genius. The news of what is happening here will go from country to country. You have rocked the cradle of reputation. The fame of O'Casey is born tonight.'[72]

Yeats did not care for O'Casey's next play, *The Silver Tassie*, which O'Casey set during World War I. In a letter to O'Casey, he argued that the earlier plays had been written 'out of your own amusement with life or your sense of its tragedy; you were excited, and we all caught your excitement; ... and you moved us as Swift moved his contemporaries'.[73]

But Yeats viewed *The Silver Tassie* as 'anti-war propaganda'. His conclusion was that O'Casey was not really interested in the war, and that his play was too abstract: 'the whole history of the world must be reduced to wallpaper in front of which the characters must pose and speak'. He asked O'Casey to 'Put the dogmatism of this letter down to splenetic old age and forgive it,'[74] but O'Casey dismissed Yeats's advice. In his *Autobiographies*, published twenty-five years after the events it describes, O'Casey took a series of shots at Yeats.

Recalling his decision to leave Ireland in 1926, O'Casey wrote that:

> He would leave Yeats on his Island of Innisfree, standing pensively at the door of his small cabin of clay and wattles made; or moving, slow and moody, between his nine bean rows, thinking of peace where there was no peace; for Ireland's red-rose-bordered hem was muddy now, and ragged.[75]

Coming from a family with a record of military service, including his brother's participation in the Boer War, O'Casey was seriously offended at being told 'by one [Yeats] who wouldn't know a Life Guard red from a Horse Guard blue, that he wasn't interested, directly or indirectly, in the Great War!'[76] Although *The Silver Tassie* was later performed at the Abbey, the two writers were never properly reconciled.

## 'The one strong intellect'

Yeats became enamoured of the new government's strong-man, Kevin O'Higgins, and was shocked when he was gunned down by the IRA in July 1927 while he was on his way to Mass near his home in Dublin. Yeats saw O'Higgins as 'the one strong intellect in Irish public life'.[77] With

O'Higgins's death, Ireland had lost 'the man it needed, its great builder of a nation'.

Yeats was pained by the remembrance of all that O'Higgins 'had still to do'.[78] This view was shared by Yeats's friend Æ, who saw O'Higgins as 'the moral architect of the new state', who, had he lived, would have 'moulded the Free State into the image of his imagination, but a state we would all have been proud of'.[79] O'Higgins had his admirers outside of Ireland too. Winston Churchill described him as 'a figure out of the antique cast in bronze'.[80]

O'Higgins ultimately made it into Yeats's poetry. In 'Parnell's Funeral' he is described as the Free State's 'sole statesman' and numbered among those who might have 'eaten Parnell's heart' and thus satisfied 'the land's imagination'. In 'The Municipal Gallery Revisited' he features alongside Casement and Griffith among those the reader can 'Ireland's history in their lineaments trace'. Here we meet:

> Kevin O'Higgins' countenance that wears
> A gentle questioning look that cannot hide
> A soul incapable of remorse or rest;

Yeats appears to have overlooked O'Higgins's role in the introduction of censorship, for he set up a Committee on Evil Literature whose proposals became law in 1929, by which time O'Higgins was two years dead. Yeats was in Galway when he heard the news of O'Higgins's death, but returned to Dublin to help pass more stringent laws, which he ardently hoped would 'take certain crimes out of the hands of jurors'.[81]

The most important consequence of O'Higgins's murder was that, threatened with being stripped of their seats, Fianna Fáil members ended their abstention-ist policy and took their seats in Dáil Éireann. Thus, as the entry on O'Higgins in the *Dictionary of Irish Biography* states, 'O'Higgins's assassination might be interpreted as the blood sacrifice that brought the major opposition into constitutional politics.'

The Censorship of Publications Bill of 1929 came as a major blow to Yeats, who feared that the bill would give the Minister for Justice control 'over our thoughts'. There would, he feared, be 'a mob censorship' driven by the prejudices of organisations such as the Catholic Truth Society. He thought that the Irish popular mind had been left 'to its own lawless vulgarity' and hoped that censorship would galvanise 'all men of intellect' to push back against censorship.[82] To some extent that is what happened as an increasingly uncompromising censorship came to be seen as the epitome of conservative Ireland's malfunctioning performance. It gave people of more liberal mind a target to aim at, and a more and more controversial policy to contest. By the 1960s, Ireland's censorship had become an embarrassing notoriety.

## Looking Back

In January 1932, on the eve of a general election that would bring de Valera's Fianna Fáil party into power, Yeats went into print in *The Spectator* to reflect on the events of the previous decade. Looking back on his ten-ure in the Senate, his experience had convinced him 'that no London Parliament could have found the time or the knowledge' for the kind of transformation that had occurred in Ireland.[83] It pleased him that 'Ireland is substituting traditions of government for the rhetoric of agitation'.[84] The eighteenth century, he believed, had regained its importance, with Berkeley and Swift, 'whose hold on Irish imagination is comparable to that of O'Connell'[85] – a highly dubious assertion.

In a final tribute to Ireland's eighteenth century, he wrote that he might 'gather together the descendants of those who had voted with Grattan against the Union that we might ask the British Government to return his body' from Westminster Abbey, where his remains are interred.[86] For Yeats, the Anglo-Irish tradition was a gift not only to modern Ireland (even if largely unheralded there), but to the modern world too. He had held the same view of Ireland's Gaelic past when he first encountered it in the 1880s and thought it could be a basis for the next 'great utterance' for which the world had been waiting.

As a Nobel Prize-winner, Yeats could have taken an extended bow in the fashionable drawing rooms of London and the stately homes of the English countryside. Instead, he threw his lot in with an emerging Irish polity and expended considerable energy on the troubled cause of the fledgling Irish Free State. He was even tipped off about plans for an army mutiny in 1924, about which he informed the government, which managed to defuse the situation.

Of course, he made his share of misjudgements, and his over-the-top lionisation of Anglo-Ireland turned out to be a cul-de-sac. He would have been better advised to push for a hybrid culture composed of Gaelic and English elements. But, vitally, his poetry profited from this sustained dabbling in politics, and the Irish Free State benefitted from having Yeats on its watch.

# 8

# 'And say my glory was I had such friends'

## Yeats in the 1930s

# The Municipal Gallery Revisited

## I

Around me the images of thirty years:
An ambush; pilgrims at the water-side;
Casement upon trial, half hidden by the bars,
Guarded; Griffith staring in hysterical pride;
Kevin O'Higgins' countenance that wears
A gentle questioning look that cannot hide
A soul incapable of remorse or rest;
A revolutionary soldier kneeling to be blessed;

## II

An Abbot or Archbishop with an upraised hand
Blessing the Tricolour. 'This is not,' I say,
'The dead Ireland of my youth, but an Ireland
The poets have imagined, terrible and gay.'
Before a woman's portrait suddenly I stand,
Beautiful and gentle in her Venetian way.
I met her all but fifty years ago
For twenty minutes in some studio.

## III

Heart-smitten with emotion I sink down,
My heart recovering with covered eyes;
Wherever I had looked I had looked upon
My permanent or impermanent images:
Augusta Gregory's son; her sister's son,
Hugh Lane, 'onlie begetter' of all these;
Hazel Lavery living and dying, that tale
As though some ballad-singer had sung it all;

## IV

Mancini's portrait of Augusta Gregory,
'Greatest since Rembrandt,' according to John Synge;

A great ebullient portrait certainly;
But where is the brush that could show anything
Of all that pride and that humility?
And I am in despair that time may bring
Approved patterns of women or of men
But not that selfsame excellence again.

V

My mediaeval knees lack health until they bend,
But in that woman, in that household where
Honour had lived so long, all lacking found.
Childless I thought, 'My children may find here
Deep-rooted things,' but never foresaw its end,
And now that end has come I have not wept;
No fox can foul the lair the badger swept –

VI

(An image out of Spenser and the common tongue).
John Synge, I and Augusta Gregory, thought
All that we did, all that we said or sang
Must come from contact with the soil, from that
Contact everything Antaeus-like grew strong.
We three alone in modern times had brought
Everything down to that sole test again,
Dream of the noble and the beggar-man.

VII

And here's John Synge himself, that rooted man,
'Forgetting human words,' a grave deep face.
You that would judge me, do not judge alone
This book or that, come to this hallowed place
Where my friends' portraits hang and look thereon;
Ireland's history in their lineaments trace;
Think where man's glory most begins and ends,
And say my glory was I had such friends.

### 'Ireland's history in their lineaments trace'

'The Municipal Gallery Revisited' is representative of Yeats's literary vitality during the 1930s. It is a magnificent poem focused on Yeats's own coterie of friends and on some of his fellow Irish public figures. The poem celebrates his two closest artistic collaborators, Augusta Gregory and John Synge, as well as others, with whom his life and preoccupations had overlapped. Augusta Gregory's nephew, art collector Hugh Lane, makes an appearance, as does her son, Robert, as well as Hazel Lavery, the glamorous American wife of the Belfast-born artist Sir John Lavery, whose image as Cathleen ní Houlihan was used as a watermark on Irish currency until 2002. Yeats came to believe that 'my glory was I had such friends'. His true glory was that he could write about his friends with such commanding eloquence.

But not everyone was impressed with Yeats's efforts. The hardheaded poet and critic Yvor Winters was scathing about Yeats's 'attempt to transform himself and his friends into legendary heroes', pointing out that few of them would be known had Yeats not written about them. An unimpressed Winters accused Yeats of being 'ridiculous' in expending 'so much hyperbole' on people of 'small importance'.[1] Surely Yeats deserves credit for celebrating the 'glory' of his friendships and for drawing insight from them. As the poet Patrick Kavanagh once wrote of his own modest locale in County Monaghan: 'Gods make their own importance.'

Fittingly, in light of Yeats's lifelong engagement with the public life of Ireland, there is also room in his gallery for three Irish political figures: Roger Casement, the last of the 'Sixteen Dead Men' Yeats wrote about in 1916, who were executed in the wake of the Easter Rising; Sinn Féin founder, Arthur Griffith; and Yeats's preferred Irish Free State politician, Kevin O'Higgins.

Yeats wrote 'The Municipal Gallery Revisited' in September 1937, just sixteen months before his death. He told his paramour, the poet Dorothy Wellesley, that he liked the poem 'exceedingly' and thought it perhaps the best he had written for some years. It is easy to agree with that assessment. As he strove to put things in order at the Abbey and at his sisters' Cuala Press, he hoped that he could then 'fold my arms and be a wise old man and gay'.[2] Perhaps he was thinking about the two Chinese figures whose image he admired in 'Lapis Lazuli':

> Their eyes mid many wrinkles, their eyes,
> Their ancient, glittering eyes, are gay.

In truth, Yeats the writer never 'folded his arms' but kept working creatively to the very end. His attitude in his final years can perhaps best be understood with reference to his poem 'What Then?'. Written in 1936, it presents the poet's view of life during his seventy-first year. It is clear from what he wrote that he was still the 'pilgrim soul' he had written about (referring of course to Maud Gonne, who else) at the beginning of his writing career. His life was arguably more of a pilgrimage than Maud's, given her perennial rootedness in advanced republican nationalism compared with Yeats's unending search for an ideological home for his 'indomitable' Irishness.

'What Then?' reviews his life as a successful poet and celebrates his personal life, his marriage and the children it produced:

Everything he wrote was read,
After certain years he won
Sufficient money for his need,
Friends that have been friends indeed; ...

All his happier dreams came true –
A small old house, wife, daughter, son,
Grounds where plum and cabbage grew,
Poets and Wits about him drew;
*'What then?' sang Plato's ghost, 'what then?'*

But would he rest on those considerable laurels? Certainly not:

'The work is done,' grown old he thought,
'According to my boyish plan;
Let the fools rage, I swerved in naught,
Something to perfection brought;'
*But louder sang that ghost 'What then?'*

In the previous two decades he had, indeed, brought 'to perfection' quite a number of fine poems, and he continued to produce new poetry of remarkable vigour and intensity. His achievement in remaining outstandingly creative to the very end of his life is a truly imposing one, exemplified in poems such as 'The Circus Animals' Desertion', 'Under Ben Bulben' and 'The Statues', with its bold assertion that:

We Irish, born into that ancient sect
But thrown upon this filthy modern tide
And by its formless, spawning, fury wrecked,
Climb to our proper dark, that we may trace
The lineaments of a plummet-measured face.

Yeats's ability to be so vigorously creative in his final years is among the reasons why his work is valued so deeply. It is fairly normal for artists to lose some of their creative energy as they age. In Yeats's case, he was still at work on a poem the day before he died.

As I am now in my own late sixties, I see Yeats as a model for energetic, intellectual ageing. I would like to be able to emulate his unshakable dedication, even if I, of course, lack the smallest modicum of his genius, and besides I have no inclination towards the amorous philandering that obsessed Yeats as he aged. Yes, he preserved that 'pilgrim soul' to the end, forever journeying, restless for wisdom and understanding.

## 'Upon an aged woman and her house'

The 1930s began with Yeats at death's door as he battled with Malta fever, a form of brucellosis that left him bedridden for months in the Italian coastal city of Rapallo near Genoa. But he survived and recovered his old vim and vigour.

With his own health woes temporarily behind him, Lady Gregory's increasing frailty began to be a concern for Yeats. In Gregory's final months, he spent considerable time keeping watch on her at Coole Park. She was grateful to him and he to her. She considered that his friendship had made her last years 'from first to last fruitful in work, in service'. 'I do think,' she wrote to him, 'that I have been of use to the country – & for that in great part I thank you.'[3] On his side, Yeats had treasured 'the friend who was my sole adviser for the greater part of my life, the one person who knew all that I thought and did'.[4]

The final part of Yeats's *Autobiographies,* entitled *Dramatis Personae* (1935), with its account of the early years of the Irish dramatic movement, was written as a tribute to Gregory even if he also exacted a belated vengeance on George Moore for the manner in which he had disparaged Yeats and Gregory years before in his autobiography, *Hail and Farewell.*

Yeats confessed that he had come to love Coole Park 'more than all other houses'. He appreciated the tradition enshrined there, a place where 'Every generation had left its memorial.'[5] Gregory, he believed, had 'never lost her sense of feudal responsibility ... of burdens laid upon her by her station and her character'.[6]

She had been 'friend and hostess, a centre of peace, an adviser who never overestimated or underestimated trouble'. Ultimately, she had become 'the founder of modern dialect literature'.[7] In an especially poignant tribute to the command she acquired of the folklore of rural Ireland, he wrote majestically that 'she was born to see the glory of the world in a peasant mirror'.[8]

His 1933 collection *The Winding Stair and Other Poems* contained two poems about Gregory and her home, which had been a source of comfort, refuge and inspiration to Yeats throughout the thirty-five years of their friendship. In 'Coole Park 1929', he meditated:

Upon an aged woman and her house,
...
Great works constructed there in nature's spite
For scholars and for poets after us,
Thoughts long knitted into a single thought,
A dance-like glory that those walls begot.
...

And yet a woman's powerful character
Could keep a swallow to its first intent; ...

His panegyric concludes with a request to 'traveller,
scholar, poet' to dedicate with:

Back turned upon the brightness of the sun
And all the sensuality of the shade –
A moment's memory to that laurelled head.

In a later poem, 'Coole Park and Ballylee, 1931', he summarises his collaboration with Gregory:

We were the last romantics – chose for theme
Traditional sanctity and loveliness;
Whatever's written in what poet's name
The book of the people; whatever most can bless
The mind of man or elevate a rhyme;
But all is changed, that high horse riderless,
Though mounted in that saddle Homer rode
Where the swan drifts upon a darkening flood.

Yes, Yeats's perennial goal was to preserve what he saw
as the romantic inheritance of the past, which, despite
a spate of vicissitudes and disappointments, he believed
could find continued residence and expression in Ireland.

## 'No loose-lipped demagogue'

Ireland was on the cusp of renewed political change in
the early 1930s as de Valera's Fianna Fáil party, founded
in 1926, came knocking on the door of high political
office. Fianna Fáil won an electoral victory in 1932 and a

more decisive one the following year. This meant that, less than ten years after the end of the Irish Civil War, its victors (who had formed the outgoing Cumann na nGaedheal government) peacefully ceded power to those they had vanquished in arms a decade earlier. That was the making of Irish democracy, for other less peaceful outcomes were certainly possible at the time, as Yeats clearly appreciated.

The 1930s also brought change for Yeats's life as, freed of his duties in the Senate, he began to spend more time outside Ireland, initially in Rapallo, where, 'When we are not lost in mountain clouds it is brilliant sunlight and blue sea which melts imperceptibly into the sky'.[9] Later, he would winter in Majorca and ultimately in the south of France while continuing to spend much of the rest of the year in Ireland.

His life in Ireland also changed with his abandonment of Thoor Ballylee, which had become impractical for the ageing, ailing poet, and the family's move from its base in fashionable Merrion Square to a house with gardens in the Dublin suburb of Rathfarnham. In spite of his persistent ill health, his spirits were often high. As he wrote in December 1930, 'I have a great sense of abundance – more than I have had for years. George's ghosts have educated me',[10] a reference to the 'philosophy' he had extracted from his wife's automatic writing.

That intense phase of the couple's marriage had passed and the many letters they exchanged have a tone that is more practical than intimate. He addressed George as 'Dear Dobbs' and signed his letters, W.B. Yeats. During the last decade of his life, an emotionally needy Yeats entered into a series of relationships with other women:

the poet Lady Dorothy Wellesley (who, in his poem 'To Dorothy Wellesley', was 'Rammed full / Of that most sensuous silence of the night'); the writer and political activist Ethel Mannin; the prominent journalist Edith Shackleton Heald; and Margot Ruddock, about whom Yeats penned three poems, 'Margot', 'A Crazed Girl' and 'Sweet Dancer':

> The girl goes dancing there
> On the leaf-sown, new-mown, smooth
> Grass plot of the garden;
> Escaped from bitter youth,
> Escaped out of her crowd,
> Or out of her black cloud.
> *Ah, dancer, ah sweet dancer!*

More telling, perhaps, was his appeal in 'Margot':

> Let me be loved as though still young
> Or let me fancy that it's true,
> When my brief final years are gone
> You shall have time to turn away
> And cram those open eyes with day ...

Ruddock's 'black cloud' resulted in her following Yeats to Majorca, where she had some sort of breakdown from which Yeats and George had to rescue her when she ended up behaving erratically in Barcelona. Yeats also underwent a Steinach operation designed to restore sexual vigour, which he believed had been a success. His friend Oliver St John Gogarty, a writer and a medical doctor, was sceptical about the procedure's efficacy and the wisdom of undertaking it.

George quietly ignored her husband's 'considerably less than clandestine adulteries of the mind and heart' and remained indomitable in her support of him, albeit in a different manner from the early years of their marriage: 'more of a mother than a wife, who came to the rescue when her ailing husband's health proved unequal to the hectic amatory pace he set himself'.[11]

Never an admirer of de Valera, Yeats worried that his ascent to power might result in a further narrowing of Ireland's public life, but he was gradually won over. When he met de Valera to discuss the Abbey's state subsidy, which the new administration continued to pay, Yeats was impressed with his 'simplicity and honesty though we differed throughout. It was a curious experience, each recognised the point of view so completely. I had gone there full of suspicion but my suspicion vanished at once.'[12]

Writing to his main correspondent at this stage in his life, his first lover in the 1890s, Olivia Shakespear, he urged her not to believe what she read about de Valera in the English newspapers. He had come to believe that de Valera had 'forced political thought to face fundamental issues'.[13] Tellingly, however, de Valera never attracted a favourable mention in Yeats's poetry.

When he wrote 'Parnell's Funeral' in 1933, he imagined the effect on contemporary politicians of eating Parnell's heart (somehow that notion brings to mind the opening line of the 'Calypso' episode of *Ulysses*: 'Mr Leopold Bloom ate with relish the inner organs of beasts and fowls. He liked thick giblet soup, nutty gizzards, a stuffed roast heart, liver slices fried with crustcrumbs, fried hencod's roes'). Here's how Yeats dealt with the then recently elected head of government:

Had de Valera eaten Parnell's heart
No loose-lipped demagogue had won the day,
No civil rancour torn the land apart.

Yeats evidently continued to blame de Valera for his part in precipitating the Civil War, but was relieved that his government turned out to be more stable and reliably conservative than many might have imagined. Always a doer, Yeats pushed the idea of an Irish Academy of Letters and toured America for the last time to raise funds for it and for his own coffers. During that visit, Yeats was often described as 'Ireland's cultural ambassador'. His stated aim was 'to substitute a cultural link' between Ireland and Irish America for the political one. The lecture he delivered most often was entitled 'The New Ireland', in which he divided Irish history into four eras, the fourth beginning with the death of Parnell in 1891. This was very much in line with the thesis he had advanced in his Nobel Prize lecture in 1923, in which he presented Parnell's fall as a turning point that unleashed cultural energies that helped pave the way for Ireland's revolution.

His urge to establish the Academy stemmed from what he saw as a need to push back against censorship, which, by excluding Irish writers from their home market, threatened to make it impossible for them to make a living by means of a 'distinctive Irish literature'.[14] Yeats was eager to recruit James Joyce, a resident of Paris since the early 1920s (he was 'the first name that seemed essential both to Shaw and myself').[15] Joyce politely but firmly declined the invitation. He wrote to the Academy and wished them every success, adding, 'I see no reason why my name should have arisen at all in connection with such an academy.'[16]

The Academy had nineteen founder members 'who have done creative work for Ireland' and eight associates (including T.E. Lawrence, aka Lawrence of Arabia, and the American playwright Eugene O'Neill). Yeats saw the Academy as a lobbyist for Ireland's literati, who felt threatened by what was turning out to be an expansive censorship. He pinned his hopes on a belief that there was in Ireland 'still a deep respect for intellectual quality'.[17]

When the Academy came under attack by the notoriously aggressive *Catholic Bulletin*, being accused of having an anti-Catholic agenda, Yeats wrote that, if he were a younger man, he would welcome years of conflict 'for it creates unity among the educated classes' and would force de Valera 'in all probability, to repudiate the ignorance that has in part put them into power'.[18] He told Olivia Shakespear that she was right to compare de Valera with Mussolini or Hitler, as 'All three have exactly the same aim as far as I can judge.'[19] Yeats was dead wrong there, for de Valera was a dedicated democrat, who saw off both the fascist Blueshirts and the extreme elements among the anti-Treaty republicans. At the same time, he altered Ireland's constitutional status by peaceful and democratic means while clinging to a conservative social ethos and lacking any clear economic ambition for Ireland.

In 1933 Yeats revealed to Shakespear that he was working with others, including an ex-cabinet minister, on a social theory, 'which can be used against Communism in Ireland – what looks like emerging is Fascism modified by religion'.[20] In reality, a deeply Catholic authoritarianism leavened by fascist ideas would have been a more likely outcome in the Ireland of the 1930s. It was a blessing for Ireland that the prosaic orthodoxies of conventional democratic politics ultimately won the day, and that the authoritarian pyrotechnics of that era largely passed the country by.

So much for any idea of Yeats as an apolitical artist. He always liked to be in the thick of things. 'Politics,' he thought, were 'growing heroic.' He saw a fascist movement forming so as 'to be ready should some tragic situation develop'. He found himself 'constantly urging the despotic rule of the educated classes as the only end to our troubles'.[21]

## 'Defending Ireland's soul'

This Yeatsian affection for 'despotic rule' brings us to the big elephant in the room that has to be tackled when looking at Yeats's life and work in the 1930s. Was he in any sense a fascist? It is impossible to run away from that question, but it needs to be explored with the 'cold eye' that he urged on those passing his grave at Drumcliff churchyard in County Sligo.

In approaching this topic, it is important to understand the particular genesis and the meagre record of Irish fascism, which has correctly been described as 'always far more Irish than fascist'.[22] Ireland's fascist moment was a residue of the Irish Civil War, which ended in 1923 with the defeat of the anti-Treaty republicans. Fianna Fáil's ascent to power in 1932, and their anti-Treaty heritage, caused supporters of the outgoing government to fear for their positions and their security.

An Army Comrades' Association (ACA) was formed in 1932 to defend the interests of those who had taken the pro-Treaty side in 1922/23, and to protect opposition political gatherings from IRA intimidation. By the summer of 1933 the ACA had been renamed the National Guard and become known as 'the Blueshirts' after the uniform they wore. In their brief heyday, they were led by dismissed Police Commissioner Eoin O'Duffy.

The whole thing fizzled out very quickly as a march on Dáil Éireann in August was banned and the National Guard declared illegal. A new political party, Fine Gael, emerged as a successor to Cumann na nGaedhael and O'Duffy became its leader. Within a year he had been ousted and Ireland's brush with fascism had passed. As one historian has pointed out, fascism's rise elsewhere in Europe depended on being able to attract young militants (who in Ireland were more likely to be attracted to the cause of Sinn Féin's radical republicanism) and secure the support of traditional conservative elites, but the Blueshirts 'failed on both counts'.[23]

In the ferment that followed de Valera's ascent to power, Yeats had his fancy tickled by the prospect of influencing the new movement and he duly met O'Duffy to explain his 'anti-democratic philosophy' to him. Yeats was not terribly impressed with O'Duffy and did not think him 'a great man though a pleasant one'. He hoped that 'his face and mind may harden or clarify'.[24] Although uncertain about the Blueshirts' prospects, Yeats was comforted by the thought that it would 'bring into discussion all the things I care for',[25] but that did not happen, as de Valera's government brought a degree of political stability that minimised opportunities for fascism to flourish.

When it comes to the charge of fascism against Yeats, the chief witness for the prosecution is Conor Cruise O'Brien, the former Irish diplomat, UN official in the Congo, University President in Ghana, Humanities Professor at New York University, Irish Cabinet minister, newspaper editor, biographer of Edmund Burke and, in his later years, an undying polemicist on issues that captured his passionate attention, including Northern Ireland and the Middle East. In an influential essay published in 1965, O'Brien presents Yeats as a writer with 'abiding, and intensifying, political interests and passions'. As it happens, I agree with that part of his argument.

Towards the end of his extended analysis of Yeats's politics, O'Brien concludes that: 'Yeats would certainly have preferred something more strictly aristocratic than Fascism, but since he was living in the twentieth century he was attracted to Fascism as the best available form of anti-democratic theory and practice.'[26] O'Brien's takedown of Yeats was influential at the time of the centenary of Yeats's birth, but it also came in for sharp criticism as 'cheap and partial political comment'.[27]

O'Brien's most compelling evidence against Yeats derives from three marching songs he wrote for the Blueshirts. At that time, Yeats expressed his conviction 'that public order cannot long persist without the rule of educated and able men'.[28] His marching songs were composed as a response to 'our growing disorder, the fanaticism that inflamed it like some old bullet embedded in the flesh'.[29] Ireland, he thought, was 'drowned in political and religious fanaticism'.[30] If someone wanted to put Ireland to right and break 'the reign of the mob', he would need 'force, marching men'. Such a venture would need to promise 'not this or that measure but a discipline, a way of life'.[31] Now that does sound suspiciously like fascism.

[245]

A few months after he wrote the above words, Yeats added a codicil where he explained that he had composed those songs because he was told that the Blueshirts (although he does not name them) could be persuaded to adopt some of his ideas, but 'Finding that it neither would nor could, I increased their fantasy, their extravagance, their obscurity, that no party might sing them'.[32] That sounds a little more like a flirtation than a full-throated endorsement of the Blueshirts.

'Three Songs to the Same Tune' (the chosen tune was the patriotic ballad 'O'Donnell Abu') are well below Yeats's gold standard as a poet, which he deployed a lot during the 1930s, but not here. These 'songs' are fairly innocuous patriotic ditties. You would need to know their backstory to make any sense of them, but they had an agenda when they were written. The first of the trio delves into Ireland's past:

> Justify all those renowned generations;
> They left their bodies to fatten the wolves,
> They left their homesteads to fatten the foxes,
> Fled to far countries, or sheltered themselves
> In cavern, crevice or hole,
> Defending Ireland's soul.

And it goes on:

> Fail and that history turns to rubbish,
> All that great past to a trouble of fools;
> Those that come after shall mock at O'Donnell,
> Mock at the memory of both O'Neills,
> Mock Emmet, mock Parnell,
> All the renown that fell.

In its original form, the third song had some lines that Yeats later dropped:

> What's equality? – Muck in the yard;
> Historic Nations grow
> From above to below.[33]

The revised version read:

> Troy backed its Helen, Troy died and adored;
> Great nations blossom above;
> A slave bows down to a slave.

In the 1920s Yeats's fascist leanings centred on his interest in Mussolini. As one critic has rightly observed, Italian fascism did not in the 1920s 'carry with it the desire to control the world, engage in genocide, and foster brutal dictatorship'. What Yeats liked about Italian fascism was what he saw as its emphasis 'on hierarchy, order, and discipline'.[34]

Another potential black mark against Yeats was his refusal of a request from his one-time lover, political activist Ethel Mannin, that he join an appeal for the release from a German concentration camp of the peace campaigner and Nobel Peace Prize awardee, Carl von Ossietzky. His response to Mannin was:

> Do not try to make a politician of me, even in Ireland I shall never I think be that again – as my sense of reality deepens, and I think it does with age, my horror at the cruelty of governments grows greater, and if I did what you want, I would seem to hold one form of government more responsible than any other, and

that would betray my convictions. Communist, Fascist, nationalist, clerical, anti-clerical, are all responsible according to the number of their victims.[35]

He pointed Mannin to his poem 'The Second Coming', which he believed 'foretold what is happening'. His letter concluded: 'I am not callous, every nerve trembles with horror at what is happening in Europe, "the ceremony of innocence is drowned".'[36] In another letter to Mannin, with whom he was at odds politically even as he pursued her romantically, he wrote of his alarm at 'the growing moral cowardice of the world, as the old security disappears' and noted that 'an ignorant form of Catholicism' was his enemy.[37] Yeats was invariably driven by a fear of disorder and an anxiety about what he saw as Ireland's imperishable Catholic ethos.

## 'Four great minds that hated Whiggery'

In the last decade of his life, Yeats continued to laud the Anglo-Irish tradition, and in particular its star turns, Berkeley, Burke, Goldsmith and Swift, on whose part he was wont to make grandiose claims. Through Swift and Burke, he argued that Anglo-Ireland had 'recreated conservative thought'.[38] Comparing the two, Yeats thought that, 'Burke is only tolerable in his impassioned moments, but no matter what Swift talks of, one delights in his animation and clarity.'[39]

The more he delved into his work, the more he became haunted by Swift. In 'The Seven Sages' he wrote of 'four great minds that hated Whiggery': Burke, Berkeley, Swift and Goldsmith, even though Burke was associated with the Whig Party in Britain for most of his career as chief adviser to the Marquess of Rockingham when he was Prime Minister. To be fair though, Burke's *Reflections on the Revolution in France* caused him to be seen as one of the fathers of modern conservatism. Yeats's solution was to observe that 'whether they knew it or not', all four 'hated Whiggery', which he defined as:

> A levelling, rancorous, rational sort of mind
> That never looked out of the eye of a saint
> Or out of a drunkard's eye.

Yeats pithily summarises the four great interests of Burke's career:

> American colonies, Ireland, France and India
> Harried, and Burke's great melody against it.

As for Berkeley, Yeats continued to see him as of 'the utmost importance to the Ireland that is coming into existence'. In his poem, Berkeley, who was Bishop of Cloyne, is 'a voice':

> Soft as the rustle of a reed from Cloyne
> That gathers volume; now a thunder-clap.

In a preface he wrote for a book on Berkeley, Yeats credited him with opposing the philosophy of Newton and Locke, which conceived 'a physical world without colour, taste, tangibility' and led on to the mechanical age and to dialectical materialism and European socialism, 'all the mischief Berkeley foretold'.[40]

In Yeats's eyes, Swift exhibited 'passion enobled by intensity, by endurance, by wisdom'.[41] Yeats credited the 'astringent eloquence' of the fourth of Swift's *Drapier Letters* with having 'created the political nationality of Ireland'[42] and saw *Gulliver's Travels* as an expression of 'an Irish hatred of abstraction'.[43]

Yeats had his own view of Swift's understanding of human liberty. 'Liberty depended upon a balance within the State, like that of the "humours" in a human body, or like that "unity of being" Dante compared to a perfectly proportioned human body, and for its sake Swift was prepared to sacrifice what seems to modern man liberty itself.'[44] As Yeats wrote in 'Swift's Epitaph', a version of the Latin inscription on Swift's tomb in Dublin's St Patrick's Cathedral:

Swift has sailed into his rest;
Savage indignation there
Cannot lacerate his breast.
Imitate him if you dare,
World-besotted traveller; he
Served human liberty.

Yeats wanted Protestant Ireland to base its contribution to Irish life on Burke, Swift and Berkeley.[45] Of course, he idealised the eighteenth century to make it serve his purposes. As one scholar put it, Yeats's portrayal of eighteenth-century Ireland was founded on 'a highly selective use of a largely arbitrary amalgam of Burke, Swift, Berkeley and Goldsmith'. Thus, Yeats 'stole from 18th century Ireland what he needed, and then sought to reincarnate his thefts into a broad fictionalised canvas'.[46] There is a sense in which his obsession with Anglo-Ireland was part of 'the great melody' of Yeats's life as he sought a distinctive Irish refrain in response to the cacophonous materialism of the late-Victorian world from which he had emerged, the brilliantly utilitarian world of his formidable father, John Butler Yeats.

In 1935 he lost another ally in his struggle against Irish orthodoxies when Æ died in Bournemouth. Æ was Yeats's oldest friend, and although he 'constantly quarrelled with him', he acknowledged that Æ 'never bore malice'. Indeed, George Yeats thought Æ the nearest thing to a saint. To her husband she added that: 'You are a better poet but no saint. I suppose one has to choose.'[47] George Yeats knew her man.


## 'To this most gallant gentleman'

In his final years, Yeats wrote poems that delved into the lives of figures from Ireland's revolutionary decade: Roger Casement and, an unusual choice, 'The O'Rahilly'. The publication of William J. Maloney's book, *The Forged Casement Diaries* (1936), put Yeats into a rage. Casement's Black Diaries detailing homosexual activities had been leaked in 1916 to discredit Casement and to derail the campaign to have his death sentence revoked.

Yeats thought Casement was 'not a very able man but he was gallant and unselfish' and had a right to 'an unsullied name'.[48] The upshot was two poems, 'Roger Casement' and 'The Ghost of Roger Casement'. The former is a bit of doggerel, which was first published in de Valera's *Irish Press* and won Yeats loud applause among more traditional nationalists:

> Come Tom and Dick, come all the troop
> That cried it far and wide,

Come from the forger and his desk,
Desert the perjurer's side;

Come speak your bit in public
That some amends be made
To this most gallant gentleman
That is in quick-lime laid.

The second Casement poem, with its repeated calling out of John Bull, shows off Yeats's persistent strain of Anglophobia:

John Bull has gone to India
And all must pay him heed
For histories are there to prove
That none of another breed
Has had a like inheritance,
Or sucked such milk as he,
And there's no luck about a house
If it lack honesty.
*The ghost of Roger Casement*
*Is beating on the door.*

The Spanish Civil War rang alarm bells for Yeats, as he feared it would encourage a Christian front by 'gathering all bigots together'. In a revealing outburst in a letter to Ethel Mannin, he wrote: 'I am an old Fenian and I think the old Fenian in me would rejoice in a Fascist nation or government-controlled Spain, because that would weaken the British empire, force England to be civil to Indians, perhaps set them free and loosen the hand of English finance in the far East'. But he added that he had 'a horror of modern politics', 'the manipulation of popular enthusiasm by false news'. That all sounds very twenty-first century, doesn't it! [49]

Breaking with his stated principle of not intervening on international issues, he signed a letter by a number of writers in solidarity with the Spanish Republic that was under assault by General Franco's anti-Republican forces.[50] His fear, one that he believed de Valera shared, was that the ex-Blueshirt supremo Eoin O'Duffy, who led an Irish Catholic contingent to fight for Franco, would return to Ireland with 'enhanced fame helping "the Catholic front"',[51] which had been inflamed by the war in Spain. A triumphant O'Duffy would leave his 'pagan' institutions, the Academy and the Abbey, 'fighting for their lives against combined Catholic and Gaelic bigotry'.[52] O'Duffy's escapade in Spain in supposed defence of 'Christian civilisation' turned out to be anything but glorious, and his already faded political career fizzled out when he returned home in 1937.

Yeats's poem about 'The O'Rahilly' is a fairly straightforward retelling of the life and death of Michael Joseph O'Rahilly, who helped persuade the titular head of the Irish Volunteers, Eoin MacNeill, to call off the Rising that Pearse and others had secretly planned for Easter Sunday and carried MacNeill's countermanding order to the south-west of Ireland. O'Rahilly returned to Dublin and took part in the Rising he had opposed when it began on Easter Monday, and was killed during a conflict that he had tried his best to abort. Yeats urges us to 'sing of the O'Rahilly' who 'told Pearse and Connolly':

He'd gone to great expense
Keeping all the Kerry men
Out of that crazy fight;
That he might be there himself

Had travelled half the night.

...

'Because I helped to wind the clock
I come to hear it strike.'

The last two lines record exactly what the O'Rahilly said to Pearse and Connolly when he turned up to fight on Easter Monday 1916. It is not clear why Yeats chose to lionise 'The O'Rahilly' twenty years after his death, but it was part of his unshakable fascination with the events of 1916.

## 'Come, fix upon me that accusing eye'

Yeats had been a fairly lukewarm supporter of Parnell, but unlike James Joyce, for whom the national despair engendered by Parnell's fall was part of the backdrop to his decision to leave Ireland in 1904, Yeats saw the post-Parnell era as one that provided scope for the rise of a different brand of politics driven by cultural forces. As he wrote in 1934, 'When Parnell was dragged down, his shattered party gave itself up to nine years' vituperation, and Irish imagination fled the scene', while he and his fellow writers 'turned to romantic dreaming, to the nobility of tradition'.[53]

By the 1930s that dream had well and truly faded, but Parnell made an extraordinary comeback in Yeats's poetry. A meeting with an old Parnell ally, Henry Harrison, who had just published a defence of Parnell, encouraged Yeats to write about Parnell, the result of which was three poems: 'Parnell', 'Parnell's Funeral' and 'Come Gather Round Me, Parnellites'. Thus, in an illustration of the remarkable staying power of Parnell's mythic image, Yeats was still writing about him more than forty years after his death.

In an essay on Parnell, Yeats argued that Katharine O'Shea's husband had known of her liaison with Parnell 'from the first' and believed that Gladstone, who in his public life was 'a tolerant man of the world', also knew. But, in Yeats's view, everyone was caught 'in that public insincerity which was about to bring such discredit upon democracy'.[54]

In 'Come Gather Round Me, Parnellites', Yeats provides a ballad-like summary of Parnell's story, identifying those who brought about his fall in 1890:

> The Bishops and the Party
> That tragic story made,
> A husband that had sold his wife
> And after that betrayed;
> But stories that live longest
> Are sung above the glass,
> And Parnell loved his country,
> And Parnell loved his lass.

'Parnell's Funeral' is founded on Yeats's premise that 'the Fourth Bell' of Irish history sounded on the day of Parnell's interment in October 1891, the other three bells having been heard with the Flight of the Earls at the beginning of the seventeenth century; the Battle of the Boyne at that century's end; and the United Irishmen's Rising of 1798. In a note on the poem, Yeats offered a sophisticated analysis of nineteenth-century Irish history:

The influence of the French Revolution woke the peasantry from the medieval sleep, gave them ideas of social justice and equality, but prepared for a century disastrous to the national intellect. Instead of a Protestant Ascendancy with its sense of responsibility, we had a Garrison, a political party of Protestant and Catholic landowners, merchants and officials – but they could give to a people they thought unfit for self-government nothing but a condescending affection ... Instead of the half medieval peasantry came an agrarian party that degraded literature with rhetoric and insincerity.[55]

Late nineteenth-century nationalist history is captured by Yeats in a provocative phrase: 'the national character changed, O'Connell, the great comedian, left the scene Parnell the great tragedian took his place' with 'his pride' and 'his apparent impassivity'.[56] The poem traverses similar ground:

When strangers murdered Emmet, Fitzgerald, Tone,
We lived like men that watch a painted stage.
... But popular rage,
*Hysterica passio* dragged this quarry down.
None shared our guilt; nor did we play a part
Upon a painted stage when we devoured his heart.

Come, fix upon me that accusing eye.
I thirst for accusation. All that was sung,
All that was said in Ireland is a lie
Bred out of the contagion of the throng,
Saving the rhyme rats hear before they die.

Yeats had written an embarrassingly average poem about Parnell at the time of his death, but this in-form return to Parnell as a subject for poetry suggests that he saw his subject as the last hurrah of Anglo-Ireland. At one level, perhaps the key one, Parnell's ascendancy was an attempt to carve out a new leadership role in Ireland for his own social class. After Parnell's demise, that prospect never returned and, despite Yeats's wishes to the contrary, no Anglo-Irish figure had any moment in the sun in twentieth-century Irish politics akin to what Parnell enjoyed during the 1880s.

## 'Under the receding wave'

For anyone concerned about Yeats's reputation, his final publication, *On the Boiler*, is deeply problematic. It is more than a bit of a rant and it would have been better had he never brought those valedictory thoughts into print. I have a strong sense that *On the Boiler* was written with a deliberate intention to shock his readers. His letters at that time convey a sense of a wicked old man cutting loose and letting them have it.

His broadside begins with a bang. 'The whole State,' he exclaims, 'should be so constructed that the people should think it their duty to grow popular with King and Lord Mayor instead of King and Lord Mayor growing popular with them'. He warned that those who try to be popular 'sink into that slow, slothful, inanimate, semi-hypocritical thinking Dante symbolised by hoods and cloaks of lead'.[57] It's hard to find an excuse for this surge of unpleasant prejudice.

Then things get worse as he disparages a number of Irish public figures and haughtily opines that 'they should not have been taught to read and write'. His outpourings dander on in a ludicrously elitist, undemocratic vein: 'Forcing reading and writing on those who wanted neither was the worst part of the violence which for two centuries has been creating that hell wherein we suffer.' Ireland's representative system had given the country to 'the incompetent'. Elected men are caricatured, emotional like 'a youthful chimpanzee, hot and vague, always disturbed, always hating something or other'.[58]

At the heart of *On the Boiler* is Yeats's embrace of eugenics. His footnotes provide an outline of his readings on the subject and record his thanks to the Eugenics Society. Although there was a vogue for eugenics at the time, that is no excuse for Yeats being taken in by such vile ideas. In his account of 'Tomorrow's Revolution', he expresses a conviction 'that the principal European nations are degenerating in body and mind'.[59]

He rattles on about 'mother-wit', arguing for the ascendancy of nature over nurture, arriving at the chilling conclusion that if everybody is able 'to procure all the necessities of life and so remove the last check upon the multiplication of the uneducatable masses, it will become the duty of the educated classes to seize and control one or more of those necessities'.[60] His brutal conclusion was that 'sooner or later we must limit the families of the unlimited classes, and if our Government cannot send them doctor and clinic it must, till it gets tired of it, send monk and confession box'.[61]

I have gone into this subject in perhaps greater detail than it deserves, but I think it is important not to white-wash Yeats's sometimes unpleasantly crazy ideas. How could someone like Yeats, while possessed with such objectionable ideas, at the very same time write such magnificent lines as:

> First that sea-rider Oisin led by the nose
> Through three enchanted islands, allegorical dreams,
> Vain gaiety, vain battle, vain repose,
> Themes of the embittered heart, or so it seems,
> That might adorn old songs or courtly shows;
> But what cared I that set him on to ride,
> I, starved for the bosom of his fairy bride?

And later in the same poem:

> I thought my dear must her own soul destroy
> So did fanaticism and hate enslave it,
> And this brought forth a dream and soon enough
> This dream itself had all my thought and love.

Those lines were published in the month of Yeats's death and written sometime during the previous year while he was concocting the obnoxious brew that appeared in *On the Boiler*. My sense is that he was a good editor when he went about putting his thoughts into poetry, but that he lost control of the rudder in some of his later prose writings, which show more of a 'fanatic heart' than a 'pilgrim soul'.

There is a poignant letter, written to Lady Elizabeth Pelham on 4 January 1939, just weeks before Yeats's death. This is part of what he wrote:

I know for certain that my time will not be long. I have put away everything that can be put away that I may speak what I have to speak ... I will begin to write my most fundamental thoughts and the arrangement of thought which I am convinced will complete my studies. I am happy, and I think full of an energy, of an energy I had despaired of. It seems to me that I have found what I wanted. When I try to put it into a phrase I say, 'Man can embody truth but he cannot know it.' I must embody it in the completion of my life. The abstract is not life and everywhere draws out its contradictions.[62]

Now that's what I call living life to the full.

## 'On Roman or on Russian / Or on Spanish politics'

Yeats backed away from his admiration for Mussolini when Italy invaded Abyssinia in 1935. As he explained to Ethel Mannin, 'All through the Abyssinian war my sympathy was with the Abyssinians, but those feelings were chilled by my knowledge that the English Government was using those feelings to help an imperial policy I distrusted.'[63] The last poem Yeats wrote with a political theme was called 'Politics':

*'In our time the destiny of man presents its meanings*
*in political terms.'*
— *Thomas Mann*

How can I, that girl standing there,
My attention fix
On Roman or on Russian

Or on Spanish politics,
Yet here's a travelled man that knows
What he talks about,
And there's a politician
That has both read and thought,
And maybe what they say is true
Of war and war's alarms,
But O that I were young again
And held her in my arms.

But, of course, Yeats when he was young did fix his attention on politics – not on Roman or Russian or Spanish politics, but on the Irish variant. Throughout his life, he engaged consistently with events in Ireland. As the country evolved politically, Yeats's responses changed. At different times, he was different things: a cultural nationalist in the 1880s; an advanced nationalist in the 1890s; a disenchanted figure in the first decade of the twentieth century; a supporter of Irish independence after 1916; a critic of the anti-Treaty republicans during and after the Civil War; a diligent senator during the 1920s; an advocate for Anglo-Ireland; an aristocratic nationalist; an admirer of able men in politics; and, yes, a flirt with fascist authoritarianism.

But how to judge anyone's politics? Am I the somewhat left-wing student activist I was in the 1970s, the social liberal eager to see conservative Ireland change utterly (as it has done in recent times), or an establishment figure in my professional life as a senior civil servant, or an advocate of centre-ground politics, as I see myself today?

Yeats's chief accuser, Conor Cruise O'Brien, is a powerful illustration of the fickleness of political positioning.

Was he the conventional Irish nationalist of his youth; the anti-colonial UN official in the 1960s; the radical professor at New York University; the social democrat of the 1970s; or the dogged apologist for a radical brand of Ulster unionism that became his final political home? Or was he all of those? But which label, if any, would describe him best?

Late in his life, Yeats wrote that 'I am no Nationalist, except in Ireland for passing reasons; State and Nation are the work of intellect, and when you consider what comes before and after them they are, as Victor Hugo said of something or other, not worth the blade of grass God gives for the nest of the linnet'.[64] Yes, he was throughout his life an Irish nationalist. As far as 'passing reasons' are concerned, his interest in Ireland was more like the thing of permanence he wrote of in 'Sailing to Byzantium':

> Once out of nature I shall never take
> My bodily form from any natural thing,
> But such a form as Grecian goldsmiths make
> Of hammered gold and gold enamelling
> To keep a drowsy Emperor awake;
> Or set upon a golden bough to sing
> To lords and ladies of Byzantium
> Of what is past, or passing, or to come.

# 9

# 'Cast a cold eye'

## Yeats's Achievement

## Under Ben Bulben

### I

Swear by what the Sages spoke
Round the Mareotic Lake
That the Witch of Atlas knew,
Spoke and set the cocks a-crow.

Swear by those horsemen, by those women,
Complexion and form prove superhuman,
That pale, long-visaged company
That air in immortality
Completeness of their passions won;
Now they ride the wintry dawn
Where Ben Bulben sets the scene.

Here's the gist of what they mean.

### II

Many times man lives and dies
Between his two eternities,
That of race and that of soul,
And ancient Ireland knew it all.
Whether man die in his bed
Or the rifle knock him dead,
A brief parting from those dear
Is the worst man has to fear.
Though grave-diggers' toil is long,
Sharp their spades, their muscle strong,
They but thrust their buried men
Back in the human mind again.

### III

You that Mitchel's prayer have heard,
'Send war in our time, O Lord!'
Know that when all words are said
And a man is fighting mad,
Something drops from eyes long blind,
He completes his partial mind,
For an instant stands at ease,
Laughs aloud, his heart at peace.
Even the wisest man grows tense
With some sort of violence
Before he can accomplish fate,
Know his work or choose his mate.

### IV

Poet and sculptor, do the work,
Nor let the modish painter shirk
What his great forefathers did,
Bring the soul of man to God,
Make him fill the cradles right.

Measurement began our might:
Forms a stark Egyptian thought,
Forms that gentler Phidias wrought.
Michael Angelo left a proof
On the Sistine Chapel roof,
Where but half-awakened Adam
Can disturb globe-trotting Madam
Till her bowels are in heat,
Proof that there's a purpose set
Before the secret working mind:
Profane perfection of mankind.

Quattrocento put in paint
On backgrounds for a God or Saint
Gardens where a soul's at ease;
Where everything that meets the eye,
Flowers and grass and cloudless sky,
Resemble forms that are or seem
When sleepers wake and yet still dream,
And when it's vanished still declare,
With only bed and bedstead there,
That Heavens had opened.

Gyres run on;
When that greater dream had gone
Calvert and Wilson, Blake and Claude,
Prepared a rest for the people of God,
Palmer's phrase, but after that
Confusion fell upon our thought.

V

Irish poets, learn your trade,
Sing whatever is well made,
Scorn the sort now growing up
All out of shape from toe to top,
Their unremembering hearts and heads
Base-born products of base beds.
Sing the peasantry, and then
Hard-riding country gentlemen,
The holiness of monks, and after
Porter-drinkers' randy laughter;
Sing the lords and ladies gay
That were beaten into the clay
Through seven heroic centuries;
Cast your mind on other days
That we in coming days may be
Still the indomitable Irishry.

## VI

Under bare Ben Bulben's head
In Drumcliff churchyard Yeats is laid.
An ancestor was rector there
Long years ago, a church stands near,
By the road an ancient Cross.
No marble, no conventional phrase;
On limestone quarried near the spot
By his command these words are cut:

*Cast a cold eye*
*On life, on death.*
*Horseman, pass by!*


## 'You were silly like us'

W.B. Yeats died at the Hotel Idéal Séjour in the town of Roquebrune on the French Riviera on 28 January 1939 in the presence of his loyal and tolerant wife, George, and two of his late-life romantic interests, Dorothy Wellesley and Edith Shackleton Heald. The following day he was buried temporarily at the local cemetery, although the outbreak of war meant that nine years would elapse before his remains were transferred to their final resting place 'under bare Ben Bulben's side'. In May 2023 I visited Yeats's first resting place, trekking laboriously up the hill on a hot day from the train station to the cemetery in the medieval village 250 metres above. It's a long way from County Sligo, but the views from the cemetery are spectacular.

George outlived her husband by almost three decades, while their daughter Anne (1919–2001) and son Michael (1921–2007) went on to have successful careers in the arts and politics, respectively. Maud Gonne, inveterate in her republican politics to the end, passed away in Dublin in 1953 at the age of eighty-six; her daughter, Iseult, the 'child dancing in the wind' in Yeats's poem, died the following year.

Yeats's passing drew from W.H. Auden a fine poem of tribute, one that Yeats would, I think, have been proud to have written:

> He disappeared in the dead of winter:
> ...
> The death of the poet was kept from his poems.
> ...
> The words of a dead man
> Are modified in the guts of the living.[1]

Yeats's words have indeed captivated the living across the generations that have passed since his death.

It was a generous effort from Auden, who had been given scant representation in the *Oxford Book of Modern Verse* (1936) that Yeats had edited. In his guise as anthologist, Yeats had taken the view that the work of Auden and his school, which perversely he professed to admire greatly, suffered from a 'lack of form and consequent obscurity'.[2] Auden, who clearly took this rebuke to heart, later described Yeats's anthology as 'the most deplorable volume ever issued' by its publisher, the Clarendon Press.[3] In his poem, Auden, who had issues too with Yeats's right-wing leanings, commented that:

> You were silly like us; your gift survived it all,
> The parish of rich women, physical decay,
> Yourself; mad Ireland hurt you into poetry.

That seems to me to be a fair assessment. Not everyone valued Yeats so highly. Yvor Winters, who dismissed the idea that Yeats was a great poet and thought much of his work to be 'pseudo poetic', had some disobliging things to say about him: 'unfortunately, the better one understands him, the harder it is to take him seriously'.[4] Readers of Yeats's poems can ignore the silliness Auden and Winters detected in him because it does not often intrude into his verse.

T.S. Eliot was someone who wrote approvingly of Yeats's literary achievement, noting that he had shown that an artist 'by serving his art with entire integrity, is at the same time rendering the greatest service he can to his own nation and to the whole world'.[5] Eliot, too, had been damned with faint Yeatsian praise as someone who wrote about 'men and women that get out of bed or into it out of mere habit', and whose poetry thus 'seems grey, cold. He is Alexander Pope working without imagination.'[6] Ouch!

## 'Ancient Ireland knew it all'

In a late radio broadcast, Yeats offered more nuanced views on the evolution of poetry during his lifetime, stretching from his own generation that 'disliked Victorian rhetorical moral fervour' to 'the most revolutionary man in poetry',[7] T.S. Eliot, who together with his contemporaries, had been shaped by the Great War.

Yeats, one of the few writers in the English language who thrived artistically both before and after 1914, correctly understood that the war had been a genuine cultural watershed. Before the war, 'All civilised men had believed in progress, in a warless future, in always-increasing wealth, but now influential young men began to wonder if anything could last or if anything were worth fighting for ... The past has deceived us: let us accept the worthless present.'[8]

Not that Yeats was inclined to go along with that advice about treating the past as a deceiver. Ireland's past continued to offer him hope and inspiration. His valedictory poem, 'Under Ben Bulben', saw him restate a belief that 'ancient Ireland knew it all' and reassert his kinship with Ireland's national struggle stretching back well beyond his now beloved eighteenth century.

Yeats's gripes were with Ireland's present, and with:

> ... the sort now growing up
> All out of shape from toe to top,
> Their unremembering hearts and heads
> Base-born products of base beds.

This is an example of Yeats as an intemperate elitist, one of his many poses, an unappealing one for sure. Fear and apprehension about the condition of the modern world had by then become a staple of Yeats's thinking, although we should remember that the state of the world in the late 1930s provided good grounds for being alarmed about the future. 'Under Ben Bulben' offers a backward look at Ireland:

> Sing the peasantry, and then
> Hard-riding country gentlemen,
> The holiness of monks, and after
> Porter-drinkers' randy laughter; ...

By the time the poem was written, in 1938, those particular country gentlemen were probably few and far between, and the word 'peasantry' had undoubtedly become an outdated description of the small tenant farmers of 1930s Ireland – and as for the holiness of monks!

He continued to be enchanted by the Irish past, and by Ireland's struggles, through:

> ... the lords and ladies gay
> That were beaten into the clay
> Through seven heroic centuries; ...

This dichotomy between the glories of ancient Ireland and the sombre realities of its contemporary situation was at the heart of Yeats's disenchantment. Yet he continued to insist on Ireland's exceptionalism. Its contemporary poetry was different from the European mainstream because, in Yeats's view, 'modern Irish poetry began in the midst of the rediscovery of folk thought' and Ireland still had 'a living folk tradition'.[9] In 'A General Introduction for my Work', which remained unpublished during his lifetime and acts as something of a prose accompaniment to 'Under Ben Bulben', he wrote that behind all of Irish history lay 'a great tapestry' on which nobody can say 'where Christianity begins and Druidism ends'.[10]

Yeats quoted approvingly from Arnold Toynbee's *The Study of History*, to the effect that 'the romance of ancient Ireland has come to an end', and that modern Ireland had made up her mind 'to find her level as a willing inmate in our workaday Western world'.[11] Yeats evidently wanted Ireland to avoid that fate. He saw literature as a means of keeping alive his indomitable version of 'Irishry'. Hence in 'Under Ben Bulben' he urges his readers to:

Cast your mind on other days
That we in coming days may be
Still the indomitable Irishry.

## 'Man lives and dies between his two eternities'

How should we assess the 'great melody' Yeats composed to accompany his meandering Irish journey? He lived through torrid times, in Ireland and in the wider world and wrote voluminously, poetry, plays, fiction, folklore and essays. He kept a hand in many pies as writer, theatre director, senator and public man. Looking back on his life, he wrote that: 'A poet is justified not by the expression of himself, but by the public he finds or creates; a public made by others ready to his hand if he is a popular poet, but a new public, a new form of life, if he is a man of genius.'[12] Part of Yeats's achievement had been to create a national literature and to find a public for it, even if his grip on the attention and sympathy of that public was not abidingly firm. In turn, he uplifted, annoyed and puzzled them, but he never lost his desire to connect with his Irish public and to be, in one sense or other, a popular poet.

In a broadcast Yeats made for Irish radio in October 1935, he looked back at the Irish literary movement that had begun forty years earlier. Yeats remembered the Dublin of that day, ungenerously I am sure, as 'a vile hole' where 'Nationalist and Unionist never met.' In fact, he was part of Dublin's Contemporary Club, where individuals drawn from those communities did meet.

In Yeats's recollection:

Unionist Ireland was a shabby and pretentious England where we would have met nothing but sneers. Nationalist Ireland was torn with every kind of political passion and prejudice, wanting, insofar as it wanted any literature at all, Nationalist propaganda disguised as literature. We wanted plays about life, not about opinions – Ireland for their sole theme.'[13]

And Ireland did become, if not his sole theme, certainly a predominant and enduring one for him. The critic Denis Donoghue goes further, asserting that Yeats 'invented a country, calling it Ireland'.[14]

One of the collections of Yeats's poetry in my personal library comes with an introduction by the much-loved Yeats scholar at University College Dublin, Augustine Martin. I never met Martin, but I know a lot of people who were taught by him and who remember him fondly. In his sparkling introduction he recalls various entries from Yeats's ledger of achievements: a poet 'infatuated with lake isles, hazel woods, spooks and fairies, the lost enchantments of the Celtic Twilight'; 'a right-wing visionary'; an adherent of 'an archaic brand of Irish nationalism'; 'a pseudo-philosopher' possessed by 'an arcane, pretentious theory of history'; and, in the words of a reviewer of a biography of Yeats, a 'Great Irish Silly-Billy'.

Martin also quotes the American mega-critic Harold Bloom's assessment of Yeats's early poetry as 'the last great manifestation of European Romanticism', and he was, in Martin's view, 'one of the foremost artistic intelligences of the twentieth century'.[15] Yes, Yeats was all of those things; his 'great melody' was at times a ballad, a tuneful song, a cacophony, an anthem and, in his later years, often a deeply profound symphony.

No other major Irish writer had such a prolonged and intensive engagement with the Ireland of his time, from the 1880s onwards when, as he recalled, he turned his back on foreign themes and 'decided that the race was more important than the individual'.[16] I struggle to think of any major writer in the English language since Milton who was as continuously involved with the public affairs of his country as Yeats was and to whom what happened in the political arena really mattered. There is scarcely a significant Irish public event or movement between the 1880s and the 1930s in which Yeats did not have an involvement or about which he did not have an opinion. Although he spent long spells living in London, there is very little of England or English themes in his writings. James Joyce, George Bernard Shaw and Samuel Beckett all warily kept a physical and intellectual distance from the awkward affairs of the Ireland they knew, but Yeats never did. He weighed in and took the fight to those who had contrasting notions of Ireland's destiny. Indeed, he appeared to draw strength from being a 'public man' in an Irish context. That is why, in a conscious echo of one of his most notable prose essays, I called this book *Pilgrim Soul: W.B. Yeats and the Ireland of His Time.* I do not think it would be so readily feasible to write a book about Joyce, Shaw or Beckett and the Ireland of their times.

I see Yeats as a great interrogator and interpreter of the Ireland of his era and, indeed, of ours, which is why we still need to take him seriously. He was a witness to Irish history at a crucial time and the reflections he bequeathed us retain their value as a window on Ireland's past and a lodestar for the 'modern, tolerant, liberal nation'[17] for which Yeats argued passionately in his Senate speech on divorce, insisting that the new Irish state should respect the liberties of its minorities.

There are ways in which Yeats was Ireland's Shakespeare, the bard of a changing country in a troubled world, leaving behind a cache of poems addressing the issues of his time, just as Shakespeare did in his history plays as the long reign of Queen Elizabeth I drew to a close. As time passes, Yeats, on account of the power and lasting appeal of his poetry, may become a prime source for our understanding of revolutionary Ireland, just as Shakespeare now is for Elizabethan England. There is, I think, an argument for naming Yeats as the greatest Irish person of the twentieth century. That type of contest is of course invidious, as we can rarely compare like with like. But in terms of the longevity of his contribution, the scale of his achievement, the international recognition he garnered and the length of time during which his renown has been sustained, there is certainly a cogent case to be made for him.

I have long been fascinated by the period of Irish history between 1890 and 1922, about which I have written extensively.[18] In my papers, I have some handwritten notes I made during my time in India in the early 1980s on lined, foolscap paper, under the heading 'The historical politics of Yeats's poetry', which could be a first draft of this book. In those notes, I wrote that Yeats entered Irish nationalism through the land of literature, and that he aspired to create a literature that would be both 'Irish and great.' I stand by that novice judgement.

I also observed that Yeats, in his later years, with his command of language and poetic imagery, could 'make powerful philosophical statements without seeming to lose touch with reality'. At that time, I thought of the 1890s as a decade of intellectual formation for Yeats, one that shaped him for life. Referring to those years, Roy Foster has written of:

> the great upward curve of Irish cultural achievement from about 1890 to 1914 and the fact that this went with an opening out of attitudes, a modernisation of nationalism, an exploration of cultural diversity, a questioning of too-readily-received forms of authority in public and indeed private life. That was the period when, in a sense, modern Irish history was 'made'.[19]

It was also when modern Irish literature was made. The turn of the century was a key moment in Yeats's Irish journey. That was when Yeats's engagement with Irish nationalism reached a crescendo and then began to fade as doubts about the country's direction of travel started to unsettle him. During those years, Yeats's infatuation with Maud Gonne hit its peak of belated sexual fulfilment, to be followed by the trough of Gonne's impulsive marriage to John MacBride in 1903. This all occurred alongside the crucial role Yeats played, as playwright and theatre manager, in the emergence and development of the Irish dramatic movement that culminated in 1904 with the founding of the Abbey Theatre.

In exploring Yeats's indomitable Irishness, I have argued that the tensions surrounding language and political identity served to give Irish writing in English a unique voice. Subsequent generations of Irish writers are all in one way or another the offspring of that revolution of the mind. It is also true that Ireland blazed a trail by demonstrating the possibility of creating a national literature in English with a distinctive flavour born of native conditions and influences.

The emergence of a national literature defied the predictions of those who, for much of the twentieth century, envisaged that Ireland's unqualified embrace of English would corrode Ireland's national identity. On the contrary, Ireland is a country that, even without the revival of its native language, has retained a notable measure of cultural distinctiveness.

## 'All that stir of thought'

What was Yeats's impact on 'that long gestation' about which he spoke in Stockholm in 1923, and that prefaced the dramatic events of Ireland's revolutionary era? It is entirely possible that Irish independence would eventually have been won without the influence of the Gaelic League, the GAA or the emotional nationalism of Yeats's *Cathleen ni Houlihan*. It may well be that the presence of three published poets among the leaders of the 1916 Rising was entirely coincidental, and that revolutionary pragmatism and opportunism were more influential than Gaelic or literary idealism as a harbinger of independence.

Whatever weight we choose to give to the political impact of cultural nationalism, modern Ireland would surely have been a very different place without what Oliver MacDonagh once described as 'the Irishing of Ireland' that occurred during Yeats's heyday as a cultural nationalist. Had Ireland been granted Home Rule under Parnell in the 1890s, where would the incentive for attempting to de-Anglicise Ireland have come from? Would the leaders of a Home Rule Ireland have invested any significant effort in seeking to revive the Irish language? Without its political overtones, would the GAA have evolved into such a core element of modern Irish identity?

Traditional music and dance were also part of that 'stir of thought' about which Yeats spoke in Stockholm in 1923. The 1916 leader Tomás Ceannt was a traditional music piper, while Sean O'Casey, during his Irish Ireland phase in the early years of the twentieth century, was a keen Irish dancer, of the social rather than the performance variety. Those elements help delineate the cultural singularity of today's Ireland.

While historians brood about the burden of culture on Irish history, not enough credit is given to the positive impact of our past on today's Ireland. For dearth of comparative perspective, there is an inclination to undervalue Ireland's possession of perhaps the strongest native culture of any advanced European nation. Where else in Europe will you find traditional music played so routinely? Is there any European country with a native sport that can match the success of hurling and Gaelic football in more than holding their own against the universal lure of internationally dominant sports such as soccer? And while the Irish language has not been revived, it remains a meaningful component of Irish identity, as reflected in the existence of TG4, Raidió na Gaeltachta and a network of Gaelscoileanna (Irish-medium schools) dotted around the country.

These enduring remnants of traditional culture, whose survival has in many ways been against the odds in the teeth of modernisation and globalisation, are all, in one way or another, legacies of Yeats's 'long gestation'. It is, therefore, as a feeder of contemporary Irish identity, rather than as a spur to political ferment, that the cultural movements Yeats lionised in his Nobel speech now deserve recognition.

My argument is that the question of identity, and the heated debate it inspired, gave Irish writing its extraordinary vigour at the beginning of the twentieth century.[20] For Irish men and women at that time, there were searching questions to be confronted now that Ireland was on the cusp of some form of self-government. What did it mean to be Irish, and how did Irishness square with the country's predominantly English-language culture? For someone of Yeats's background, from a Protestant and traditionally English-oriented community, this issue was especially taxing. Despite drawing on Irish history and mythology, Yeats was often subjected to searing criticism for failing to pass all the tests for inclusion in the nationalist fold.

Joyce and Yeats scholar Richard Ellmann argued that Yeats's:

> Irishism is of a very special kind. Like Joyce's prose, his poetry makes use of national and local boundaries only to transcend them. He is Irish; he is also anti-Irish in an Irish way; and his interest in Irishmen is always subordinated to an interest in men ... Ireland is his symbol for the world, and he is caught between estrangement and love for both.'[21]

Yes, Yeats was a transcendent Irish poet, anchored by his understanding of Irish history, literature, folklore and mythology, and by his variegated Irish experience.

This points to Yeats's complex, convoluted engagement with Ireland. There was a relentlessness to his involvement in Irish affairs that weathered every setback and kept him coming back for more. His endurance is perhaps best captured in 'Remorse for Intemperate Speech':

Out of Ireland have we come.
Great hatred, little room,
Maimed us at the start.
I carry from my mother's womb
A fanatic heart.


## 'Cast your mind on other days'

It is hardly surprising that the 1920s and 30s witnessed a passionate dispute about Irish history and culture as the new state sought to make its way in the world in the wake of the War of Independence and a dangerous, debilitating Civil War. Nor should it surprise anyone to discover that questions of identity generated agitated exchanges between competing views.

After all, this was the first time in several hundred years that the Irish people had an opportunity to try to shape their own future. There were many who sincerely wanted the emerging Ireland to be genuinely Gaelic and devotedly Catholic. Most of our leading writers, Yeats included, were offended by the conservative, Catholic dispensation ushered in by independence. They ought not to have been surprised, even if their disappointment was understandable.

The historian F.S.L. Lyons has argued that there was a divisive clash between the Gaelic and Anglo-Irish cultures during the half-century between the death of Parnell in 1891 and the death of Yeats in 1939. Lyons's influential thesis was that 'in Ireland culture – or rather, the diversity of cultures – has been a force which has worked against the evolution of a homogenous society and in doing so has been an agent of anarchy rather than of unity' and that 'the co-existence of several cultures, related yet distinct, has made it difficult, if not impossible, for Irishmen to have a coherent view of themselves in relation to each other and to the outside world'.[22]

I can readily understand why Lyons thought in this way, for he wrote in the late 1970s in the teeth of the Troubles in Northern Ireland and his pessimism about the malign influence of culture on Irish affairs was at that time a credible, understandable conclusion. But at this remove, it may be time to beg to differ. Looking back, you have to ask if there was any alternative to the kind of cultural 'war' in which Yeats became engaged? Lyons identifies four warring cultures in early twentieth-century Ireland – the English, the Gaelic, the Anglo-Irish and the Ulster Unionist.

The last of those was the only one with which Yeats did not engage, except in 1912–13, when he had tried to reassure Unionists that their rights would be protected in a Home Rule Ireland. The other three were part of his intellectual territory. He was, after all, a distinguished inhabitant of the English literary tradition, someone who had been seen at one time as a potential poet laureate. As far as Gaelic Ireland was concerned, Yeats drew on it and saw ancient Ireland as having a lot to offer to the modern world. Yet he could not accommodate the Gaelic League's revival project, for, as he explained, Irish was not a language in which he could express himself creatively.

In truth, Yeats's enthusiasm for Anglo-Ireland was a bit of a cul-de-sac. No amount of idealising of the Ireland of Berkeley, Burke and Swift was likely to win over the descendants of the 'Hidden Ireland' of the Penal Laws and the Protestant Ascendancy. F.S.L. Lyons was undoubtedly closer to the truth when he wrote that the Anglo-Irish:

> lived the sort of lives that landlords lived everywhere. Shooting, fishing and hunting, interspersed with hospitality frequently more lavish than they could afford – this was the framework of their lives. Worship of the horse was universal and the late Brendan Behan when he christened them 'the Horse Protestants' hit the nail exactly on the head. Books, unless they had to do with angling or the turf, were not widely read in their households, though some had splendid libraries dating mainly from the eighteenth century.[23]

In the early years of Irish independence, there were inevitably many who harboured resentment against remnants of the old Irish establishment. This surfaced in some overly aggressive critiques of Anglo-Irish literature. In 1932, for example, the *Irish Catholic* carried a long article disparaging those who had become members of the newly established Irish Academy of Letters, arguing that 'their relationship with Ireland lies for the most part in the mere accident of birth'. They were not real Irishmen but 'embittered émigrés brooding on imaginary wrongs'.[24]

Yet this remained essentially a battle of ideas with limited wider impact. As Lyons himself conceded, the Protestant minority in the Irish Free State was 'enervated by the almost repressive tolerance shown to it by the majority'.[25] There were many places in Europe where, in those tempestuous times, such cultural conflicts went well beyond the realm of ideas, and with destructive consequences for the lives of many who found themselves in hostile ethnic and linguistic locales.

In Ireland, political stability prevailed to the extent that it was possible to have a peaceful change of government in 1932 less than a decade after the end of a bitter civil war. This stability, albeit that it was coupled with very modest material advancement, served to minimise social upheaval to the benefit of a minority that remained relatively privileged in economic terms. Anglo-Irish identity was ultimately incorporated into a more inclusive Irish identity, which is Anglo-Irish in the sense that its principal medium is the English language. Irish people no longer feel a need to use the word Anglo-Irish except in historical contexts.

Despite his oftentimes pushy and exaggerated endorsement of the minority Anglo-Irish identity, and the dismissive things he said about modern Irish Catholicism, Yeats was afforded the equivalent of a state funeral when his remains were brought back from France in 1948. His body returned on board an Irish naval vessel, *Macha*, which, with its tribute to the ancient Irish settlement at Emain Macha, recalled lines from an early Yeats poem, 'The Madness of King Goll':

> My word was law from Ith to Emain,
> And shook at Inver Amergin
> The hearts of the world-troubling seamen,
> And drove tumult and war away
> From girl and boy and man and beast; ...

By 1940, the mid-point between the deaths of Yeats and Joyce, new intellectual currents could be detected in Ireland with the emergence of *The Bell*, a literary magazine edited by Sean O'Faolain, who had taken part in

Ireland's independence struggle, but became progressively disenchanted with 'the dreary Eden' represented by the Irish Free State.[26] O'Faolain, who had been an admirer of Yeats – but not an uncritical one – reproached contemporary Ireland for its failure to realise its pre-independence promise.

Narrowness was presented as the culprit. As O'Faolain put it in his first editorial, appealing for a pluralist approach: 'Whoever you are, O reader, Gentile or Jew, Protestant or Catholic, priest or layman, Big House or Small House – *The Bell* is yours.'[27] Signing off as editor six years later, he urged Irish writers to avoid the Gaelic Mind, the Catholic Mind and the Irish Mind. A parochial Ireland, he insisted, 'has no part in our vision of the ideal nation that will yet come out of this present dull period'.[28] O'Faolain spent the rest of his long life more than a little disgruntled with the Ireland he had fought to bring into being during the War of Independence.

The disputes about Irish identity that marked Yeats's latter years have now faded. The image Yeats had of Ireland as an Anglo-Gaelic hybrid has more currency today than the preferences of those advocates of an Irish Ireland, who upbraided Yeats in the opening years of the twentieth century. Modern Ireland's identity is a compound of traditional and contemporary elements. Perhaps neither Daniel Corkery, nor D.P. Moran, nor W.B. Yeats would be fully pleased with this outcome, but Ireland's cultural patrimony, including the achievements of our leading writers whose works were once subjected to censorship, is now seen as a source of strength and pride.

With the passage of time, the tension between Irish and Anglo-Irish identity has happily faded. We are more likely today to debate the intersections between Irish, European and Anglo-American identities. Positive developments in Northern Ireland since the 1990s and improvements in Anglo-Irish relations have removed some of the contemporary sting from Irish history although strains surrounding Britain's departure from the European Union has put some of it back.

It is now possible to 'cast a cold eye' on the Irish past, to savour the country's achievements and to acknowledge its failings. We can now admire the literary and architectural achievements of eighteenth-century Ireland without displaying the 'characteristic latter-day Irish cringe' that D.P. Moran once attributed to admirers of Swift.[29] There is no longer any barrier to a simultaneous appreciation of Anglo-Irish literature and the Gaelic poets of the 'Hidden Ireland'.

Although Yeats entered into a wholehearted and somewhat uncritical embrace of Anglo-Ireland, he deserves credit as the chief intellectual architect of the idea of a national literature for Ireland in the English language, an idea that has stood the test of time. Ireland is, and no doubt will always be, an English-speaking country, but it is one that has a voice of its own and a cultural patrimony that is neither Gaelic nor Anglo, but Irish.

## 'An Ireland the poets have imagined'

At a Cambridge Irish Studies seminar at Magdalene College in the early summer of 2023, I was asked to put a date on when today's Ireland had been born. As the seminar had just heard a paper on Seamus Heaney, in an off-the-cuff remark I suggested that the origins of contemporary Ireland could be traced back to 1995, when Heaney became the fourth Irish-born writer to be awarded the

Nobel Prize for Literature. The more I think about it, the more I see arguments to sustain that chronology of contemporary Ireland's gestation.

In his 1995 Nobel lecture, Seamus Heaney reminded his listeners that when Yeats received his prize, 'Ireland was emerging from the throes of a traumatic civil war that had followed fast on the heels of a war of independence', and that was 'bloody, savage and intimate, and for generations to come it would dictate the terms of politics within the twenty-six independent counties of Ireland'. Heaney recalled that Yeats 'came to Sweden to tell the world that the local work of poets and dramatists had been as important to the transformation of his native place and times as the ambushes of guerrilla armies'.

Heaney made reference to Yeats's poem 'The Municipal Gallery Revisited' and the sudden realisation captured there to the effect that something truly epoch-making had occurred during Yeats's lifetime:

'This is not', I say,
'The dead Ireland of my youth, but an Ireland
The poets have imagined, terrible and gay.'

Heaney argued that, like Yeats, the Ireland that he inhabited in 1995 was one that his fellow Irish poets had in the preceding decades 'helped to imagine'. Although this is almost certainly not what Heaney had in mind, in 1995 the country in which Dublin-based Heaney lived was as he spoke in Stockholm being shaped by the decisions taken in 1992 at the Edinburgh European Council, which doubled the size of the EU's structural funds, to Ireland's immense benefit.

At that time, Ireland was also profiting from the establishment of the European Single Market in 1993, which turned out to be an economic game-changer for an open, trade-dependent Irish economy. And then there was the first IRA ceasefire of August 1994, which pointed the way forward towards the Good Friday Agreement of 1998. Divorce, an issue that had galvanised Yeats during his time in the Irish Senate, was the subject of a referendum in 1995 that removed the constitutional ban that had been in place since the Irish Constitution was adopted in 1937. That referendum legalising divorce, which passed by an extremely narrow margin, set in train the emergence of a more liberal and tolerant nation in the two decades that followed. Yes, Ireland was definitely on its feet and moving forward when Heaney collected his prize, just as it was when Yeats travelled to Stockholm in 1923 from a country with its independence secured and the Civil War behind it.

W.B. Yeats was not the only person awarded a Nobel Prize by the Swedish Academy in December of 1923. An Austrian scientist, Fritz Pregl (1869–1930), won an award for his work on the microanalysis of organic substances. A Canadian and a Scottish researcher, Frederick Banting (1891–1941) and John Macleod (1876–1935), were honoured for the discovery of insulin, thereby leaving a legacy of more immediate worldly value than Yeats's oeuvre, for theirs was a discovery that has no doubt saved countless lives during the intervening decades.

Nonetheless, the names Pregl, Banting and Macleod have dropped out of our collective memory, while, in testimony to the enduring power of literature, Yeats's reputation continues to shine, and looks set to retain its lustre, in sturdy defiance of the passage of time and of changing cultural tastes. That pilgrim soul's posthumous journey continues, driven by the 'masterful images' he conjured up from his well-stocked imagination and the material provided by the Ireland of his time. The poet whose work I have journeyed with throughout my life, and in the pages of this book, was a deeply complex and immensely accomplished writer who, as I have shown, was inveterately, unconventionally and indomitably Irish, but along distinctive lines that he marked out for himself and, through his poetry, for 'Ireland in the Coming Times' too.

# Acknowledgements

I wrote much of this book in 2022/23 during my time as Global Distinguished Professor of Irish Studies at Glucksman Ireland House, New York University, and as Parnell Fellow at Magdalene College, Cambridge, although, to use Yeats's words, its 'long gestation' stretches back to my years at University College Cork and even to my schooldays at Mount Sion in Waterford.

During my forty-four years with Ireland's Department of Foreign Affairs, I often had occasion to talk about Yeats's life and work, especially during the 150th anniversary of the poet's birth in 2015, when I was Ambassador in London and gave innumerable talks about him at universities, arts festivals and Irish centres all over Britain. All of those activities have undoubtedly shaped my understanding of Yeats and his importance as an Irish writer.

At New York University I was fortunate to have the support of Loretta Brennan Glucksman, Ted Smyth, Kevin Kenny and Caroline Heafey. It was a great pleasure to spend a semester there following my retirement from the Department of Foreign Affairs in August 2022. My thinking about Yeats was deepened by being able to teach a course at NYU on 'Literature as History: Ireland 1880–1940'. I thank my students there for the willingness with which they engaged with me on the literary/historical themes that are at the heart of this book.

I thank the Master of Magdalene College, Christopher Greenwood, its President, Brendan Burchell, and the Fellows of the College for the warm welcome they extended to me during my time in Cambridge. My particular thanks go to Professor Eamon Duffy, who had the bold idea of offering the College's annual Parnell Fellowship to a retired diplomat. Eamon has become, and will always be, a dear friend.

I owe a debt of gratitude to my Washington-based friend Joe Hassett, lawyer and literary scholar extraordinaire, for his astute comments on earlier drafts of a couple of chapters I shared with him.

Part of my rationale for writing this book comes from the fact that, since November 2019, I have been Honorary President of the Yeats Society Sligo. I thank the society for the work it does in honouring the life and literary legacy of Ireland's preeminent English-language poet.

Last but certainly not least, I want to record my deepest appreciation to my loving wife, Greta, for having had the forbearance to accompany me on life's journey, including on this journey through Yeats's life. Greta has scrupulously proofread every word I have ever published and, although I have taken her suggestions on board, like all of those who have discussed Yeats with me over the years, she carries no responsibility for the content of this book. This is my effort to put on paper some of what I have learned over the years about Yeats and the Ireland of his time.

# Bibliography

## Writings by W.B. Yeats

*The Celtic Twilight: Men, Women, Dhouls and Faeries* (Lawrence & Bullen, 1893)

*Essays and Introductions* (Palgrave Macmillan UK, 1961)

*Explorations* (MacMillan & Co., 1962)

*Mythologies* (Macmillan, 1959)

*A Tribute to Thomas Davis* (Cork University Press, 1965)

*Writings on Irish Folklore, Legend and Myth*, edited by Bruce Welch (Penguin Books, 1993)

Peter Allt & Russell K. Alspach (eds), *The Variorum Edition of the Poems of W.B. Yeats* (Macmillan, 1957)

George Bornstein & Hugh Witemeyer (eds), *The Collected Works of W.B. Yeats Vol. VII, Letters to the New Island* (Macmillan, 1989)

Edward Callan (ed.), *Yeats on Yeats: the last introductions and the 'Dublin' edition* (Dolmen Press, 1981)

Denis Donoghue (ed.), *Memoirs* (Macmillan Papermac, 1988)

John P. Frayne (ed.). *Uncollected Prose by W.B. Yeats: Volume I, first reviews and articles 1886–1896* (MacMillan, 1970)

John P. Frayne & Colton Johnson (eds), *Uncollected Prose by W.B. Yeats: Volume II, reviews, articles and other miscellaneous prose, 1897–1939* (Macmillan, 1975)

Warwick Gould, John Kelly & Deirdre Toomey (eds), *The Collected Letters of W.B. Yeats, Vol. II, 1896–1900* (Clarendon Press, 2005)

A. Norman Jeffares (ed.), *W.B. Yeats Selected Criticism* (Pan Books, 1976)

A. Norman Jeffares (ed.), *W.B. Yeats Selected Prose* (Macmillan, 1964)

Colton Johnson (ed.), *The Collected Works of W.B. Yeats, Vol. X: Later Articles and Reviews* (Scribner, 2000)

John Kelly & Eric Domville (eds), *The Collected Letters of W.B. Yeats, Vol. 1, 1885–1895* (Clarendon Press, 1986)

John Kelly & Ronald Schuchard (eds), *The Collected Letters of W.B. Yeats, Vol. III, 1901–1904* (Clarendon Press, 1994)

John Kelly & Ronald Schuchard (eds), *The Collected Letters of W.B. Yeats, Vol. IV, 1905–1907* (Oxford University Press, 2005)

John Kelly & Ronald Schuchard (eds), *The Collected Letters of W.B. Yeats, Vol. V, 1908–1910* (Oxford University Press, 2018)

Anna MacBride White & A. Norman Jeffares (eds), *Always Your Friend: the Gonne-Yeats Letters, 1893–1938* (Hutchinson, 1992)

W.K. Magee (ed.), *Literary Ideals in Ireland* (T. Fisher Unwin, 1899)

Donald R. Pearce (ed.), *The Senate Speeches of W.B. Yeats* (Prendeville, 2001)

Ann Saddlemyer (ed.) *W.B. Yeats and George Yeats: The Letters* (Oxford University Press, 2011)

Allan Wade (ed.), *The Letters of W.B. Yeats* (Rupert Hart-Davis, 1954)

## Biography

*The Dictionary of Irish Biography (www.dib.ie)*

Keith Aldritt, *W.B. Yeats: The Man and the Milieu* (John Murray, 1997)

Douglas Archibald, *Yeats* (Syracuse University Press, 1983)

Terence Brown, *W.B. Yeats: A Critical Biography* (Gill & Macmillan, 1999)

Stephen Coote, *W.B. Yeats: A Life* (Hodder and Stoughton, 1997)

Denis Donoghue, *Yeats* (Fontana/Collins, 1971)

Richard Ellmann, *James Joyce* (Oxford University Press, 1959)

Richard Ellmann, *The Identity of Yeats* (Faber & Faber, 1964),

Richard Ellmann, *W.B. Yeats: The Man and the Masks* (Norton, 1978)

Richard J. Finneran, George Mills Harper & William M. Murphy (eds), *Letters to W.B. Yeats* (The Macmillan Press, 1977)

R.F. Foster, *W.B. Yeats: A Life: I: The Apprentice Mage 1865–1914* (Oxford University Press, 1997)

R.F. Foster, *W.B. Yeats: A Life: II: The Arch-Poet 1915–1939* (Oxford University Press, 2003)

R.F. Foster, *Words Alone: Yeats and his Inheritances* (Oxford University Press, 2010)

R.F. Foster, 'The Irish Literary Revival' in Thomas Bartlett (ed.), *The Cambridge History of Ireland, Vol. IV, 1880 to the Present* (Cambridge University Press, 2018)

Maud Gonne MacBride, *A Servant of the Queen* (Colin Smythe, 1994)

Joseph Hone, *W.B. Yeats* (Pelican Books, 1971)

Joseph Hone (ed.), *Letters of J.B. Yeats* (Faber & Faber, 1999)

A. Norman Jeffares, 'Yeats as Public Man' in *Poetry* (Vol. 95, No. 4, July 1961)

A. Norman Jeffares, *W.B. Yeats: A New Biography* (Arrow Books, 1990)

John S. Kelly, *W.B. Yeats: A Chronology* (Palgrave Macmillan, 2003)

Horatio Sheafe Krans, *William Butler Yeats and the Irish Literary Revival* (McClure, Phillips & Co, 1904)

Micheál Mac Liammóir & Eavan Boland, *W.B. Yeats* (Thames & Hudson, 1971)

Brenda Maddox, *George's Ghosts: A New Life of W.B. Yeats* (Picador, 1999)

Patrick Maume, *D.P. Moran* (Historical Association of Ireland, 1995)

E.H. Mikhail (ed.), *W.B. Yeats: Interviews and Recollections, Vols 1 & 2* (Macmillan, 1977)

William M. Murphy, *Prodigal Father: The Life of John Butler Yeats (1839-1922)* (Cornell University Press, 1979)

Ulick O'Connor, *The Yeats Companion* (Pavilion Books, 1990)

Colm Tóibín, *Lady Gregory's Toothbrush* (University of Wisconsin Press, 2002)

Colm Tóibín, *Mad, Bad, Dangerous to Know: the Fathers of Wilde, Yeats and Joyce* (Penguin Books, 2018)

Katharine Tynan, *Twenty-five Years: Reminiscences* (Devin-Adair, 1913)

## Literature and Literary Criticism

Brian Arkins, *The Thought of W.B. Yeats* (Peter Lang, 2010)

Harold Bloom, *Yeats* (Oxford University Press, 1970)

Terence Brown, *The Literature of Ireland: Culture and Criticism* (Cambridge University Press, 2010)

Matthew Campbell, *Irish Poetry under the Union, 1801–1924* (Cambridge University Press, 2015)

Daniel Corkery, *Synge and Anglo-Irish Literature* (Mercier Press, 1966)

Elizabeth Cullingford, *Yeats, Ireland and Fascism* (Macmillan, 1981)

Seamus Deane, *Small World: Ireland, 1798–2018* (Cambridge University Press, 2021)

Denis Donoghue (ed.), *The Integrity of Yeats* (Mercier Press, 1967)

Lady Augusta Gregory (ed.), *Ideals in Ireland* (At the Unicorn, 1901)

Daniel A. Harris, *Yeats, Coole Park and Ballylee* (St John's University Press, 1974)

Joseph M. Hassett, *W.B. Yeats and the Muses* (Oxford University Press, 2010)

Joseph M. Hassett, *Yeats Now: Echoing into Life* (The Lilliput Press, 2020)

T.R. Henn, *The Lonely Tower: Studies in the Poetry of W.B. Yeats* (Methuen & Co., 1979)

Herbert Howarth, *Irish Writers, 1880–1940* (Rockliff, 1958)

Marjorie Howes, *Yeats's Nations: Gender, Class and Irishness* (Cambridge University Press, 1996)

Marjorie Howes (ed.), *Irish Literature in Transition, 1880–1940* (Cambridge University Press, 2020)

Marjorie Howes & John Kelly (eds), *The Cambridge Companion to W.B. Yeats* (Cambridge University Press, 2006)

A.N. Jeffares & K.G.W. Cross, *In Excited Reverie: A Centenary Tribute to W.B. Yeats* (Macmillan, 1965)

A. Norman Jeffares, *A New Commentary on the Collected Poems of W.B. Yeats* (Macmillan, 1984)

Niall MacMonagle (ed.), *Windharp: Poems of Ireland since 2016* (Penguin, 2016)

Sean MacMahon (ed.), *The Best from The Bell* (O'Brien Press, 1978)

Vivian Mercier, 'Literature in English, 1891–1921' in W.E. Vaughan (ed.), *A New History of Ireland VI: Ireland under the Union, II, 1870–1921* (Clarendon Press, 1996)

William H. Pritchard (ed.), *W.B. Yeats: A Critical Anthology* (Penguin, 1972)

Joseph Ronsley (ed.), *Myth and Reality in Irish Literature* (Wilfrid Laurier University Press, 1977)

Sonja Tiernan (ed.), *Eva Gore-Booth: Collected Poems* (Arlen House, 2018)

Robert Welch (ed.) *The Oxford Companion to Irish Literature* (Oxford University Press, 1996)

Thomas R. Whitaker, *Swan and Shadow: Yeats's Dialogue with History* (Catholic University of America Press, 1989)

Yvor Winters, *The Poetry of W.B. Yeats* (Alan Swallow, 1960)

Michael Wood, *Yeats & Violence* (Oxford University Press, 2010)

## History

Thomas Bartlett (ed.), *The Cambridge History of Ireland, Vol. 4, from 1880 to the present day* (Cambridge University Press, 2018)

J.C. Beckett, *The Anglo-Irish Tradition* (Faber & Faber, 1976)

Eugenio Biagini & Daniel Mulhall (eds), *The Shaping of Modern Ireland: A Centenary Assessment* (Irish Academic Press, 2016)

Terence Brown, *Ireland: A Social and Cultural History, 1922–1985* (Fontana Press, 1985)

Pat Cooke, *The Politics and Polemics of Culture in Ireland, 1800–2010* (Routledge, 2022)

Daniel Corkery, *The Hidden Ireland: A Study of Gaelic Munster in the Eighteenth Century* (Gill & Macmillan, 1989)

Patricia Craig (ed.), *The Oxford Book of Ireland* (Oxford University Press, 1998)

Ruth Dudley-Edwards, *Patrick Pearse: The Triumph of Failure* (Victor Gollancz, 1977)

Sean Farrell Moran, *Patrick Pearse and the Politics of Redemption: Mind of the Easter Rising, 1916* (Catholic University America Press, 1998)

Diarmaid Ferriter, *Between Two Hells: The Irish Civil War* (Profile Books, 2022)

R.F. Foster, *Modern Ireland: 1600–1972* (Allen Lane, 1988)

R.F. Foster, *Vivid Faces: The Revolutionary Generation in Ireland, 1890–1923* (Penguin, 2015)

Niamh Gallagher, *Ireland and the Great War: a Social and Political History* (Bloomsbury, 2019)

Martin Gilbert, *A History of the Twentieth Century; Vol. 1, 1900–1933* (HarperCollins, 1997)

Liam Harte (ed.), *A History of Irish Autobiography* (Cambridge University Press, 2018)

J.R. Hill (ed.), A *New History of Ireland VII: Ireland 1921–1984*, (Oxford University Press, 2003)

F.S.L. Lyons, *Culture and Anarchy in Ireland, 1890–1939* (Oxford University Press, 1982)

Dorothy Macardle, *The Irish Republic* (Victor Gollancz, 1937)

Daniel Mulhall, *A New Day Dawning: A Portrait of Ireland in 1900* (Collins Press, 1999)

Daniel Mulhall, *Irish Literature and the Making of Modern Ireland* (Marburger Universitätsreden Band 28, 2011)

Conor Cruise O'Brien, *Ancestral Voices: Religion and Nationalism in Ireland* (Poolbeg Press, 1994)

William I. Thompson, *The Imagination of an Insurrection: Dublin, Easter 1916* (Oxford University Press, 1967).

W.E. Vaughan (ed.), *A New History of Ireland VI: Ireland under the Union, II, 1870–1921* (Clarendon Press, 1996)

# Notes

## Chapter 1 'Those masterful images': Yeats's Ireland

1. Yeats was an inveterate reviser of his poems and I have used the final versions that appear in Allt & Alspach (eds), *The Variorum Edition of the Poems of W.B. Yeats*.

2. 'Thoor' was Yeats's transliteration of the Irish word for tower, *túr*.

3. That line comes from one of his earliest poems, 'The Song of the Happy Shepherd', but could serve as a motto for the poet's life.

4. Throughout this book I refer to William Butler Yeats as 'Yeats'. Other members of his family are referred to as John Butler Yeats (1839–1922), his father, Jack B. Yeats (1871–1957), his brother, Lily, Susan Mary Yeats (1866–1949) and Lollie, Elizabeth Corbet Yeats (1868–1940), his sisters. His mother was also Susan Mary Yeats, *née* Pollexfen (1841–1900).

5. Foster (2003), p. 245.

6. Tony Gray, *Mr Smyllie, Sir* (Gill & Macmillan, 1994), p. 101.

7. SC, pp. 195–6.

8. Quoted in *Chron.*, p. viii.

9. R.F. Foster, *Modern Ireland: 1600–1972* (Allen Lane, 1988), p. 532.

10. Ronan McGreevy, *Great Hatred: The Assassination of Field Marshal Sir Henry Wilson* (Faber, 2022).

11. A. Norman Jeffares (ed.), *W.B. Yeats Selected Poetry* (Pan Books, 1974), p. xiii.

12. Seamus Deane, 'Yeats and the Idea of Revolution' in Jonathan Allison (ed.), *Yeats's Political Identities* (Michigan University Press, 1996), p. 133.

13. A. Norman Jeffares (ed.), *W.B. Yeats Selected Plays* (Pan Books, 1974), p. 231.

14. 'Introduction' in *Ibid.*, p. 15.

15. Vijaya Lakshmi Pandit, *The Scope of Happiness: A Personal Memoir* (Outlet, 1979), pp. 60–1.

16. *One Hundred Favourite Poems: Poems for All Occasions, Chosen by Classic FM Listeners* (Hodder & Stoughton, 2009).

17. Æ, 'The Winding Stair' in Monk Gibbon (ed.), *The Living Torch A.E.* (Macmillan, 1938), pp. 90–4.

18. Coote (1997), p. 111.

19. Hassett (2010), p. 212.

20. Quoted in Maddox (1999), p. xv.

21. In modern Irish, *turas* is the word for both pilgrimage and journey.

22. *NC*, p. 146.

23. Lyons (1982), p. 1.

## Chapter 2 'That sang, to sweeten Ireland's wrong': Yeats and the Literary Revival

1. For an account of the Literary Revival, see R.F. Foster, 'The Irish Literary Revival' in Thomas Bartlett (ed.), *The Cambridge History of Ireland, Vol. 4, 1880 to the Present* (Cambridge University Press, 2018), pp. 168–95.

2. Pat Cooke, *The Politics and Polemics of Culture in Ireland, 1800–2010* (Routledge, 2022), p. 41.

3. Vivian Mercier, 'Literature in English, 1891–1921' in W.E. Vaughan (ed.), *A New History of Ireland VI: Ireland Under the Union, II, 1870–1921* (Clarendon Press, 1996), p. 357.

4. *Letters*, p. 215.

5. William M. Murphy, 'The Ancestry of William Butler Yeats' in *Yeats Studies*, Number 1 (Dublin, 1971), pp. 1–19.

6. *Au*, p. 14.

7. Foster (1997), p. 1.

8. Hone (1971), p. 29.

9. Quoted in John McGahern's Introduction to Joseph Hone (ed.), *Letters of J.B. Yeats* (Faber & Faber, 1999), p. 4.

10. *Au*, p. 6.

11. Entry on 'John Butler Yeats' in the *Dictionary of Irish Biography* (www.dib.ie).

12. Letter to Katharine Tynan quoted in Jeffares (1990), p. 28.

13. Nicholas Allen, 'Autobiography and the Irish Literary Revival' in Liam Harte (ed.), *A History of Irish Autobiography* (Cambridge University Press, 2018), p. 156.

14. Mikhail (ed.) (1977), vol. 1, pp. 3–7.

15. *Ibid.*, p. 2.

16. *Ibid.*, p. 6.

17. Peter McDonald (ed.), *The Poems of W.B. Yeats: Volume One, 1882–1889* (Routledge, 2020) p. 281.

18. Tynan (1913), p. 299.

19. Declan Kiberd, 'Yeats and Criticism' in Howes & Kelly (eds), *The Cambridge Companion to W.B. Yeats*, p. 127.

20. *CL1*, p. 11.

21. *Ibid.*, p. 35.

22. *Ibid.*, p. 191.

23. Tynan (1913), p. 289.

24. *Ibid.*, p. 291.

25. Quoted in *NC*, p. 3.

26. 'Autobiography' in *Mem.*, p. 52.

27. *Au*, pp. 95–6.

28. *Ibid.*, pp. 101–2.

29. John O'Leary, *Recollections of Fenians and Fenianism*, Vol. 1 (Downey and Company, 1896). p. 3.

30. Mulhall (1999), p. 159.

31. *UP1*, p. 81.

32. *Ibid.*, p. 82.

33. Campbell (2015), p. 70.

34. Deane (2021), p. 116.

35. *UP1*, p. 147.

36. W.B. Yeats, *Writings on Irish Folklore, Legend and Myth*, Bruce Welch (ed.), (Penguin, 1993), p. 3.

37. Quoted in William H. Pritchard (ed.), *W.B. Yeats: A Critical Anthology* (Penguin, 1972), p. 30.

38. *W.B. Yeats, Poems Selected by Seamus Heaney* (Faber & Faber, 2000).

39. *Mem*, p. 40.

40. Hassett (2010), p. 65.

41. *Mem*, p. 72.

42. *Ibid.*, p. 63.

43. *CL1*, p. 154.

44. *LNI*, p. 61.

45. *CL1*, p. 290.

46. Quoted in E.H. Mikhail (ed.) (1977), *Vol. 2*, pp. 280–1.

47. *YGL*, p. 53.

48. *CL1*, p. 237.

49. *UP1*, p. 207.

50. *Au*, p. 199.

51. *CL1*, p. 297.

52. *Ibid.*, pp. 298–9.

53. The letter was published on 6 September 1892 and is reproduced in CL1, pp. 310–12.

54. *Au*, p. 194.

55. *UP1*, p. 89.

56. *Ibid.*, p. 104.

57. *CL1*, p. 15.

58. *Ibid.*, p. 231.

59. Mikhail (ed.) (1977), Vol. 1, p. 41.

60. *Au*, p. 218.

61. *CL1*, p. 338.

62. *Ibid.*, pp. 339–40.

63. *UP1*, p. 248.

64. *Ibid.*, p. 249.

65. *Ibid.*, p. 250.

66. Pritchard, (1972), pp. 32–3.

67. Yeats, *The Celtic Twilight*, p. ix.

68. *Ibid.*, p. 6.

69. Declan Kiberd, 'Literature and Politics' in Margaret Kelleher & Philip O'Leary (eds), *The Cambridge History of Irish Literature Vol. II: 1890–2000* (Cambridge University Press, 2006), p. 10.

# Chapter 3 'The noisy set': Yeats at the Turn of the Century, 1896–1904

1.  Yeats in Magee (ed.) (1899), p. 19.
2.  Mulhall (1999), p. 158.
3.  *CL3*, p. xliii.
4.  Quoted in Dudley-Edwards (1977), p. 30.
5.  'Introduction to the Oxford Book of Modern Verse' in *SC*, p. 217.
6.  *Letters*, p. 397.
7.  Maud Gonne, *Servant of the Queen*, pp. 328–30, quoted in *NC*, p. 78.
8.  Francis MacManus (ed.), *The Yeats We Knew* (Mercier Press, 1965), pp. 13–15.
9.  Horatio Sheafe Krans, *William Butler Yeats and the Irish Literary Revival* (McClure, Phillips & Co., 1904), p. 10.
10. *Mem*, p. 72. See also Hassett (2010), pp. 11–34, for a full account of Yeats's lifelong association with Shakespear, a woman he probably ought to have married in the 1890s.
11. Tóibín (2002), p. 35.
12. *Mem*, pp. 160–1.
13. Tóibín (2002), p. 33.
14. *Mem*, p. 101.
15. Brown (1999), p. 107.
16. 'Cuchulain of Muirthemne' in *Exp.*, p. 3. In the 'Scylla and Charybdis' episode of *Ulysses*, James Joyce has Buck Mulligan jokingly quote those words as an example of 'the Yeats touch' in arch flattery of his literary friends.
17. *E&I*, p. 188.
18. *Myth*, p. 1.
19. *CL2*, p. 117.
20. George Moore, *Hail and Farewell*, pp. 190–1.
21. *Chron.*, p. 43.
22. Quoted in Foster (1997), p. 193.
23. Quoted in *Chron.*, p. 54.
24. *UP2*, pp. 149–52.
25. *Au*, p. 235.

26. *Mem*, p. 84.
27. Quoted in Jeffares (1990), p. 80.
28. *Letters to W.B. Yeats: Volume 1*, p. 45.
29. Cited in Brown (1999), p. 120.
30. *UP2*, p. 199.
31. *Ibid.*, p. 200.
32. *Ibid.*, p. 184.
33. *CL3*, p. 119.
34. *Letters*, p. 319.
35. *Ibid.*, pp. 336–7.
36. *Ibid.*, p. 338.
37. *Ibid.*, p. 339.
38. *CL3*, p. 187.
39. *Letters*, p. 294.
40. Quoted in Mulhall (1999), p. 23.
41. *CL2*, p. 102.
42. *Ideals*, p. 11.
43. *Ibid.*, p. 88.
44. *Ibid.*, p. 102.
45. *Ibid.*, p. 105.
46. *Ibid.*
47. The Moran quotes are taken from D.P. Moran, *The Philosophy of Irish Ireland* (University College Dublin Press, 2006). See also Daniel Mulhall, 'George Russell, D.P. Moran and Tom Kettle' in Biagini & Mulhall (2016), pp. 124–38.
48. *UP2*, p. 237.
49. *Ibid.*, p. 238.
50. *Ibid.*
51. Quoted in *CL3*, p. 10, fn. 5.
52. *CL3*, p. 19.
53. *Ibid.*, p. 71.
54. *UP2*, pp. 303–7.
55. *Letters to W.B. Yeats, Vol. 1*, p. 96.
56. *Ibid.*, p. 115.
57. *CL3*, pp. 166–7.
58. Quoted in Howarth (1958), p. 127.

59. Tóibín (2002), pp. 48–9.
60. *UP2*, p. 288.
61. *Ibid.*
62. *UP2*, p. 290.
63. *CL3*, pp. 315–17.
64. *Ibid.*, p. 389.
65. *Ibid.*, pp. 398–9.
66. *Ibid.*, p. 356.
67. *Ibid.*, p. 346.
68. *Ibid.*, pp. 377–8.
69. *Ibid.*, p. 396.
70. See Daniel Mulhall, 'Did James Joyce get a tip for the horses from W.B. Yeats?' in *The Irish Times*, 2 February 2023.
71. *UP2*, pp. 310–11.
72. *Ibid.*, p. 315.
73. *Ibid.*, pp. 318–19.
74. *Ibid.*, p. 313.
75. *Ibid.*, p. 320.
76. *Ibid.*, p. 326.
77. *Ibid.*, p. 321.
78. Quoted in Donald T. Torchiana, *W.B. Yeats and Georgian Ireland* (Northwestern University Press, 1966), pp. 4–5.
79. De Valera's St Patrick's Day Broadcast 1943, quoted in Patricia Craig (ed.), *The Oxford Book of Ireland* (Oxford University Press, 1998), p. 13.
80. *YGL*, p. 178.

## Chapter 4 'For men were born to pray and save': The Strange Death of Romantic Ireland

1. See Mulhall (1999) and 'Preface' in Biagini & Mulhall (eds) (2016), pp. xiii–xxi.
2. See Daniel Mulhall, 'The Strange Death of Romantic Ireland' in The *Irish Times*, 30 August 2012.
3. For an account of Farr's relationship with Yeats see Hassett (2010), pp. 37–63.

4. *YGL*, pp. 274–5.

5. Pritchard (1972), p. 165.

6. 'An Introduction to my Plays' in *YY*, p. 84.

7. *CL4*, p. 9.

8. Coote (1997), p. 253.

9. Quoted in Foster (1997), p. 342.

10. *Letters*, p. 447.

11. *Letters to W.B. Yeats*, p. 155.

12. *Letters*, p. 466.

13. *Mem*, p. 148.

14. Quoted in Foster (1997), p. 323.

15. Quoted in *CL4*, p. lii.

16. Howes (1996), p. 97.

17. *CL4*, p. 10.

18. *Ibid.*, p. 8.

19. *YGL*, p. 174.

20. *E&I*, p. 303.

21. *Ibid.*, p. 299.

22. *Ibid.*, p. 311.

23. *CL4*, p. 866.

24. Quoted in Coote (1997), p. 260.

25. *YGL*, p. 241.

26. *UP2*, p. 349.

27. Quoted in Hone (1971), p. 220.

28. Conor Cruise O'Brien (1994), pp. 82–5.

29. Quoted in Coote (1997), p. 262.

30. Quoted in Foster (1997), p. 365.

31. *Letters*, p. 448.

32. *E&I*, p. 313.

33. Denis Donoghue's 'Introduction' in *Mem*, p. 11.

34. *Mem*, p. 139.

35. *Ibid.*, p. 144.

36. *Ibid.*, pp. 212–13.

37. *UP2*, pp. 378–9.

38. Quoted in Hone (1971), p. 254.

39. Foster (1997), p. 393.

40. *YGL*, pp. 258–9.

41. *NC*, p. 85.

42. Quoted in *NC*, p. 90.

43. *Ibid.*, p. 106.

44. *Ibid.*, p. 107.

45. Quoted in Foster (1997), p. 481.

46. *Exp.* p. 239.

47. *UP2*, pp. 406–7.

48. Foster (1997), p. 378.

49. Quoted in *CL4*, p. 842.

50. *Letters*, p. 490.

51. *CL4*, p. 561.

52. *Ibid.*, p. 671.

53. *E&I*, p. 246.

54. Robert Saunders, 'A Nation in an Age of Anxiety' in *Financial Times*, 7/8 January 2023, *FT Weekend*, p. 9.

55. *E&I*, p. 260.

56. Ezra Pound, 'The Later Yeats' in Pritchard (1972), p. 63.

57. T.S. Eliot in Pritchard (1972), p. 159.

## Chapter 5 'A terrible beauty': Yeats's Easter Rising

1. Bloom (1970), p. 126.

2. Arkins (2010), p. 174.

3. *Var,* p. 320.

4. Bloom (1970), p. 172.

5. *NC*, p. 112.

6. *Au*, p. 433.

7. *Ibid.*, p. 364.

8. Foster (1997), p. 460.

9. Brown (1999), p. 204.

10. Gallagher (2019), p. 18.

11. W.B. Yeats, *A Tribute to Thomas Davis* (Cork University Press, 1965), p. 12.

12. *Ibid.*, p. 15.

13. *Letters*, p. 588.

14. Quoted in Foster (2003), p. 5.

15. Hone (1971), p. 292.

16. *Ibid.*, p. 276.
17. *Letters*, pp. 596–97.
18. *Ibid.*, p. 599.
19. *Ibid.*, p. 601.
20. Ellmann (1959), p. 405.
21. *Letters*, p. 605.
22. *Ibid.*, p. 604.
23. *Ibid.*, p. 605.
24. *Ibid.*, p. 612.
25. *Ibid.*, p. 613.
26. *YGL*, p. 375.
27. *Letters*, p. 614.
28. *Ibid.*, p. 614.
29. Bloom (1970), p. 314.
30. R.F. Foster used Yeats's words for his group portrait of the generation that supported Ireland's independence struggle, *Vivid Faces: the revolutionary generation in Ireland, 1890–1923* (Penguin, 2015).
31. *Letters*, p. 612.
32. Quoted in Mulhall (1999), p. 160.
33. Farrell Moran (1998), p. 117.
34. Foster (2003), p. 46.
35. *Mem*, pp. 177–8.
36. *YGL*, p. 384.
37. Brown (1999), p. 229.
38. Brown (2010), p. 46.
39. Hassett (2010), p. 33.
40. *Letters*, p. 633.
41. Maddox (1999), p. 73.
42. *Letters*, p. 633.
43. *Ibid.*, p. 634.
44. Hassett (2010), p. 133.
45. Cooke (2022), p. 42.
46. *Au*, p. 106.
47. William I. Thompson, *The Imagination of an Insurrection: Dublin, Easter 1916* (Oxford University Press, 1967).

# Chapter 6 'We had fed the heart on fantasies': Yeats on the Irish War of Independence and Civil War, 1918–1923

1. Hassett, *Yeats Now*, p. 132.
2. Ellmann, (1978), p. 223.
3. *Letters*, p. 643.
4. *Ibid.*, p. 644.
5. See Daniel Mulhall, 'James Joyce, W.B. Yeats and the Horses' in *The Irish Field*, 25 March 2023.
6. From Kettle's poem, 'To my daughter Betty, the Gift of God' in Niall MacMonagle (ed.), *Windharp: Poems of Ireland since 1916* (Penguin Random House, 2016), pp. 8–9.
7. *Letters*, p. 649.
8. Foster (2003), pp. 123–4.
9. *Ibid.*, p. 127.
10. *Letters*, p. 651.
11. Hone (1971), pp. 348–9.
12. *Letters*, p. 655.
13. *Ibid.*, p. 651.
14. *Ibid.*, p. 679.
15. *Ibid.*, p. 698.
16. Arkins (2010), p. 84.
17. Cullingford (1981), p. 121.
18. Welch (ed.) (1996), p. 588.
19. Coote (1997), p. 397.
20. *NC*, p. 203.
21. Gilbert (1997), pp. 529–30.
22. *Ibid.*, pp. 532–3.
23. *Letters*, p. 656.
24. *Ibid.*, p. 659.
25. E. Engelberg, 'The New Generation and the Acceptance of Yeats', in *W.B. Yeats 1865–1965: Centenary Essays* (Ibadan: Nigeria, 1965), p. 95.
26. *Letters*, p. 851.
27. Wood (2010), p. 23.

28. Saddlemyer (ed.) (2011), pp. 70–1.
29. Coote (1997), p. 448.
30. *Letters*, p. 668.
31. Hone (1971), p. 327.
32. Conor Cruise O'Brien, 'Passion and Cunning: An Essay on the Politics of W.B. Yeats' in Jeffares & Cross (eds), *In Excited Reverie* (1965).
33. *Letters*, p. 675.
34. *Ibid.*, p. 678.
35. Foster (2003), p. 207.
36. *Letters*, p. 676.
37. *Ibid.*, p. 680.
38. *Ibid.*, p. 681.
39. *Ibid.*, p. 682.
40. *Ibid.*, p. 690.
41. *Ibid.*, p. 696.
42. *NC*, p. 223.
43. *Au*, pp. 579–80.
44. Yeats, *The Oxford Book of Modern Verse*, p. xxxiii.

## Chapter 7 'We the great gazebo built': The Anglo-Irish Yeats

1. Brown (1981), p. 14.
2. F.S.L. Lyons quoted in Vivian Mercier, 'Literature in English, 1891–1921' in Vaughan (ed.) (1996), p. 35.
3. Anne Dolan, 'Politics, Economy and Society in the Irish Free State, 1922–1939' in Bartlett (ed.) (2018), p. 323.
4. Brown (1985), p. 28.
5. *UP2*, p. 488.
6. Donald T. Torchiana, 'Senator Yeats, Burke and Able Men' in *The Newberry Library Bulletin*, Vol. V, No. 8, July 1961, p. 275.
7. See Tiernan (ed.) (2018).
8. MacMonagle (2016), p. 11.
9. Beckett (1976), p. 63.
10. 'Introduction to the Words upon the Window-Pane', in Jeffares (ed.) (1964), p. 213.

11. *UP1*, pp. 351–3.

12. *Ibid.*, pp. 382–7.

13. *Ibid.*, p. 360.

14. *Ibid.*, p. 408.

15. *CPl*, p. 601.

16. Macardle (1937), pp. 34–5.

17. Quoted in Craig (ed.) (1998), p. 216.

18. Lyons (1982), p. 168.

19. Corkery (1966), pp. 6–7.

20. *Ibid.*, p. 21.

21. *Ibid.*, p. 25.

22. Colton Johnson (ed.) *The Collected Works of W.B. Yeats, Vol. X: Later Articles and Reviews* (Scribner Book Company, 2000), p. 257.

23. *Sen*, pp. 143–4.

24. Quoted in Thompson (1967), p. 144.

25. *Letters*, p. 701.

26. Quoted in Aldritt (1997), p. 288.

27. *Au*, p. 536.

28. *Ibid.*, pp. 539–40.

29. *Ibid.*, p. 556.

30. *Ibid.*, p. 546.

31. *Ibid.*, p. 554.

32. Hone (1971), p. 362.

33. *Letters*, p. 692.

34. *Ibid.*, pp. 698–9.

35. *Ibid.*, p. 693.

36. Ellmann (1999), p. 249.

37. Hone (1971), p. 369.

38. *UP2*, p. 452.

39. Quoted in Aldritt (1997), p. 286.

40. *Letters*, p. 694.

41. Edward MacLysaght, 'The first Senate's last senator' in the *Irish Press*, 13 December 1982, p. 9.

42. *Sen*, p. 8.

43. *Letters*, p. 705.

44. *Sen*, p. 18.

45. *Letters*, p. 696.

46. *Ibid.*, pp. 107–8.
47. *Sen*, p. 22.
48. *Letters*, p. 697.
49. See Ferriter (2022), pp. 111–12.
50. *Ibid.*, p. 112.
51. *Sen*, p. 38.
52. *Letters*, p. 706.
53. *UP2*, p. 439.
54. *Sen*, p. 58.
55. *Ibid.*, p. 64.
56. *Ibid.*, p. 63.
57. Jeffares (ed.) (1976), p. 265.
58. *UP2*, pp. 439–49.
59. A. Norman Jeffares, 'Yeats as Public Man' in *Poetry* (Vol. 95, No. 4, July 1961), p. 260.
60. *Sen*, p. 150.
61. Jeffares, 'Yeats as Public Man', p. 261.
62. *Sen*, p. 102.
63. *Ibid.*, p. 104.
64. *Ibid.*, p. 98.
65. *Ibid.*
66. *Ibid.*, pp. 80–1.
67. *Ibid.*, p. 8.
68. From 'The Child and the State', a speech delivered at the Irish Literary Society on 30 November 1925, reproduced in *Sen*, pp. 156–62.
69. See Clare Marie Moriarty, 'A Library by any other name?' in *History Ireland*, Vol. 31, No. 3, May/June 2023, pp. 16–17.
70. *Sen*, p. 142.
71. *GYL*, p. 439.
72. Quoted in Ann Saddlemyer & Robert Skelton (eds), *The World of W.B. Yeats*, p. 107.
73. *Letters*, p. 741.
74. *Ibid.*, p. 742.
75. Sean O'Casey, *Inishfallen, Fare Thee Well* in *Autobiographies Vol. 2*, p. 245.

76. *Ibid.*, p. 275.
77. *Letters*, p. 727.
78. *UP2*, p. 476.
79. *Ibid.*, p. 477.
80. Aldritt, p. 291.
81. *Letters*, p. 727.
82. *UP2*, p. 484.
83. *Ibid.*, p. 488.
84. *Ibid.*, p. 489.
85. *Ibid.*
86. *Ibid.*, p. 490.

## Chapter 8 'And say my glory was I had such friends': Yeats in the 1930s

1. Winters (1960), p. 6.
2. Hone (1971), p. 465.
3. Quoted in Foster (2003), p. 437.
4. *Ibid.*, p. 438.
5. *Au*, p. 389.
6. *Ibid.*, p. 395.
7. *Ibid.*, p. 455.
8. *Ibid.*, p. 457.
9. *Letters*, p. 773.
10. *Ibid.*, p. 781.
11. Brown (1999), p. 347.
12. *Letters*, p. 809.
13. *Ibid.*, p. 811.
14. *Ibid.*, p. 801.
15. *Ibid.*, p. 800.
16. Ellmann (1959), p. 673.
17. *Letters*, p. 801.
18. *Ibid.*, p. 805.
19. *Ibid.*, p. 806.
20. *Ibid.*, p. 808.
21. *Ibid.*, pp. 811–12.

22. Cullingford (1981), p. 200.
23. Brian Girvan, 'The Republicanisation of Irish Society, 1932–1948' in Hill (ed.) (2003), p. 134.
24. *Letters*, p. 813.
25. *Ibid.*, p. 814.
26. Conor Cruise O'Brien, 'Passion and Cunning: an essay on the politics of W.B. Yeats' in Jeffares & Cross (eds) (1965), p. 260.
27. Patrick Cosgrave, 'Yeats, Fascism and Conor O'Brien' in *The London Magazine* (July 1967), p. 41.
28. *Var*, p. 497.
29. *NC*, p. 498.
30. *Ibid.*, p. 499.
31. *Ibid.*, pp. 499–500.
32. *Ibid.*, p. 500.
33. *Var*, p. 547.
34. Arkins (2010), p. 78.
35. *Letters*, p. 851.
36. *Ibid.*
37. *Ibid.*, p. 873.
38. *Exp*, p. 292.
39. *Ibid.*, p. 293.
40. *E&I*, p. 401.
41. *Letters*, p. 776.
42. *E&I*, p. 348.
43. *Ibid.*, p. 351.
44. *Ibid.*, p. 356.
45. *Letters*, p. 779.
46. Arkins (2010), p. 69.
47. *Letters*, p. 838.
48. *Ibid.*, p. 867.
49. *Ibid.*, p. 881.
50. Foster (2003), p. 575.
51. *Letters*, p. 881.
52. *Ibid.*, p. 885.
53. *Exp*, p. 372.
54. *E&I*, p. 488.

55. *NC*, pp. 333–4.

56. *Ibid.*, p. 335.

57. *Exp*, p. 410.

58. *Ibid.*, pp. 412–13.

59. *Ibid.*, p. 420.

60. *Ibid.*, p. 425.

61. *Ibid.*, p. 426.

62. *Letters*, p. 922.

63. *Ibid.*, p. 872.

64. *E&I*, p. 526.

## Chapter 9 'Cast a cold eye': Yeats's Achievement

1. Pritchard (ed.) (1972), p. 143.

2. A.N. Jeffares (ed.) (1976), p. 227.

3. Pritchard (ed.) (1972), p. 137.

4. Winters (1960), p. 3.

5. *Ibid.*, p. 165.

6. Jeffares (ed.) (1976), p. 223.

7. *Ibid.*, p. 245.

8. *Ibid.*

9. *Ibid.*, p. 252.

10. *Ibid.*, p. 259.

11. *Ibid.*, p. 261.

12. Yeats,'Introduction to Essays' in *YY*, p. 80.

13. Johnson (ed.) (2000), p. 254.

14. Donoghue (1971), p. 14.

15. W.B. Yeats, *Collected Poems* (Vintage Books, 1992), p. xxiii.

16. Yeats,'I became an author' (1938) in Johnson (ed.) (2000).

17. *UP2*, p. 452.

18. See Mulhall (1999) and Biagini & Mulhall (eds) (2016).

19. Quoted in Margaret Kelleher, 'Introduction', *Irish University Review*, Vol. 33, No. 1 (Spring/Summer 2003), p. viii.

20. See Mulhall (1999), pp. 147–74.

21. Ellmann (1964), pp. 4–5.

22. Lyons (1982), p. 2.

23. Lyons (1979), p. 21.
24. *The Irish Catholic*, 3 December 1932.
25. Lyons (1982), p. 163.
26. See Dan Mulhall, 'Sean O'Faolain and the Evolution of Modern Ireland' in *The Irish Review* (No. 26, Autumn 2000), pp. 20–9.
27. Sean O'Faolain, 'This is your magazine' (*The Bell*, October 1940) in McMahon (ed.) (1978), p. 16.
28. Sean O'Faolain, 'Signing off' (*The Bell*, April 1946) in McMahon (ed.) (1978), p. 123.
29. Moran was writing in the *New Ireland Review* in December 1899. His uncomplimentary view of Swift is quoted in Robert Mahony, 'Jonathan Swift as the Patriot Dean' in *History Ireland*, Vol. 3, No. 4 (Winter 1994), p. 27.

# Index

Yeats's defence of 109–12